FOREWORD For many years I have been asked if there was a record of my father's stories and have always had to say No. He maintained that, when printed, many stories lost their impact. Because of this, nothing was ever done. At last this book not only tells some of his many stories, but gives a good coverage of the various facets of his long life. As a young man, Father spent a short time in business with his brother. Later, having qualified as a minister of religion, he applied himself to pastoral work for some sixty-four years. Being gifted with a talent for public speaking and recounting stories, he gave good service to the Ulster Farmers' Union, especially in their formative years, when they were not so well organized as they are today. Brought up on a farm, he never lost his love for the land and, as there was a wee farm attached to the manse in Dervock, he always kept some livestock, concentrating on a small flock of Border Leicester sheep.

My best thanks go to the Rev Robert Hanna, Mr Eull Dunlop and many others for all their efforts in providing, arranging and editing all the data which came to hand. I hope this life-story will give to many a deeper understanding of my father's work and that, as you read, you will be transported back to the happy hours spent listening to him preach, lecture or tell stories. **Vincent H McIlmoyle**

Mr Samuel Black, Coleraine Road, Portstewart, the well-known breeder, exhibitor and judge, has learned that the Rev RJ McIlmoyle joined the Society of Border Leicester Sheep Breeders in 1915 and purchased his first sheep from Mr Robert Bell and Mr Tom Stokes. This photograph appeared in the Belfast Telegraph, 4 February 1963.

INTRODUCTION At the Mid-Antrim Historical Group's bus outing to the Kells and Connor area on Friday, 15 June 1990, Miss Jane Megaw, Markstown, Cullybackey, after referring in appreciative terms to *The Armoy Athletes*, dropped the hint that "the next story from North Antrim which should be undertaken is that of the Rev RJ McIlmoyle of Dervock". I must admit that not much earnest thought was given to the idea until Mr Eull Dunlop, Secretary of the Mid-Antrim Historical Group, began to speak on the same subject before the summer holidays. I replied that I would give my decision in September. After I had made contact, in the meantime, with a son of the Rev RJ McIlmoyle, Mr Vincent H McIlmoyle of Limavady, and obtained his kind permission, the way ahead seemed clear. Indeed Vincent has been very enthusiastic and co-operative in forwarding family photographs and relevant material. He has also been very generous in practical terms to the Mid-Antrim Historical Group, so that this biography might be published and his hope realized that "the final effort is something of which we can all be proud". Vincent has recalled that his father was in great demand at public meetings. Some nights he would have two engagements, if the venues were not far apart. Sometimes he had to refuse invitations. There were some organizers of meetings whom he advised to contact him first, before they set a date or booked a hall and in that way they had a better chance of having him present. But distance and a late hour were no problem to the Rev RJ. It is well known that he left even Enniskillen at midnight to travel home to Dervock and, if the weather was too foggy or if he himself felt too sleepy to proceed any farther, he would have parked at the side of the road and gone to sleep for the night. Then he drove home in the morning when conditions were improved and he was refreshed! Vincent recalls that "Mother never knew when to expect him". Each year RJ stayed one night at Ayr Show and one night at the Highland Show. He flew for the first time in 1961 to be honoured by Her Majesty the Queen and to receive the MBE for services to agriculture. The outward flight to London was rather poor, but the homeward one was so good that he wished that in future he could fly to Ayr. As to his father's story-telling, Vincent has said that with a new story he would tell it once and if it was not a great success he would try it again somewhere else, in case it was badly told. If there was no improvement with the story, he would drop it altogether.

The Rev RJ McIlmoyle's was a household name, for more than half-a-century, across the North of Ireland and further afield. He was as well-known on the public platform in Enniskillen as in Islandmagee, as well-known at the sheep sale-ring in Lanark, Scotland, as among the exhibitors at the Royal Ulster Agricultural Show, Balmoral, Belfast. But the Rev RJ was first and foremost an able preacher of the Everlasting Gospel and a faithful and beloved pastor of those committed to his care. I heard him preach several times in the Kilraughts Reformed Presbyterian Church, where I was brought up. Strangely enough, I can remember only one of the texts he used: "Now in the place where He was crucified there was a garden, and in the garden a new sepulchre wherein was never man yet laid" (John 19:41). The date was Sabbath, 24 October 1954. The Rev RJ and the minister of Kilraughts, the Rev James Blair, had officially exchanged pulpits for the day, prior to the Northern Presbytery's visitation of Kilraughts. Fellow ministers have lately been recalling to me that for special services RJ delighted in expounding the Saviour's words, "Launch out into the deep", while another favourite theme was "The mountain-top experiences". A perusal of my diaries then reminds me of the wireless broadcasts made

INTERNATIONAL FUND FOR IRELAND

PO Box 2000 Belfast BT4 3SA
Telephone: Belfast 768832
Fax: Belfast 63313

PO Box 2000 Dublin 2
Telephone: Dublin 780655
Fax: Dublin 712116

Rev Robert Hanna BA
38 Grove Road
Kells
Ballymena
BT42 3LR

28 May 1991

Dear Mr Hanna

Thank you for your letter of 21 May referring to your research of the Rev R J McIlmoyle. I do have vague personal recollection of Rev McIlmoyle but I am afraid that I have no documents which are relevant.

I have however sent a copy of your letter and cutting to my cousin Alastair McGuckian of Masstock, who is a son of Sandy McGuckian and may be able to help you.

Your project is a very worthy one and I wish you every success.

Yours sincerely

JOHN B McGUCKIAN

FARMING LIFE

Saturday, June 8, 1991

- J B McGuckian, the new president of Ballymena Show, with Robert Orr, chairman of the executive committee.

from time to time by RJ McIlmoyle. The programme, "For Northern Ireland Farmers", broadcast on the Northern Ireland Home Service, quite frequently included Sandy McGuckian of Cloughmills, the expert on pigs, and the Covenanting minister of Dervock, the expert on sheep. Sandy McGuckian died in 1952 and the *AA McGuckian Memorial Volume*, edited by Prof AE Muskett, was a fitting tribute to his memory. More than twenty-six years have passed since the Rev Robert John McIlmoyle of Dervock died, on 18 May 1965. Of late I have found great pleasure in researching this biography and I trust that readers old enough to remember him, as well as younger ones, will find a story to amuse them and something from one of the sermons to challenge them as to their relationship to God.

Lives of great men all remind us
We must make our lives sublime
And departing leave behind us
Foot-prints in the sands of time

ACKNOWLEDGEMENTS Material has been taken from *The Minutes of the Synod of the Reformed Presbyterian Church of Ireland, The Covenanter, The Reformed Presbyterian Witness*, the *Fasti of the Reformed Presbyterian Church of Ireland*, the *Memorial Volume of the Tercentenary of the National Covenant of Scotland*, the *Northern Whig*, the *Belfast News Letter, Belfast Telegraph, Ballymena Observer, Londonderry Sentinel* and *Mid-Ulster Mail*. I appreciated greatly the help given by Neil Johnston ('Ulster Diary') in the *Belfast Telegraph* and 'Roamer' (the one and only Louis Malcolm) in the *News Letter*, also by the *Ballymena Guardian*, the *Ballymena Times*, the *Ballymoney Times*, the *Coleraine Chronicle* (Mr W "Speedy" Moore) and the *Northern Constitution* in appealing to readers for material such as newspaper cuttings, photographs *etc*. On Radio Ulster's "Sunday Sequence" (28 April 1991) the life and work of the late Rev RJ McIlmoyle were well featured by the Rev Dr Bert Tosh, senior producer of religious programmes, and to him we are indebted. The scrapbooks lent by Miss Eileen Kerr and Mr W Norman McConaghie proved very useful, as did materials, including photographs, from Messrs Vincent H McIlmoyle (son), Mr Robert J Bleakly and George Wright; also from Miss Margaret White, Mrs Anne Smith, Mrs J Graham and Mrs S McGregor. Many others responded with different contributions, such as McIlmoyle stories, and these are acknowledged elsewhere in these pages. I have appreciated the help of the Linen Hall Library, Belfast; also Coleraine Library and Ballymena Library for microfilm facilities and print-out copies. Assistance in various ways has also been given by Messrs James Donnelly, John Hanna, Verdun Wright, Dr Haldane Mitchell (RJ's grandson), Mrs Hilda Cusick, Mrs A Smith, James Gribben and Samuel Johnston; and not forgetting my wife Isa for her continuing patience and understanding.

Finally, sincere thanks from myself and the denomination in which Rev RJ McIlmoyle was the longest serving minister go to the Mid-Antrim Historical Group, where I have enjoyed the company of many friends over the last three seasons, for undertaking this second publication and in particular to its energetic and efficient Secretary, Mr Eull Dunlop, for editorial work. With any errors of omission or commission we crave your tolerance. **RH**

Kellswater Manse, 38 Grove Road, Kells, Ballymena, Co Antrim,
BT42 3LR

"Which reminds me Robert – you have not been evident amongst MY flock recently"

EDITORIAL "The denomination, with ideas born of other ages, still preserves a lingering but a decaying existence in the locality." Thus the hardly sympathetic judgment of Thomas Camac, when discussing the Covenanters of Carnaff in his 'History of the Parish of Derrykeighan', first published in 1908 (reprinted in 1930). How long, then, did Camac expect RJ McIlmoyle, the lately-installed pastor of that little flock, to retain a congregation? At the other end of the twentieth century we look back and marvel at both McIlmoyle's length of ministry and also at his parallel involvement in the community to an extent of which Camac, in other remarks, seems not to have believed a Covenanter capable. A new history of the parish would therefore have to include the very material found hereafter, even if, after an excursion into Armoy athletics in 1990, the Mid-Antrim Historical Group has again transgressed its natural boundaries, has strayed from the immediate fold, so to speak. But Robert Hanna, a regular supporter of our various activities, has once more urged us to look north. Doubly qualified, as a presbyter who is also a son of the northern soil, he has researched with relish one of his illustrious predecessors in the Reformed Presbyterian ministry, so much so that this slow-footed writer has sometimes had difficulty in keeping up with one who claims an athletic past; indeed, at one point, I had temporarily to 'stay proceedings', until other mountains were duly moved. But the job has now got done and, without doubt, has been very well worth doing. Exploits of another County Antrim 'character' have been committed to paper, "while it is day". And that, after all, is our essential business.

Already in 1991 our local historical activity (in happy association with Antrim & District Historical Society) has highlighted the differing personalities of Bonar Thompson, who grew up to clod swarry-breed in the Eastern Reformed Meeting House at Eskylane, and John Carey, whose reputation still provokes intense debate in and around Duneane. If, as Bob Foy reports, his fellow enthusiast, Nelson Montgomery, always salutes the Covenanting church at Dervock, in memory of the sheep farmer who was long its incumbent, then let a wider company, within and without that denomination, now also accord him posthumous honour. For McIlmoyle was obviously a rare character, as many contributors (to whom hearty thanks!) here bear unanimous witness. This editor was both amused and moved by sections of their cumulative testimony. It is fervently hoped, therefore, that the spirit of the whole man has been accurately reflected in what Robert Hanna's way of working requires us to call this scrapbook. For while the Mid-Antrim Historical Group, as such, has no theological opinions, and this, of course, is not an official publication of the Reformed Presbyterian Church, the fair-minded student of local history (he who will happily permit others to be distinctive in a day when too simple comprehensivism is more frequently required) will recognise that our subject (who obviously had his own variation on a theme) must be read in context. Here, inter alia, is a compendium of Covenanting cultural heritage, not its first reflection in a growing corpus of publications. As already explained in 'Mid-Antrim, Part 2', the volume of essays published earlier this year, out of Adam Loughridge's lecture (1985) on "The Covenanters in County Antrim" came my edition of the late Superintendent Robert Buchanan's 'Short History' of Kellswater, 'Capital of Covenanting', published by the congregation in 1989. And it was there, near the Shankbridge, that our bus-runs on 30 June 1989 and 15 June 1990 were made more than welcome. It was perhaps because of that harmony that Robert Hanna felt moved to request publication of his tribute to Steve and Charlie McCooke. Now follows this compilation which gives much information about a man of whom I had heard a little from my former colleague in Cambridge House Boys' GS, Elizabeth McMaster (nee Donnelly), whose father makes his own very literate contribution hereafter. And the whole has made me think of a kinsman's words in defence of the Rev Samuel Dill (1772-1845) of Donoughmore: "I am well aware of the prevalent impression that farming is incompatible with the full and faithful execution of the ministerial office; and this impression, it must be admitted, is not altogether groundless. There have been, unfortunately, some notable instances of ministers who have allowed themselves to be dragged down to a lower level by the rude associations and coarse secularities with which farming operations had brought them into contact. The official dignity being lowered, the ministerial influence was correspondingly lessened; their minds lost, by degrees, much of that aptitude for the higher intellectual pursuits which are proper to their calling, and becoming, it may be, also somewhat impaired in the tone of spiritual feeling, were so far forth unfitted for the peculiar functions of the ministerial office. Still, ministerial farming has been condemned by many without reason, and without discrimination; often, I apprehend, because it is considered undignified, rather than because it hinders ministerial efficiency. It is not, however, so much the thing itself, as the manner of doing it, that will be found to be objectionable. In the case before us, I have no hesitation in affirming that Mr Dill's occupation of a large farm did not tend in the least to lower his social position or to detract from his ministerial efficiency." Consider, then, RJ McIlmoyle as pastor of two flocks.

Once again it is a more than pleasant duty to return thanks to Sylvia Hamilton, Ballymena Borough Council, for processing as much as possible of what was very diffuse material, before the rest was put into the hand of our usual printer. Special thanks must also be returned to our advertisers and other sponsors, and very especially to Mr Vincent McIlmoyle, Limavady. We trust that he finds that all here has been done decently and in order. So, shall any good thing come out of Dervock? In 1810 John Smith of Ballymena, a poet upon whom Ivan Herbison, a contemporary of Carnaff's present pastor loci, keeps a constant eye, found its one long street tedious ("from the uniformity of its houses, the eye of the traveller is fatigued before he reaches the end of it"), but it is hoped that, on Friday, 8 November 1991, Dervock will not be the least of all the towns of North Antrim. Will all roads lead, that night, to the launch scheduled for 8 o'clock? **ED**

NOBODY KNOWS MY AGE ..... or do they? Even in death, RJ was a step ahead, so to speak. On 11 July 1991, when the Editor, briefed by Robert Hanna, consulted the index of births (1875) in the General Register Office, Dublin, there was our man promised at 6/490. But then a hiccup. There was no such name at that number; which is where the native wit of the attendant, James Gunning, was all important. Someone had long since made a slip, but in 1991 Robert John McIlmoyle was found by a chance check at 6/940.

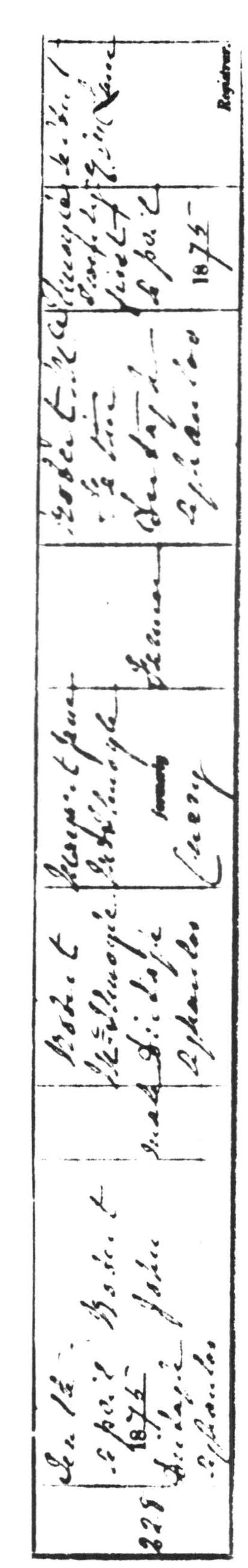

DOYEN OF DERVOCK

Stupid are sheep, they oft times stray,
Even with shepherds present,
Though without, one can fall a prey
To wolves, which is not pleasant.
All we like sheep have gone astray,
Though Shepherd Good is ours,
If we persist on our own way,
What should be sweet oft sours.
Shepherd indeed, RJ McIlmoyle,
Of flocks and congregations,
He patiently with both did toil,
And that for generations.
The RP Church recorded lore,
Anent that renowned servant,
Installed Dervock 1904,
His zeal for duty fervent.
Professor Adam Loughridge, did
Fasti compile and edit,
A calendar where naught is hid
Of detail that brings credit.
And so for three-score years, RJ
Till nineteen and sixty-four,
Kept Border Leicesters, that many's a day
At shows would often score.
His congregation he tended well,
For all of that time forby,
And very many records tell
Of a worth none dare decry.
Great Ulster Farmers' Union man,
Involved from its very founding,
To meetings here and yonder ran,
Gave those opposed a pounding.
He championed the farmers' lot,
In those lean years a blessing;
They were his care, and so why not
Their welfare be assessing?
A pastor who proclaimed the Word
With steadfastness and feeling,
Did faithfully declare his Lord
With messages appealing.
In all the varied roles he filled,
The one where most folk knew him,
Was when as chairman, then he thrilled
The crowds who came to view him.
Those were the days, I should say nights,
When rural halls heard laughter,
As tales were told that brought delight,
Whiles sore sides morning after.
Thus wisely Robert Hanna got
Eull Dunlop's assistance,
To bind this tribute in one lot,
Preserving its existence.
Herein then for posterity,
Are yarns that great man spun,
Tell them again in verity,
They are wisdom every one.
RJ McIlmoyle footprints left,
Plain on the sands of time;
Although we be of him bereft,
Recollections are sublime.
James G Kenny, "The Cottage",
Ballygarvey, Ballymena, 15 December 1990

ROBERT McILMOYLE & FAMILY
about the turn of the century?

Back (left): Andrew Ferguson, died aged 80; Sarah Moore, died aged 96; Robert John, died aged 90; Jane Hall, died aged 98; **front**: Matthew, died 1941; Mrs Margaret Jane McIlmoyle, died aged 95; Elizabeth, died 1929; Mr Robert McIlmoyle, died aged 92; William Payne, died 1919; Thomas Alfred, died aged 83; **sitting**: Margaret, died aged 90

1896-1898

At the first International Convention of the Reformed Presbyterian Churches, held in Edinburgh from 27 June to 3 July 1896, the name of RJ McIlmoyle, Limavady, was in the list of members in attendance. He was then a student at Magee College, Londonderry and would graduate GAMC in 1897 and commence his studies at the Reformed Presbyterian Theological Hall that autumn. He was then 22 years of age, having been born (as we now know) on 10 April 1875.

THE COMMITTEE OF SUPERINTENDENCE OF THE THEOLOGICAL HALL.

Your Committee met in the Library, College Street South, Belfast, on 9th November, 1897. Only one Student presented himself for examination, viz., Mr. R. J. M'Ilmoyle, who had obtained the Certificate of Arts in Magee College, Londonderry. Mr. M'Ilmoyle is a member of the Limavady Congregation, and is under the care of the Western Presbytery. The examination being sustained, he was enrolled as a Theological Student of the first year.

Owing to the ill-health of Professor Houston, and in order to give him further time for the preparation of his lectures, as well as to save time and expense, your Committee decided that the Student should meet with Professor Dick at his residence during the first term, and with Professor Houston at his residence during the second term.

In the evening of the day on which the Committee met, the opening lecture of the Session was delivered in the Hall by the Moderator of Synod, the Rev. William Russell, M.A., the subject being, "*Submission to Christ, the Note of the True Church.*" Mr. Russell has since complied with the request of his audience by publishing the lecture in the "Covenanter."

CLOSE OF THE SESSION.

The Session ended on 8th March, when Mr. M'Ilmoyle was examined orally before the Committee by the Professors; and he was, by written examination, awarded the Mawhinney Bursary.

Report to Synod, 1898

It will be of interest to take a look at the Roll of Synod in 1900.

MINUTES OF THE PROCEEDINGS

—OF—

THE REFORMED PRESBYTERIAN SYNOD

IN IRELAND

MDCCCC.

SESSION I.

At Belfast, the 28th day of May, 1900.

Constitution

THE Synod of the Reformed Presbyterian Church in Ireland met, and, after a discourse by the Moderator, the Rev. Ezek. Teaz, founded on John vi. 15—"When Jesus therefore perceived that they would come and take him by force to make him a king, he departed again into a mountain himself alone"—was constituted with prayer, by the Moderator, the Rev. Ezek. Teaz.

Roll

The Commissions of Ruling Elders having, according to Synodical arrangement, been sent to the Clerk, a Roll was formed as follows:—

NORTHERN PRESBYTERY.

Ministers.	*Elders.*	*Congregations.*
J. Ramsey, LL.B.	Jas. Warnock	Ballymoney
J. D. Houston, A.B.	R. J. M'Afee	B'clabber, Coleraine
A. M. Thompson, A.M.	Ephraim M'Fall	B'laggan, B'money
J. A. S. Stewart	Saml. Chestnutt, *alt.* D. Taggart	Dervock
H. K. Mack, A.B.	Wm. Mayberry	Drimbolg & Magherafelt, Portglenone
	Jas. Warwick	Kellswater
J. M'C. Cromie	Thos. Loughridge	Kilraughts, B'money
		Cloughmills
		Garvagh
	Wm. M'Aleese	Ringrash, Coleraine
*S. H. Kennedy, A.B		Antioch, Syria

* Absent from all the Sessions.

SOUTHERN PRESBYTERY.

Ministers.	*Elders.*	*Congregations*
Wm. M'Knight		Ballylane, Markethill
Wm Russell, A.M.		Ballenon, Poyntzpass
A. Holmes	Thomas Scott	Crievagh, Ballybay
		Fairview, C'blayney
Gawin Douglas	Richd. Copeland	Loughbrickland
A. S. Lyons	Robert Long	Newry
J. T. Potts, A.B.	Jas. S. Moffet	Rathfriland
*W. S. Ferguson		Grange, Stewartstown

EASTERN PRESBYTFRY.

Ministers.	*Elders.*	*Congregations*
S. R. M'Neilly, A.B.	Wm. Martin, *alt.* Saml. Graham	Bailiesmills, Lisburn
A. M. Stavely	Saml. Kennedy	Ballyclare
John Lynd, D.D.	S. Agnew, *alt.* John Donnelly	Belfast, Dublin Road
Torrens Boyd	Wm. Corry, *alt.* Saml. Douglas	Dromara
*Matthew Hodge	Wm. Donaldson	Killinchy
Geo. Benaugh, D.D.	Wm. J. Millikin, *alt.* Wm. Reid	Knockbracken, Belfast
S. G. Kennedy, LL.D.	Saml. MacKeown, *alt.* W. M'Coubry	Belfast, College St. S.
Robert Allen		Newtownards
Ezekiel Teaz	J. J. Draffin	Liverpool
James Dick, A.M.	Thos. Hutchinson, *alt.* John Potts	Belfast, Trinity Street
*Jas. Martin, A.M., M.D.		Antioch, Syria
*Walter M'Carroll		Geelong, Australia
		Dromore, Co. Down
	James M'Dowell	Larne

WESTERN PRESBYTERY.

Ministers.	*Elders.*	*Congregations*
Joseph M'Ewen	Jas. Buchanan, *alt.* Joseph Sayers	Bready, Strabane
Wm. Scott	Jas. Galbraith	Convoy
S. Ferguson, A.B.	Joseph M'Eldowney	Faughan
S. Kennedy, A.B.	Wm. S. Wilson	Limavady
R. H. Davidson	Joseph Hall, *alt.* Thos. Mathers	Londonderry
*R. A. M'Farlane, B.D.		Stranorlar
Wm. Dick, A.M.	Jas. Marshall	Mulvin

* Absent from all the Sessions.

Moderator addresses the Court

I. The Moderator addressed the Court, and requested the brethren to choose a successor to him in the Moderator's Chair.

Report of the Committee of Superintendence of the Theological Hall submitted to Synod in 1900: It is the pleasant duty of your Committee to report that four students attended our Hall during the Session 1899-1900. Of these, two were enrolled at the opening of the Session in November, viz

Mr. Samuel Hanna, B.A., of Kilraughts Congregation; and Mr. James Edgar, of Dublin Road, Belfast, Congregation. Mr. T. A. M'Ilfatrick, B.A., has completed two Sessions; and Mr. M'Ilmoyle, having completed the prescribed Theological course, has been recommended to his Presbytery for Licence to preach the Gospel. A Licentiate of the United States Covenanter Church —Mr. J. M. Johnston—also attended.

The Entrance and Bursary Examinations were held in the first week in November. Mr. Hanna gained the Mawhinney Bursary; and prizes of £4, £3, and £3 were given to Mr. M'Ilfatrick, Mr. M'Ilmoyle, and Mr. Edgar respectively. At the close of the Session the Archibald Bursary was awarded to Mr. M'Ilfatrick, and a prize (two-thirds Archibald Bursary) to Mr. Hanna.

The Professors' Reports are as follow :—

Professor Dick's Report—

"In the Department of Hebrew, the first-year students engaged in the study of grammar mainly. The exercises in this included translation and retranslation of sentences from the Scriptures. Toward the close of the Session the first and second Psalms were read in the Hebrew. The more advanced students, in addition to grammar lessons, read Psalms 25th to 29th inclusive.

"In Greek Exegesis the Gospel according to John, chapters 8 to 15 inclusive, formed the subject of reading and of prelections critical and expository.

"In Systematic Theology, the subjects taken up were—the Imputation of Adam's sin, the Covenant of Grace, the Person of Christ, His Mediatorial Offices, with special reference to the *nature* and *extent* of the Atonement, to His Intercession, and to His Reign over the Church and over all things for the Church, Effectual Calling, Regeneration, Faith, Justification, Perseverance of the Saints, and Subjects and Mode of Baptism.

"Some attention was given to the framing of outlines of discourses on subjects which were, for the most part, prescribed at the time.

"The attendance of the Students was regular, save for an occasional absence through indisposition, and their attention to the work of the department was highly satisfactory.

"The Public Exercises required by the Book of Government and Order were delivered.

"The conduct of the Students was marked by uniform courtesy both to me and to one another.

"JAMES DICK."

Professor Houston's Report :—

"In regard to the work of the Session, 1899-1900, I have to report—

"In the Department of Homiletics and Pastoral Theology thirteen lectures were delivered, treating various branches of the subjects. The Students read Shedd's treatise on Pastoral Theology, and the greater part of Shedd's treatise on Homiletics, and were carefully examined thereon.

"In the Department of Church History, thirteen lectures were delivered on subjects that presented themselves in the Course. The Students read and were carefully examined on the period extending over the thirteenth, fourteenth, fifteenth, and sixteenth centuries, particular attention being paid to the time of the Reformation. The text book used was Dr. Mosheim's Ecclesiastical History.

"During the Session the Students prepared skeletons of sermons and essays on alternate weeks. These were read and criticized.

"The Exercises prescribed by the Code were delivered in public by the Students, and afterwards criticized by the Professors and Students.

"The Students throughout the entire Session gave diligent attention to their work, and their conduct was in the highest degree praiseworthy.

"J. D. HOUSTON."

The closing Lecture of the Session was given, on the 13th March, by the Rev. Ezekiel Teaz, Moderator of Synod.

The
Reformed Presbyterian Church of Ireland

II. The Rev. Wm. Dick proposed, and the Rev. R. H. Davidson seconded, "That the Rev. Saml. Kennedy, A.B., Limavady, be appointed Moderator for the ensuing year." Passed unanimously. Mr. Kennedy took the Chair, and addressed the Court.

Rev. S. Kennedy, B.A chosen Moderator

MODERATOR:

REV. SAMUEL KENNEDY, A.B., Limavady.

CLERK:

REV. PROF. J. D. HOUSTON, A.B., Coleraine.

PROFESSORS:

Systematic Theology, Hebrew and Biblical Criticism—Rev. James Dick, A.M., Belfast.

Church History and Pastoral Theology—Rev. J. D. Houston, A.B., Coleraine.

TRUSTEES OF SYNOD'S FUNDS:

Rev. Prof. Dick, A.M., Belfast	Mr. Wm. Reid, Newtownards
Mr. John Porter, Belfast	Mr. James Macdonald, Waterside, Londonderry
Mr. S. Graham, Bailiesmills	

GENERAL TREASURER:

MR. WILLIAM REID, Newtownards.

HONORARY SOLICITOR TO THE SYNOD:

MR. T. C. HOUSTON, LL.B., Belfast.

COMMITTEE OF SUPERINTENDENCE OF THE THEOLOGICAL HALL:

The Professors	Rev. John Lynd, D.D.
Rev. Wm. Dick, A.M.	Rev. A. M. Thompson, A.M.
Rev. J. M'C. Cromie	Rev. H. K. Mack, A.B.
Rev. S. G. Kennedy, LL.D.	Rev. J. T. Potts, A.B.
Rev. R. A. M'Farlane, B.D.	Rev. S. R. M'Neilly, A.B., Con.

1900 On 2 May the Western Presbytery had licensed Robert John McIlmoyle to preach the gospel. He soon accepted a unanimous call to Ballyclare congregation.

—**Ordination of Mr. R. J. M'Ilmoyle. Ballyclare.** —The Eastern Presbytery met at Ballyclare on Thursday, September 6th, for the purpose of ordaining Mr. R. J. M'Ilmoyle, Licentiate of the Western Presbytery, to the ministry of the Gospel. After preliminary exercises, conducted by the Rev. Dr. Kennedy, the Rev. E. Teaz preached an appropriate sermon from the text Isaiah l. 4. The Rev. Prof. Dick then explained and defended Presbyterian ordination. The narrative of the steps leading to the ordination having been given by the Rev. R. Allen, the Rev. Dr. Benaugh proposed the usual formula of questions, and led in the ordination prayer. The Rev. Dr. Lynd then addressed the newly-ordained minister, and the Rev. T. Boyd the congregation. Afterwards the members of the Presbytery and a number of friends were entertained by the congregation to dinner in the Central Dining Rooms, Ballyclare. The Rev. Dr. Benaugh, Moderator of Presbytery, presided. In the evening a social meeting of the congregation, to welcome Mr. M'Ilmoyle, was held in the church. Dr. Lynd occupied the chair. Addresses were delivered by the following:—Revs. A. M. Stavely, E. Teaz, and Prof. Dick, of the Eastern Presbytery; S. Kennedy, of the Western Presbytery; R. J. M'Ilmoyle, the newly-ordained minister; D. Cummins, H. C. Meeke, and J. T. Doherty, of the General Assembly. Solos were given by Messrs. Thomas Bailie and Andrew Cunningham. A recitation was given by Mr. David Kennedy. A most enjoyable meeting was brought to a close by the singing of the 133rd Psalm and the pronouncing of the benediction.

Reformed Presbyterian Church, Ballyclare
(photograph courtesy of the Rev Samuel L Reid)

In making reference to the ordination and installation, the Eastern Presbytery report, signed by George Benaugh (Moderator) and Robert Allen (Clerk), to the 1901 Synod stated: "It is to be hoped that our young brother will be honoured in carrying on the work in that field where his faithful and devoted predecessors, Rev William Russell and Rev AM Stavely, laboured so long and successfully".

On 24 July 1901 the marriage of Robert John McIlmoyle and Matilda Louise Hopkins took place in Limavady Reformed Presbyterian Church. The officiating minister was the Rev Samuel Ferguson, minister (1881-1928) of Faughan RP Church, although the minister of Limavady at that time was the Rev Samuel Kennedy who served there from 1896 to 1924.

No.	When Married.	[illegible]	[illegible]	Condition.	Rank or Profession.	Residence at the Time of Marriage.	Father's Name and Surname.	Rank or Profession [illegible]
31	24th July 1901	Robert John McIlmoyle	Full	Bachelor	Presbyterian Clergyman	Dirtagh Parish of Aghanloo	Robert McIlmoyle	Farmer
		Matilda Louise Hopkins	Full	Spinster	—	Bolea Parish of Drumachose	David Hopkins	Farmer

Married in the above registered building according to the Usages of the Reformed Presbyterian Church, by licence, by me, Saml Ferguson, Officiating Minister.

This Marriage was solemnized between us: Robert John McIlmoyle, Matilda Louise Hopkins
in the Presence of us: Matthew McIlmoyle, Katie M. Cresswell

Presented to the Annual Meeting of Synod, 1902

CAUSES OF HUMILIATION AND THANKSGIVING.

The Rev. R. J. M'Ilmoyle presented the Draft of Causes of Humiliation and Thanksgiving. The Draft was accepted by Synod, on the motion of Rev. G. Douglas, seconded by Prof. Lynd.

CAUSES OF HUMILIATION.

1. We would humble ourselves in the presence of Almighty God on account of our many sins and shortcomings. Our opportunities for doing God service have been many and great, but too often we have let them slip. We have not regarded as we should the saying of Christ, "Herein is My Father glorified, that ye bear much fruit."

2. We lament, as a Church, the little advantage to which we have used the heritage of Divine truth handed down to us through the instrumentality of faithful, covenanted forefathers. God has revealed to us great and glorious truths, but we have not been as active as we ought to have been in making these truths known to others.

3. We lament the fact that the time-honoured and scriptural practice of meeting together for social worship is fast dying out among the members of our congregations. Many are thus denying themselves what is an appointed means of grace, and, at the same time, a source of joy and comfort. "Then they that feared the Lord spake often one to another: and the Lord hearkened, and heard it, and a book of remembrance was written before Him for them that feared the Lord, and that thought upon His name. And they shall be Mine, saith the Lord of hosts, in that day when I make up My jewels; and I will spare them as a man spareth his own son that serveth him."

4. We lament a growing disregard on the part of many for the claims of the Sabbath; and deplore the fact that the example of the King, in visiting picture galleries and places of amusement on the Lord's Day, is not likely to increase reverence for the Day of Rest on the part of his subjects.

5. We mourn over the fact that while the servants of Christ are not altogether neglecting their duty to be witnesses for Him unto the uttermost parts of the earth, there are still so many of the world's inhabitants living in gross darkness as to the things divine.

6. It is great cause for sorrow that our own nation, although suffering for almost three years, through the war in South Africa, what we believe to be the merited punishment of heaven on account of the rejected claims of Christ, shows no signs of repentance.

CAUSES OF THANKSGIVING.

1. We thank God, the Giver of all good, for His greatest gift—the Son of His love, Christ Jesus; for the Word of Truth that reveals the person and work of the Saviour; and for the Holy Spirit that gives the truth effect.

2. We thank God for the spiritual privileges we enjoy. The means of grace are dispensed in our midst. We can worship the God of our fathers in the closet, in the social gathering, and in the public assembly, there being none to make afraid or annoy.

3. We thank God for His goodness to our Church in ennabling her to adhere firmly to her testimony for the truths of Revelation, when there are so many enticements to desert the ground she has occupied so long and so honourably; for such an increase in the number of candidates for the ministry as we have experienced of late; and for the fact that our ministerial ranks have been unbroken by death during the past year.

4. We rejoice that while devoted members of the Church are called away, from time to time, from the labours and sufferings of earth, there is still a seed to do God service; that it cannot be said of the new generations that arise that they do not know our spiritual Joseph; that the children are coming forth instead of the fathers, and taking upon themselves the vows of God, pledging them to the faithful service of the Master.

5. We thank God for increasing interest, on the part of our own and other Churches, in the cause of Missions. The Churches in general are laying more to heart than formerly the command of Christ, "Go ye into all the world, and preach the Gospel." The good seed is being carried into far-off lands, and in many cases God is rewarding the labourers with an abundant harvest. The kingdom of Christ is being extended. The Redeemer is seeing of the travail of His soul. It is an increased ground of gratitude that we have such encouraging reports in relation to the success of our home missionaries in the work of carrying the Gospel to our benighted fellow-countrymen.

6. We thank God for temporal blessings—for the measure of health and strength we enjoy, for domestic and social comforts that are ours, and for the liberty (civil as well as religious) experienced in our land.

1904

Dervock—Installation of Rev. R. J. M'Ilmoyle.—On Wednesday, August 31st, the Northern Presbytery installed the Rev. R. J. M'Ilmoyle to the ministry and pastoral charge of the Congregation of Dervock. The Rev. A. Holmes preached. Rev. J. Ramsey, LL.B., expounded Presbyterian Ordination, and emphasised the right of the Reformed Presbyterian Church to dispense the ordinance. Rev. Prof. Houston, B.A., gave a narrative of the steps leading up to the installation, and addressed a charge to the newly-ordained minister, who was solemnly set apart with prayer by the Rev. Prof. Dick, M.A. A charge was given to the congregation by Rev. T. E. M'Elfatrick, B.A. All the members of Presbytery were present, and the other Presbyteries of the Church were represented by Revs. S. R. M'Neilly, B.A.; S. Kennedy, B.A., Limavady; and S. Hanna, B.A., Larne.

After the close of the service the congregation entertained the members of Presbytery and a large company of friends to dinner. The Moderator of Presbytery (Rev. J. M'C. Cromie) presided. At the close of the dinner, Rev. Profs. Dick and Houston expressed the thanks of the Presbytery for the repast so hospitably provided, and spoke in highest terms of praise of the spirit which has always prevailed in this historic congregation of our Church. Mr. Robert M'Kinney replied on behalf of Dervock Congregation.

In the evening the newly-installed minister was welcomed in the meeting-house by a large and enthusiastic assembly. Rev. J. Ramsey, LL.B., presided, and the addresses given were worthy of the occasion. All present greatly enjoyed the meeting, and high hopes are entertained regarding the happy settlement effected.

The meeting house at Carnaff, Dervock

As a background to the new pastorate, we turn gratefully (with permission given) to *A Covenant Heritage, the Historical Sketch of Dervock Reformed Presbyterian Church, 1783-1983*, by the Rev Trevor McCauley:

The fifth minister of Dervock was Rev. James Alexander Smyth Stewart who had served in Limavady for eight years. Brought up in the Drimbolg congregation and educated at Queen's College and the Theological Hall, Belfast, Mr. Stewart was installed on 21st August, 1895.

Rev. James A. S. Stewart.

Mr. Stewart was the first minister to come to Dervock with some pastoral experience. All the previous ministers had been licentiates. Bringing with him what he had learned in his former charge, he made an immediate impact on the congregation, and contributed greatly to its work and witness. The same was also true of Mrs. Stewart.

Mrs. Stewart, having rendered valuable service to the Woman's Missionary Association in Limavady, was a welcome addition to the ranks of the Dervock W. M. A., which was just two years old. Providing wise and useful leadership in those early and formative years, she helped establish a strong W. M. A. in the congregation. The generous giving to Mission Work in the years following is evidence of this.

Mr. Stewart, while an earnest and gifted preacher and an attentive pastor, exerted greatest influence among the young people in the congregation. Being closely associated with the Covenanters' Union, a society set up by Synod in 1893 with the aim : "the spiritual education of the young and their instruction in the principles and position of the Covenanting church," he encouraged those in the Dervock Sabbath School to study the course set by the Covenanters' Union and enter for the annual examination held every November. In the years around the turn of the 20th century, Dervock was usually well represented in the examination, and it was not uncommon for them to be awarded the highest honours.

As a member of the Presbytery, Mr. Stewart never spared himself in helping his fellow ministers. If through illness any of them were unable to preach, he never failed to come to their assistance, even if it meant personal sacrifice. As the Minute on his death that was read to Synod, noted, "he kept our pulpits supplied and the doors of our mission stations open when otherwise they could have been closed."

His sudden death on 6th June, 1902, at the age of thirty-six, came as a great shock, not only to the congregation of Dervock, but to the whole Church. The week before Synod, which was to be held in Belfast from 26th May, 1902, he contracted a flu virus. With characteristic devotion to duty he travelled to Kellswater to preach on Sabbath, 25th May, however, instead of being able to go on to Synod, he had to return home being in a rather weak condition. On Wednesday, 28th May, he rose and made an effort to attend the meeting of Synod in Belfast, but was unable to go farther than the railway station at Dervock. He was again out on Thursday, and for the last time. He developed pneumonia, and from this he never recovered. On Friday morning, 6th June, he passed away.

He left a widow and four children "for whom he had been able to make no temporal provision." Such was the concern for their welfare that within days of his death a fund, known as The Stewart Fund, was set up "with the object of helping the widow to bring up and educate her children." Almost immediately, subscriptions amounting to £200 were received. The Executive Committee of this fund, whose duty it was to administer it, was comprised as follows : Chairman - John Baxter, County Councillor, Ballymoney; Vice-Chairman - Rev. John McC. Cromie, Pinehill Manse, Knockahollet, Ballymoney; Treasurer - Joseph Lamont, Cabra, Ballymoney; Secretary - Rev. John Ramsey, Ballymoney; Members - Rev. J. B. Armour, Ballymoney; William Moffett, Ballymoney; James Gardner, Ballynahone; James McKee, Ballylaggan.

The Rev Trevor McCauley, in his bicentenary sketch, continues:

A "Diamond Jubilee" Ministry

Following the sudden and unexpected death of Rev. James A. S. Stewart in 1902, the congregation had a two-year vacancy. In seeking a successor, Dervock turned to the minister of Ballyclare, the Rev. Robert John McIlmoyle. Brought up in Limavady, Mr. McIlmoyle had been in business for a number of years before entering the gospel ministry. Upon completing his studies at Magee College, Londonderry, and the Theological Hall, Belfast, he gave four years service in Ballyclare. He was installed as pastor of the Dervock congregation on 31st August, 1904, and began a ministry that was to last sixty years. This wrote the name of Dervock indelibly in the record books in that it, in only 181 years of existence, had two sixty-year ministries — Rev. William J. Stavely (1804 — 1864) and Rev. Robert J. McIlmoyle (1904 — 1964).

(see the list of ministers of Dervock RP Church)

1905 The annual soirée was held on 6 December. There was a splendid attendance and an enjoyable and profitable evening was spent. Rev RJ McIlmoyle presided. Addresses were delivered by Revs E Ritchie (Original Secession), J Pyper, J Colhoun, A Crothers (Presbyterian) and J Ramsay. Miss Davidson sang very acceptably. Recitations were given by Mr JN McFall and selections on the gramophone by Mr AS Ross. A note of thanks was passed on the motion of Mr R Clarke, seconded by Mr John Rea.

1906 On 9 January the Northern Presbytery ordained Mr James A Lyons BA to the pastorate of Cullybackey congregation. Rev RJ McIlmoyle preached. In the April issue of *The Covenanter*, Dervock Church News reported that "some time ago a cow was driven into the Manse yard and has been supplying the minister and his wife and family with milk and butter since. The gift, quietly and unostentatiously made, is a strong testimony to the good feeling existing between the Rev RJ McIlmoyle and his devoted and spirited congregation." The Sabbath School in connection with the congregation had its annual excursion to Ballycastle on Friday, 15 June. The weather was all that could be desired. Accompanying the excursion were Mr RJ Carswell and Miss Carswell and Master John Nevin Carson (nephew of Mr Robert Carson, elder in Dervock congregation) from Denver congregation, USA.

On Wednesday evening, August 29, a deputation from the Bible Class and Sabbath School teachers of Dervock Sabbath School waited on Miss Carson and Miss Lizzie Carson at the home of their father, Mr Robert Carson, elder in Dervock congregation, and presented them each with a Bible and a silver-backed brush and comb, on the eve of their departure for America. On 11 September 1906 Rev William McCullough BA was ordained in Ballylaggan.

The Dervock Manse in RJ McIlmoyle's time (with modern renovations)

1907

THE COVENANTER

March 1907

CHURCH NEWS

—Miss Mary Gilmore, a member of Dervock Congregation, died some time ago after a brief illness. She had many times during her lifetime expressed it as her intention to bequeath some money to the Dervock Congregation and some to its minister. Her illness was very brief, and she had not made a will. Her brother and sisters, however, respected her wish, and handed over some time ago £15 to the congregation and £5 to the minister.

———

—On the evening of 20th November, the Moderator of Dervock Session, Rev. R. J. M'Ilmoyle, with Messrs. Clarke and Taggart, waited on Rev. J. M'C. Cromie at his residence at Kilraughts manse, and on behalf of the Session and congregation of Dervock, presented him with a cheque, in recognition of his services rendered the congregation when left without a pastor, and on account of his attention to their claims on the Estate of the late Mr. Samuel Patton, of Portrush, when the will of the deceased was being construed by the Court of Chancery and the monies bequeathed were being allocated.

Portrush.—The Interim Session met in the Lecture Hall on the evening of the 4th December. With the Session were associated Rev. Prof. Houston and Rev. R. J. M'Ilmoyle. The Moderator of Session, Rev. J. M'C. Cromie, preached, and explained the steps which had been taken in connection with the election of the elders, put the questions in the formula, and by prayer and with the laying on of hands ordained Mr. W. J. Young to the office of the eldership ; and by prayer installed in office Messrs. Hugh M'Conaghy and Hugh Kennedy. On the request of the Session Mr. William Smith, an elder of Drimbolg Session, and Mr. M'Dowell, an elder of Ballyclabber Session, joined in the act of ordination. A solemn and impressive charge was afterwards addressed to the elders, who had just been set apart to office, by Rev. Prof. Houston, A.B. The concluding exercises were conducted by Rev. R. J. M'Ilmoyle, Dervock. After the close of the meeting, the Session and those associated with it in the work of ordination, with the newly-installed eleders, were hospitably entertained by Mrs. Close, Portrush, to whom was formally conveyed the best thanks of the company for the generous repast provided for them. It is the earnest desire of all who took part in these services that the work done, in the Name of the Head of the Church, may have resting upon it the Divine blessing.

———

1908 Relationships by family or ministerial ties across the Covenanting Church have always been affected by times of joy and rejoicing, as well as by sorrow and loss, even when there is the distance of South Down from North Antrim. For example, Alexander McLeod Stavely Lyons of Ballygan, Ballymoney, was ordained to the Gospel ministry and installed minister of Riverside, Newry, congregation on 12 June 1872. He later married Margaret Nevin, daughter of John Nevin of Carnaff, Dervock. Rev Prof T B McFarlane, in the centenary sketch of the congregation, 1845-1945, recorded that, after a fruitful ministry,

——————— on the 7th September, Mr. Lyons was called home with startling suddenness and in a most unexpected way. He was going to visit a family of the congregation at Jerrettspass, and while walking along the line from Goraghwood, owing no doubt to the noise of an approaching train, he did not observe a motor train coming behind him. He was struck by it, and instantaneously killed. He was not, for God took him. How mysterious the Providence! In a moment, and without warning, the call came, and yet it was as he would have wished, with his hands full of work in the Master's service. That same evening he was to have preached in a country School-house, on Tuesday evening he was advertised to lecture in Riverside, on "The Distinguishing Features of Evangelical Religion". On the following Sabbath he was to have conducted Communion services in Dublin but ere the Sabbath came he was called to the Marriage Supper of the Lamb. What a tragedy it would be to some, if with equal suddenness they were summoned into the presence of the King! But to him so quickly taken, it was the Master's appointed time, and way. Happy are all who can, as he could, breathe the spirit of those words :–

"Just when Thou wilt, no choice for me,
Life is a gift to use for Thee.
Death is a hush'd and glorious tryst,
With Thee my King, my Saviour, Christ".

The news of the death of Mr. Lyons quickly spread filling hearts with sadness. To Riverside congregation, to a wide circle of friends, and to the whole Christian community, it brought consternation. We can but dimly imagine the heart-breaking sorrow of Mrs. Lyons, and the stricken family. Amid manifestations of sorrow on every hand, Mr. Lyons was buried in the Meeting-House Green, in the place which he himself had chosen, near to the building in which he had preached the Gospel, there to rest, with many members of his flock, who had fallen asleep, until the trumpet sounds.

Sympathetic and touching tributes to the memory of Mr. Lyons were made in the local Churches and throughout the congregations of the Covenanting Church, in this land, and in Scotland.

1909: A Purse of Sovereigns

THE COVENANTER

Church News

Dervock.—Address and Presentation.—The Annual Social Meeting of the Dervock Congregation was held on January 6th. There was a large attendance. After tea, Rev. R. J. M'Ilmoyle, Pastor, took the chair, and introduced the programme. When a few items had been disposed of, Rev. John Ramsey, LL.B., was called to the chair. He explained that he had been put in that position to give the Congregation an oppostunity of giving expression of their good will to their Pastor. Mr. Robert Carson then read an address, which spoke in high terms of the faithfulness and efficiency of Mr. M'Ilmoyle in the pulpit, the Bible class, and pastoral visitation, and also bore testimony to the interest shown in the congregation by Mrs. M'Ilmoyle. Mr. Taggart read the presentation. The Pastor replied, reciprocating the kindly feelings expressed. After the remainder of an enjoyable programme was gone through the benediction brought the proceedings to an end.

Church News

Northern Presbytery.—This Presbytery met in Ballymoney on Tuesday, 3rd November. The Moderator, Rev. J. A. Lyons, A.B., presided, and there was a large attendance of ministers and Elders Various matters of public interest were under discussion. The subject of Congregational Aid was considered, and a communication from the Convener of the Foreign Mission Committee, asking Presbytery to hold a Missionary Conference, was dealt with sympathetically. The Convener of the Temperance Committee brought under the notice of the Court, by letter, Synod's request to hold a series of meetings with the view of creating a healthier public opinion in favour of the total suppression of the liquor traffic. The question of rendering pecuniary aid to the members of the Drimbolg Congregation, in their endeavour to clear off the debt incurred by them in procuring their Manse, was fully discussed, and the action of Synod's Committee in taking steps to have an appeal to the members of the Church, on behalf of this object, put widely into circulation, at an early date, was cordially approved of. Special attention was called to Synod's resolution asking all the Congregations of the Church to engage in special prayer for an increase of faithful Gospel ministers, and the members of the Court were asked to put forth an earnest endeavour to increase the contributions annually sent in from their respective Congregations for the support of the Theological Hall. A Deputation from the Congregation of Portrush presented a Petition praying Presbytery to send four ministers [each minister to be sent for a period of three months] for a period of twelve months to labour amongst the members of the Congregation. The Deputation was authorized to promise the sum of £100 to cover the cost of carrying this arrangement into effect. Presbytery received the Petition sympathetically, and asked Rev. R. J. M'Ilmoyle, of Dervock, to take the matter into consideration and (provided his Congregation is willing to release him for three months) to undertake the pastoral over sight of the Congregation of Portrush, at the beginning of the New Year. Rev. A. Holmes, who has had three months' leave of absence, asked for six weeks' additional leave. His request was granted, and the hope was expressed that he would be able to return to his Congregation early in January. Presbytery experienced great difficulty in making arrange ments for the supply of vacant pulpits ; but ministers and Elders alike showed their willingness to deny themselves to help their brethren in their time of need. As it was impossible to finish the business, the Court agreed to stand adjourned till the second Tuesday in December.

The McIlmoyle family relaxing at the seaside (around 1910): Lewis, Vincent (on his father's knee), Mrs McIlmoyle (nursing Kathleen), and in the front Enid and Elvina

1910

Portrush.—The Northern Presbytery has made arrangements by which the Rev. R. J. M'Ilmoyle and the Rev. William M'Cullough supply the Congregation here constantly with Gospel Ordinances. The attendances, especially at the Evening Service, are on the increase, and Miss M'Crea has shown a great practical interest in the welfare of the Congregation by promising to contribute fifty pounds annually as soon as the Congregation secures a pastor. Miss M'Crea has already paid over to Rev. J. M'C. Cromie the sum of £50 to supplement the Congregation's contributions.

Northern Presbytery Conference.—A Missionary and Temperance Conference was held in the Ballymoney Meeting-house on July 26th, beginning at 2 p.m. Rev. J. M'C. Cromie, B.D., was Chairman, who, after devotional exercises, delivered an Address, which gave a high-toned introduction to the proceedings. Excellent papers were then read, Rev. W. M'Cullough, B.A., taking as his subject "Christian Temperance," Rev. John Ramsey, LL.B., "The British Covenants applied to the Temperance Question," and Rev. R. J. M'Ilmoyle "The application of Temperance Principles by the R.P. Church." The programme for the evening meeting included a Missionary Address by Rev. S. H. Kennedy, B.A., Alexandretta, and one from Rev. J. C. M'Feeters, D.D., Philadelphia. The presence and help of both these gentlemen and also of Miss Metheny* was very much appreciated. The Conference, like that of last year, was in every respect a great success. Details may be expected later on.

*** missionary from Alexandretta**

1911

Dervock.—The annual soiree was held on the evening of January 11th. Though the weather was exceedingly inclement, the house was well filled. Tea was dispensed by a number of the ladies of the Congregation. The Chairman, Rev. J. M'Elmoyle, then introduced the programme for the evening. Speeches were delivered by Revs. J. Colhoun, A. Crothers, and J. S. Pyper of the General Assembly, and Rev. F. Davidson of the O.S. Church. Apologies for non-attendance were received from Revs. J. Ramsey and W. M'Cullough. There were also recitations and musical items. An interesting variasion in the programme was the presentation of a gold watch-chain to each of the Precentors—Mr. Robert Carson and Mr. David Taggart. Mr. Robert Clarke, who has for many years acted in the capacity of Clerk of Session, was also presented with a gold watch-chain. The Chairman intimated that the cups and saucers in use that night (24 dozen in all) were the gift of the Carson Brothers to the Congregation. The meeting was brought to a close by the pronouncing of the benediction.

1911 In June/July *The Reformed Presbyterian Witness* (editor: Rev AC Gregg BA) reported as follows on the Irish delegates to the Synod of the Reformed Presbyterian Church of Scotland, held in the Christian Institute, Bothwell Street, Glasgow, on Monday 8 & Tuesday 9 May 1911:

Moderator—Rev. John M'Donald, B.D., Airdrie.
Clerk, pro tem.—Rev. A. C. Gregg, B.D., Loanhead.
Treasurer—Mr. John Irwin, 1 Hinshelwood Drive, Ibrox, Glasgow.

" The Irish Reformed Presbyterian Church's deputies, Rev. R. J. M'Ilmoyle and Mr Robert Holmes, being present, were introduced to the Court by Rev. H. Paton, and proceeded to address the meeting.

By Rev. R. J. M'ILMOYLE, Dervock.

MODERATOR, FATHERS, AND BRETHREN,—In the name and on behalf of the sister Church in Ireland we bring you greeting. Indeed, sometimes we in Ireland are apt to regard you in Scotland not so much as a sister Church, but as a part of ourselves. Your Church magazines, *The Witness* and *The Morning Watch*, are read and prized in many of our homes. *The Morning Watch* is a household word in thousands of homes in the Emerald Isle. *The Witness* brings us into close touch with your organizations and associations and Church work generally, through its "Church News," besides supplying us with much valuable family and social religious literature.

Another year has come and gone since last our delegates stood before you. At that time our representatives bore to you tidings of our sorrow and loss sustained through the death of Rev. Prof. J. D. Houston. To-night we tell you of another death, not so sudden perhaps, yet more or less unexpected. The Rev. Robert Allen, who during the whole of a long active ministerial life was never out of his pulpit a single Sabbath through ill-health, is now no more. But if we bring sad news, we are also the messengers of good tidings. During the past year we have had our ministerial ranks strengthened through the ordination of Mr A. Gilmour, M.A. The late Prof. Houston's place in the school of the prophets—a place which he adorned ever since his appointment as Professor of Church History and Pastoral Theology—has been filled by the appointment of Rev. S. G. Kennedy, LL.D. The Rev. W. J. Moffett, B.A., has taken up Prof. Houston's duties as Clerk of Synod.

The fact that you are now in session in your annual meeting of Synod reminds us of the flight of time. As the business man occasionally takes stock in order to ascertain how he stands and where he is, so Churches as well as individuals should betimes take bearings so that they may see in what relation they stand to the rocks and the quicksands. If we would be loyal and consistent members of the Church to which we belong, a knowledge of her principles on the one hand, and the application of these principles on the other hand, are absolutely necessary. Our Church has certain root principles blood-bought, which she holds dear. There are those who make little of and even despise principle, who are continually saying, "Principle or no principle, he can't be wrong whose life is in the right." With the second part of this statement we are in thorough agreement—a man whose life is right cannot be in the wrong. But that a man can be right as to his life whose principles are wrong is an impossibility. We may have principle without practice, but we cannot have God-honouring practice unless the life is governed by God-given principles.

Some seem to go on the assumption that the individual or the Church that gives to principle its proper place is thereby and on that account crippled and handicapped as regards practice. The Covenanting Church has always made much of principle, and with what results? Has she always been behind the times? Has she always reluctantly entered upon certain work only when other Churches have led the way? A Covenanter is sometimes defined as a person who doesn't vote, sometimes as a person who is old-fashioned, antiquated, behind the times. As regards the first definition we admit that with certain qualifications it is a correct definition. A Covenanter is a person who cannot by voting under present conditions in the political world deny to Christ and His law His and its proper place. As to the second definition we repudiate it in whole and altogether. We cannot be accused of a boasting spirit when we say that according to the testimony of past history Covenanters and the Covenanting Church have always taken the lead in any and every movement for good. Take the political platform. At one time the Covenanters were considered fanatics and madmen because they advocated certain principles, and in fifteen years afterwards the whole nation adopted these very principles, many sealing their testimony with their blood. The Covenanters were in the forefront. Again, take the slave trade in America. The Covenanters led the van. They were the first to lift their testimony against the evil of trafficking in human flesh and blood. So with the drink problem. More than sixty years ago the Irish Synod passed the following resolution:—"Synod unanimously disapprove of the traffic in ardent spirits, and declare that no member of the Church who opens a house for carrying on the trade shall be entitled to Church privileges." In acting thus Synod took a step far in advance of public opinion at the time. Now after sixty years the Evangelical Churches of the land generally are beginning to wake up to a consciousness of the advisability of excluding those connected in any way with the traffic from the privileges of Church membership. These are but a few of the many instances that might be adduced to show that if our Church has paid a good share of attention to principle, she has not been altogether lacking in practice.

As to our dinstinctive principles, in the forefront there is the supremacy of Christ over the nations. This is the distinctive principle that is at all events most prominently before the public. Him hath God the Father exalted to be a Prince. Civil government is an ordinance of God. "Let every soul be subject to the higher powers. There is no power but of God." This does not mean that every power that is is of God and rightly demands obedience; but that no power except it be of God or exercised in accordance with God-given rules has any just claim upon us, or any authority over us. "Wilt thou then not be afraid of the power? Do that which is good and thou shalt have praise of the same." Or, in other words, the power is ordained or ordered of God to ensure that those who are under its control do that which is good. Or, in other words still, a power or nation that comes up to the Divine standard is responsible for the conduct and actions of those who are subject to it. The constitution of such a nation should be moulded in accordance with the Word of Him who is King of kings. Civil government is an institution of God. It is not a mere fabric to the construction of which eminent statesmen have contributed from time to time. It is said that when heathen tribes converted to Christianity set about forming a

constitution or government they never think of taking anything else than the Bible as their standard. As Reformed Presbyterians we hold that civil government is of God, and that its purpose is not merely that of worldly expediency, but to secure righteousness on the part of subjects.

It is the duty of the Church to remind the nation of its responsibility and to witness against its unfaithfulness. The true Church of Christ on earth has not only something to say for herself in relation to great moral questions; it is also her function to tell the State as such what it ought to do in relation to these questions. God has given her the right, and not only so, but has laid it upon her as an obligation, to speak His Word to kings. The Church is ever praying, "Let Thy will be done on the earth even as it is done in heaven"; and it is alike her duty and privilege to call upon kings and nations to aid her as she strives for the bringing about of the time when this prayer shall be fully answered.

One of our distinctive principles then is the headship of Christ over nations as such. Now, what about the application of this principle? Is it a principle that can be applied? Is it a great principle that we can reduce to practice in our everyday lives as individuals and as nations? Some say No. The majority agree. But what does God say? This doctrine is not a mere theory, beautiful in appearance but unworkable. It has its place firm and sure in the Word of God, and demands that it be applied to the nation's everyday life. It demands that the constitution be shaped in accordance with the will of the King. It demands that the constitution be administered in accordance with the will of the King.

Again, it demands that rulers possess the qualifications prescribed by the King of kings. "He that ruleth over men must be just, ruling in the fear of God." The governmental level regarding qualification for civil rule is low, exceedingly low. The last thing that is looked for in a statesman nowadays is Scriptural qualification, which includes every qualification. When a candidate for Parliamentary honours is before the public many questions are asked. For instance—What good will he do his party's cause? Is he a progressive Liberal or a strong Conservative? Is he a staunch Unionist or a Home Ruler? But what about Scriptural qualification? What about religion? And in order to justify such conduct it is said that politics has nothing to do with religion, and religion has nothing to do with politics. Taking such premises as these, how would the matter work out, say, in relation to the drink problem—the evil of intemperance? There are many good Christian men and women who are doing a great deal for the overthrow of intemperance, but who say that religion is one thing and politics another; that the two are separate and ought to remain so. Under which head then—politics or religion—

would they put the drink problem? Is it politics? or is it religion? If it is politics, then the brewer, from the government's point of view—and this is also the temperance worker's point of view who identifies himself with the government—the brewer may be a good politician; leave it to the brewer. That, you see, would be absurd. Temperance legislation left in the hands of the brewer! Yet there is nothing unreasonable in such a course if the brewer may be regarded as a good politician. If, on the other hand, it is religion, then, as religion has nothing to do with politics, leave it out of Parliament altogether; it must be taken somewhere else. As Covenanters we say that religion has to do with everything, politics included. Let the people of a country look for and demand Scriptural qualifications on the part of its rulers. Then there would be no need for special parties in Parliament to promote this or the other moral question. Every question would then get a due share of attention.

Covenanters are true patriots, they are the keenest of politicians. The fact that their political principles do not manifest themselves in the shape of casting a vote at Parliamentary elections is not due to thoughtlessness, carelessness, or indifference. They desire to exalt Christ the King, and, as a result, to promote their country's good.

It was moved by Rev. W. Russell, seconded by Rev. J. P. Struthers, and heartily agreed to, that the cordial thanks of Synod be given to the Irish brethren for their interesting and stimulating addresses. It was agreed that the Moderator and Mr Matthew Kirkwood, elder, be appointed to visit the centenary meeting of the Irish Synod, to be held at Cullybackey on 26th June next and following days, and convey the fraternal congratulations of the Scottish Synod to the brethren there assembled.

1911

Mr. R. Holmes

ADDRESSES TO SCOTTISH SYNOD BY DELEGATES FROM IRISH SYNOD.

I.—By Mr R. Holmes, Elder, Ballymoney.

Moderator, Fathers, and Brethren,—We come laden with greetings from the Irish Church, which we convey to you now in the heartiest manner. We do not need to assure you of our deep affection. The ties which bind us together are many and varied, and it is our earnest wish that they may grow stronger with the years. This annual interchange of salutations is one of the most pleasing features of our ecclesiastical life. It is well to see the mother and daughter on terms of intimacy and mutual esteem.

Permit me to speak for a short time on a question which I think is of great importance. I refer to leakage. Now, what is the cause of the prevailing religious indifference from which every Church seems to suffer, even the most zealous? Is it not to be found in the neglect of the ordinances of religion, public, social, family, and personal? Are these attended to as they ought to be, and as they once were? We do believe that there are no better church-goers than Covenanters, and that none attend more faithfully to the observance of family worship, but we are not to compare ourselves with others. The question is not what others do, but what is our duty. Let us remember that one of the greatest wrongs inflicted upon a minister, and one of the greatest sins against God and one's own soul, is that of carelessly absenting oneself from the public ordinances of God's house. Another fruitful source of leakage is ignorance of Covenanter principles and traditions. When the Jews came into Canaan, freed for ever from the Egyptian oppressor, they were enjoined to set up memorial stones that succeeding generations might not forget what the Lord had showed His people. The young as well as the older should be conversant with a Covenanter testimony, and should be perfectly familiar with the history of the Church, especially from the First Reformation till the Revolution Settlement. What a noble biography and martyrology our Church inherits! Our portrait gallery of martyrs and confessors should be familiar to all eyes, and these characters should be hallowed names in every household.

Then another fruitful source of leakage is the practice of parents, often against the expressed wish of their minister, to whom they have sworn to render all loving obedience in the Lord, sending their children to Sabbath Schools of other denominations where our principles are not only not taught, but practically assailed. The children become fascinated with sensuous forms of worship, and enjoy and prefer being in an atmosphere which is freer from self-restraint than they would have in an old-fashioned Cameronian Sabbath School.

We have considered some of the causes of leakage; let us try to discover the remedies. Perhaps we might glance at one or two spurious remedies. We are constantly being twitted by outsiders with our diminution in numbers. "If you would cease driving away your members by the rigorous enforcement of discipline, how your Church would flourish!" Well, we are bound to admit that the Covenanter Church still keeps a close watch over the moral conduct of her members, with this as one result, that many flee from discipline and as a rule are received into some other Church without a question. But the matter of discipline is greatly misunderstood. Some regard it only as an instrument for expelling offending members. That is wholly an incorrect view. Discipline is rather an instrument for preventing anarchy in the Church, arresting law-breakers in the path of ruin, and restoring to Church privileges again after brotherly admonition, and when the transgressor shows signs of genuine sorrow and repentance. We may cause leakage by exercising discipline, but leakage caused in this way will be more than compensated for by the fact that a higher standard of character is maintained. And this in itself is a power of incalculable magnitude. "For if the salt have lost its savour, wherewith shall it be seasoned?" But we must hasten on to the consideration of a few genuine antidotes for leakage. They are three in number:—(1) organization; (2) co-operation; (3) loyalty.

(1) Organization. We should like every congregation thoroughly organized, with a healthy, well-manned Association vigorously maintaining and spreading broadcast our distinguishing principles. If we succeeded in perfecting organization, then, instead of the proclamation and dissemination of the truth of God, as apprehended by the Covenanter Church, being left to our ministers and to a layman here and there, our entire membership would be actively engaged in the noble work. True, "not by might nor by power, but by My Spirit, saith the Lord of Hosts"; yet if the "effectual, fervent prayer of a righteous man availeth much," may we not reasonably conclude that the effectual, fervent prayer of 10,000 righteous men will avail more? Still further; besides having the Synods of the various sections of our Church in close touch with all the congregations under their jurisdiction, might we not have an International Council, whose chief business would be to select suitable fields in which to organize new congregations; and also to assist in the distribution of our forces. If such a scheme as we have sketched were put into practice, we think very few of our members would wish to wander at haphazard into far countries, or if they should, the International Council would soon be on their track. Think of the hundreds of Covenanters who have left the British Isles during the last five decades, whom the Church has *not* followed with her literature and her prayers! That is one of the saddest facts on record, and a mistake which we trust will never be repeated. A well-organized, Spirit-filled, and praying Church will naturally foster a spirit of unanimity.

(2) And this brings us to our second specific, Co-operation. The enemy co-operate. We must adopt similar tactics in order to repel successfully their onslaughts. "United we stand, divided we fall." That is the testimony of history. That was the experience of the Church when in the fires of persecution. The battles of Drumclog and Bothwell Bridge are striking illustrations. It will be remembered that on the first flush of victory many joined the Covenanters. But in this multitude were found many half-hearted advocates of the cause at the battle of Bothwell. The heroes of Drumclog took their stand at the fiercest post, on the bridge, which was the key of the situation, but the new recruits slunk back at the crucial moment and allowed the enemy to mow them down like grass. At Drumclog, then, we have loyalty, unanimity, courage, victory; at Bothwell, disloyalty, discord, cowardice, defeat. As a Church we need all the stimulus and encouragement which co-operation can give. Our Church is so small that we can ill afford to waste time and energies and talents on needless controversies, when they are all needed to cope with our inveterate foes. Rather let us "provoke one another to love and to good works."

(3) Our third preventative for leakage, Loyalty. We would have fewer cases of disloyalty in our Church if our members realized and better understood the terms of our Covenant. We are partners in an ecclesiastical concern. The articles of association and the rules by which we are governed are written in our Testimony, and summed up in our terms of Communion. Every member when joining the Church gives an unqualified and perfectly voluntary assent to these regulations. They are, we believe, in the highest degree Scriptural. The key-note of the Church, then, is loyalty to those principles. That is what the Covenanter Church demands from her sons and daughters. It covers the whole field of Christian duty. Being faithful to God implies obedience to His revealed will, and to be faithful to one another we must fulfil the solemn engagements of our mutual Covenant. I think that our differences are unnecessarily accentuated, and, we fear, often magnified. How can this sore be healed? How can this source of leakage be prevented? Will it be by summoning a meeting of the entire Church, and discussing the elements of discord? We think not; but by the exercise of common sense. We have just one set of principles. We have only one set of terms of Communion. These are so Scripturally framed, so orderly arranged, and so plainly, tersely, and minutely stated that by no amount of ingenious twisting can they admit of two reasonable interpretations. Someone says, "I think I could be more loyal, and work more harmoniously, if it were not for bitter memories of the past—memories of slights and wrongs done to me by my brethren." But why cherish these for ever in your heart? The surgeon who has dressed the wound of a patient does not on each succeeding visit open up the wound, but applies non-irritant and healing remedies. If we expose discord and its forerunner, disloyalty, to love's rays, we detect selfishness. A splendid specific for the internal disorders which are distracting the Church is Love co-operating with her good friend Time. Let these perform their natural functions, and selfishness, the mother of discord and disloyalty, will melt as snowflakes under the rays of an Eastern sun.

> Love took up the glass of Time, turned it in his glowing
> hands;
> Every moment, lightly shaken, ran itself in golden sands.
> Love took up the harp of Life, and smote on all the chords
> with might,
> Smote the chord of Self, that trembling passed in music
> out of sight.

Now, in thinking of our leakages, we must not be unduly discouraged. They who remain are always more than they who draw back; they who are with us are more than those who are against us; one with God is a majority. Christianity always seems to be dying. Voltaire prophesied that in another generation Christianity would be a thing of the past. That generation has gone, and many others, and Christianity is still with us; and the very house where Voltaire wrote these words is now a Bible-house. The Covenanter Church is always a dying Church—in the estimation not only of the world, but also of other Churches, but still she lives, and she does not mean to die just yet to please either the Churches or the world. She has lived through two and a half centuries of cloud and sunshine, and by God's grace she will live for centuries yet to come.

This question of leakage, so many-sided, so intricate in all its aspects, and involving issues of the gravest import, is surely of sufficient magnitude to demand the most careful consideration of your revered Court. In the great name of Jesus Christ, by whose authority you are constituted, we beseech you take the case in hand. Make it the subject of your devotions, and when you reach the heights and your spirits commune with the Unseen, in the greatness of your faith and in the intense earnestness of your souls ask God what He would have you do in this matter on which hang issues of living moment for the little struggling Church of the Covenant.

Is not the time ripe for a great forward movement? We are a very small army indeed, and the opposing forces are the deadliest combination with which a single army has ever been confronted. But, unlike a nation, while we may seek to ascertain our equipment, we must despise the cost.

The tribute paid to our American brethren by Abraham Lincoln is worth quoting. He said: "I know these Covenanters well. They have made two demands of this nation—submission to God, and freedom for the slave. One of their demands has been granted during my first administration, and perhaps during my second they may obtain the other." We have two demands to make of this nation—submission to God, and freedom from the shackles of Romanism. Let us try to realize our responsibilities. I am not one of those who say that our Church has been doing nothing. Notwithstanding the defects to which I have referred, she has been fighting a noble battle. And the fact that, in these days of declension and apostasy, she has maintained her position with dignity and honour to this very hour is proof that she has done much. But we have not done as much as we should have done. As the best way to banish bad thoughts from the heart is to fill it with good thoughts, so one of the best ways to prevent leakage is to get all our members actively engaged in public Christian warfare. We require to be more on the aggressive. Why should *you* not lead in a grand crusade against the enemies of our Lord? Your name, Reformed Presbyterian Church of Scotland, is of great significance. It takes us back in thought to the noble contendings of our martyred ancestors, back to memorable scenes of strife and carnage. Although our enemies are growing bolder and bolder, and the war drum sounds louder and louder, let us enter the ever-deepening conflict with increased zeal and determination and plant the standard of the Covenant on every hill-top of the world.

The Centenary Meeting of the Synod of the RP Church of Ireland, at Cullybackey, 26 June 1911

Back: Rev AM Thompson, Rev JR Wright, ?, ?, Rev Joseph McEwen, Rev JMcC Cromie, Rev John Ramsey, Rev Thomas Dick, Rev James Blair, Rev TB McFarlane; **fourth standing**: Mr Samuel McKay, ?, ?, ?, ?, ?, Prof SG Kennedy, Rev RJ McIlmoyle, Rev Wm Dick, ?, Mr Thomas Hill, ?, ?, ?, ?, Mr William Shaw; **third standing**: ?, ?, ?, ?, Rev A Holmes, Rev SR McNeilly, Rev SH Kennedy, Rev WJ Moffett, Rev JA Lyons, ?, Prof James Dick, Rev Samuel Kennedy, Rev James Buchanan, ?, ?; **second seated**: Mr Hugh Wright, ?, Rev Gawn Douglas, Rev S Ferguson, Rev Torrens Boyd, Rev Dr Speers (USA), Rev Wm Scott, Rev William McCullough, ?; **front**: ?, Mr J Stavely Brown, Rev Ezekiel Teaz, Rev RH Davidson, Rev Wm Warnock, Rev A Gilmour, Mr R Holmes, ?, ?, Rev WH Pollock, ?

1911

—The Annual Open-air Service was held at Laymore, Cullybackey, on Sabbath evening, 25th June, the evening before the opening of the Synod. This is the district where the Covenanters met for worship before 1789, when the Cullybackey Meeting-house was built, and it is possible to go back as far as 1670 in tracing the history of the societies that met here.

Although the evening was unpleasant for an open-air gathering, there was a good attendance of members of the Church and friends.

Rev. J. N. Lyons spoke from Job xix. 25—" For I know that my Redeemer liveth." Special reference was made to the facts connected with the history of the Covenanter Church in the locality.

Church News

Our Centenary Meeting of Synod.—Our Synod met on June 26th last in Cullybackey Meetinghouse, where it had been constituted 100 years ago. Up till May 1st, **1811**, our Supreme Ecclesiastical Court was the Reformed Presbytery, which had itself been constituted 1763, and after being disorganized in 1779, reorganized in 1792. Synod could not but enter on its recent proceedings with a sense of the Divine goodness, and of very considerable progress of the best kind. And good work was, we believe, done at Synod. The forms for Covenant-renovation, which is to take place in October 3rd, 1911, were passed with unanimity, and would, we think, have been considered faithful by the Covenanters of 100 years ago. That is surely a great matter in an age of such general and shameful disregard of Reformation attainments. The Historical Testimony was unanimously ordered to be reprinted to meet the urgent need of the members of the Church, and this too was a Confession, up to date, of Scriptural but most unpopular " contendings for the faith." The routine work of Synod, in all its departments, was carefully attended to, and much progress reported,—all this in such a brotherly spirit, that there was no division of votes during the whole time of the sittings of Synod.

The Congregation of Cullybackey made matters very pleasing for members of Synod. No expense of time, thoughtfulness, or generous liberality was spared, whether at the meeting-house, where an abundant and varied menu was provided in their school-room for the entertainment of their Synodical guests at dinner and tea, or in the homes of the people. Such large-hearted hospitality of minister and people will not soon be forgotten. It harmonised with the beautiful weather to make the visit of Synod to Cullybackey a most enjoyable one.

Synod was adjourned till October 3rd.—Ed.

Dervock.—The Congregation having become aware of the fact that their minister and his wife were about to leave for a few days' holiday, a number of the young ladies of the Congregation paid a surprise visit to the Manse a few evenings ago and handed Mr. and Mrs. M'Ilmoyle a cheque for a handsome amount to defray their holiday expenses.

The Covenanter.

NEW SERIES VOL. XXI. NOVEMBER-DECEMBER, 1911. No. 11-12

Minutes of the Reformed Presbyterian Synod of Ireland, 1911.

SESSION I.

R.P. MEETING-HOUSE, CULLYBACKEY, JUNE 26th, 1911, 6 P.M.

The Synod of the Reformed Presbyterian Church of Ireland met, and, after a discourse founded on 1 Samuel xvii. 58—"Whose son art thou, thou young man?" was constituted by the Moderator, Rev. R. J. M'Ilmoyle, with prayer.

I. As to changes in the Roll, the Clerk of the Southern Presbytery reported that, at a Special Meeting of the Southern Presbytery, held in Newry on 28th March, the Rev. J. R. Wright, B.A., accepted a Call from the Ballyclabber Congregation, and was transferred to the Northern Presbytery.

The Clerk of the Northern Presbytery reported that on the 14th March, Mr. Alexander Gilmour, M.A., had been ordained to the office of the Gospel Ministry, and inducted to the pastorate of the Drimbolg Congregation, and also, that the Rev. J. R. Wright had, on the 25th April, been inducted to the pastorate of the Ballyclabber Congregation.

The Clerk of the Eastern Presbytery reported that Rev. Robert Allen, Senior Minister of Newtownards, died on 28th November, 1910.

These changes were made in the Roll.

II. The Clerk of Synod presented the Report on Elders' Commissions. The Report was adopted. But some Commissions being found technically incorrect, Rev. W. Dick moved, Mr. H. Wright seconded, and Synod agreed that all the Commissions in question be regarded as valid, but that the divergencies from strict form be not drawn into a precedent.

The Roll of Synod was then made up as follows:—

NORTHERN PRESBYTERY.

MINISTERS.	ELDERS.	CONGREGATIONS.
S. H. Kennedy, B.A.	...	Alexandretta, Syria
J. R. Wright, B.A.	Robert James Macafee ...	Ballyclabber
W. M'Cullough, B.A.	John Kelly ...	Ballylaggan
John Ramsey, LL.B.	J. Warnock *alt.* S. Lyons	Ballymoney
...	J. Chambers *alt.* J. F. Taylor	Cloughmills
J. A. Lyons, B.A. ...	H. Wright *alt.* R. M'Keivey	Cullybackey
R. J. M'Ilmoyle ...	J. M'Fall *alt.* Robt. Clarke	Dervock
A. Gilmour, M.A. ...	William Workman ...	Drimbolg & Magherafelt
...	...	Garvagh
Archibald Holmes ...	R. Moffatt *alt* J. Duncan	Kellswater
J. M'C. Cromie, B.D.	T. Hill *alt* Wm. Finlay ...	Kilraughts
...	Hugh M'Conaghy ...	Portrush
...	John M'Clements ...	Ringrash

EASTERN PRESBYTERY.

MINISTERS.	ELDERS.	CONGREGATIONS.
*J. Martin, M.A., M.D.	...	Antioch, Syria
S. R. M'Neilly, B.A. ...	James A. Hanna	Bailiesmills
James Blair ...	R. Blair, sen. *alt.* S. Kennedy	Ballyclare
James Paterson ...	...	Belfast, Botanic Av.
Prof. Kennedy, LL.D.	J. B. O'Neill *alt* J. Stewart	Belfast, College St. S.
Wm. Dick, M.A. ...	J. Black, *alt.* W. Martin ...	Belfast, Cregagh Rd.
Prof. Lynd, D.D. ...	T. Martin, *alt* J. M'Dowell	Belfast Dublin Road
Prof. Dick, M.A., D.D.	P. Wasson *alt.* W. Martin	Belfast, Trinity St.
W. Warnock, B.A. ...	J. A. Archer *alt.* G. Corry	{ Dromara { Dromore
*H. K. Mack, B.A. ...	...	Geelong, Australia
*Geo. Benaugh, D.D.	John Lowe ...	Knockbracken
*Matthew Hodge ...	S. Morrow *alt* J. Fulton ...	Killinchy
Wm. H. Pollock, B.A.	H. Snoddy *alt* J. M'Cluggage	Larne
Ezekiel Teaz ...	Robert Lamont ...	Liverpool
Torrens Boyd ...	William M'Coubrey ...	Newtownards

SOUTHERN PRESBYTERY.

MINISTERS.	ELDERS.	CONGREGATIONS.
...	...	Ballenon
William M'Knight	...	Ballylane
...	T. Scott *alt.* T. J. Moffett	Creevagh
Joseph M'Ewen ...	John Henry ...	Fairview
...	...	Grange
Gawin Douglas ...	Richard Copeland ...	Loughbrickland
T. B. M'Farlane, B.A.	J. M'Gladdery *alt.* R. Long	Newry
James Buchanan ...	Samuel Benaugh ...	Rathfriland

WESTERN PRESBYTERY.

MINISTERS.	ELDERS.	CONGREGATIONS.
...	James Armstrong ...	Bready
William Scott ...	...	Convoy
S. Ferguson, B.A. ...	J. M'Donald *alt.* D. Longwell	Faughan
S. Kennedy B.A. ...	Robert M'Ilmoyle ...	Limavady
R. H. Davidson ...	*R. Blair *alt.* *J. C. Dick	Londonderry
W. J. Moffett, B.A. ...	S. Young *alt.* R. M'Causland	Milford
...	...	Mulvin
A. M. Thompson, M.A.	...	Stranorlar & Donegal

III. The Moderator addressed the Court, and requested the brethren to choose his successor.

IV. It was moved by Rev. W. Dick, seconded by Rev. J. Ramsey, and passed unanimously, "That the Rev. S. R. M'Neilly, B.A., be appointed Moderator for the ensuing year." Mr. M'Neilly took the Chair, and addressed the Court.

NOTES ON THE CENTENARY MEETING OF THE IRISH SYNOD.

By the Rev. W. J. Moffett, B.A.

The annual meeting of the Irish Reformed Presbyterian Synod was held this year in Cullybackey, on the invitation of the Session and Committee of the congregation which worships there. And as one looks back upon the Synod of 1911 there can be nothing but the most fragrant memories remaining with every member who was privileged to be in Cullybackey during the last week of June, not only because of the harmony and brotherly love which pervaded every sederunt and every discussion, but because of the exceedingly kind, courteous, and bountiful hospitality of the Cullybackey congregation and friends of the congregation in the vicinity.

We met in Cullybackey to commemorate the first constitution of the Reformed Presbyterian Synod of Ireland, which took place a hundred years ago in the same church and on the same spot where we assembled this year. And as Synod met again in Cullybackey, after the interval of a century, one could not but think of the stalwarts of the faith who composed the membership of the first Synod—William Stavely, minister of Cullybackey and Kellswater, the apostle of the Covenanter Church in Ireland, father of the Synod and its first Moderator; William John Stavely, son of William Stavely, minister of Dervock and Kilraughts, and Clerk of the 1811 Synod; Hutchinson M'Fadden of Newtownards; John Alexander of Derry; Josias Alexander of Knockbracken and Belfast; Smith of Convoy; Boggs of Ballylane and Rathfriland; Cathcart of Creevagh and Muckney (now Fairview); John Paul of Loughmourne; and William Gamble of Ballygay (now Milford) and Letterkenny. These were the ministerial members of the first Synod. They were few in number, it is true, but they were giants in intellect, men of lofty principles and evangelical fervour. Do we not hear the tone of the first Synod of the Reformed Presbyterian Church of Ireland, and the keynote too, of the lives of its members, in the words of the text which Stavely chose for his Moderator's sermon in Cullybackey in 1811—"But Christ as a son over His own house; whose house are we, if we hold fast the confidence and the rejoicing of the hope firm unto the end?"

It is to such men as these were, who held fast the confidence and the rejoicing of the hope firm unto the end, that we really owe, under the providence of God, our existence and progress as a Synod during a century of changeful history. The wonderful increase in the activities of the Church, and the multiform schemes of work which are now under the care and

superintendence of the Synod, may truthfully be said to have all grown out of the seed planted by the Synod of 1811.

In these brief notes we can only glance at the most important items of business which came before the Centenary Synod in Cullybackey.

Synod met on the Monday evening (26th June), which, according to long-established custom, is always given to the outgoing Moderator's sermon and the appointment of the Moderator for the ensuing year. Rev. R. J. M'Ilmoyle, the retiring Moderator, preached a very helpful and practical sermon from the words—"Whose son art thou, thou young man?" and then constituted the Court. Synod unanimously appointed as its Moderator for this year the Rev. S. R. M'Neilly, B.A., of Bailiesmills, who by reason of his devoted and successful work as Convener of Synod's Committee on Foreign Missions is one of the best-known members of the Court.

On Tuesday morning Synod entered upon its work in earnest, and the first report before the Court was that on the Theological Hall, presented by Rev. J. M'C. Cromie, who brought forward a report that was satisfactory and encouraging to all who are interested in the maintenance and diffusion of the principles of the Second Reformation. The Hall is now well past its half-century, and it was never better equipped than it is to-day for the training of heralds of the Cross who shall be worthy successors of the men who formed the Synod of 1811. The urgent need of our Hall is a larger number of students, increased liberality, and more fervent prayer to Him who is Lord of the harvest and the Controller of human hearts and human lives.

The event of the Tuesday evening sederunt was, as it is indeed each year, the Scotch deputation. This year, to the great regret of every member of the Court, Mr Matthew Kirkwood and Rev. J. M'Donald, B.D., the official deputies, were unable to come to Ireland, the former through urgent business in Norway, and the latter through serious illness. Mr M'Donald, however, though not able to be present himself, sent us by letter from his sick chamber the warmest greetings and most inspiring sentiments. In addition, he sent an exceedingly able substitute in the person of the Rev. A. C. Gregg, B.D., who gave, in the unanimous opinion of the Court, one of the strongest, most hope-inspiring, and faithful addresses ever delivered in Synod. One could see how every member, and especially the younger members, of the Synod were impressed with Mr Gregg's able arguments for the continued maintenance of a full Covenanted Testimony, and his insistence that the only ground and inspiration for such a testimony was the Cross of Christ. How clearly Mr Gregg put the case for the position of the Church and its only foundation will be seen and noted by readers in another magazine of the Church.

On Tuesday evening also Synod had the rare pleasure and privilege of seeing and hearing the Rev. Dr Meyer, a Reformed Presbyterian minister from the United States of America, who, himself a Hebrew of the Hebrews, having seen that God had made that same Jesus who was crucified both Lord and Christ, is now a most zealous and devoted ambassador for the claims of King Jesus. Synod was deeply impressed with Dr Meyer's able and eloquent appeal for a fuller recognition of the urgent need of Abraham's seed for the Evangel of Christ. And it is hoped that the members of the Church will respond to the appeal in that way which is open to all—using the privilege of remembering the Jew at the Throne of Grace.

On Wednesday morning the Court considered the reports of the different Presbyteries, which showed nothing unusual in the work and life of the Church for the past year. The death of the Rev. Robert Allen, senior minister of Newtownards, was reported. He had served the Church long and faithfully. He died in a good old age, full of years, and, we believe, was gathered to his people in the rest that remaineth for the people of God.

One addition to the ranks of the ministry was reported by the Northern Presbytery through the ordination of Mr Alexander Gilmour, M.A., in Drimbolg, where doubtless in that historical congregation Mr Gilmour, with the gifts and training which God has granted him, will worthily uphold the banner of the Covenant.

The Rev. R. H. Davidson presented the report on the General Widows' and Orphans' Fund, which showed that the Church as a whole is endeavouring to follow the example of Christ in His pity and care for the lonely and needy. But the report showed also that this spirit of love is not as evident throughout the congregations of the Church as it ought to be.

On the Wednesday evening Synod always settles down, and a large general audience gathers in, wherever Synod meets, to hear two of the most important reports on the Church's work. First came the report on Irish Evangelization, read by the new convener, Rev. T. B. M'Farlane, who gave a most interesting and encouraging review of the work done by the colporteurs in Dublin and Newry during the year. Mr M'Farlane, in moving the adoption of the report, gave the Synod, in a most racy and informing speech, facts which show that Irish Mission work does pay, and does deserve a more loyal support from the members and friends of the Church.

Then came the great—some would say the greatest—report on the programme of Synod, that of the Foreign Mission Board, presented by Rev. S. R. M'Neilly. During the year the work

of the Lord in Syria has been faithfully carried on, with many evidences of the Divine blessing resting upon it. Our missionary in the field, Dr Martin, has been wonderfully sustained through arduous work and trying experiences by the grace that faileth never; and at home, through the visits and addresses of Mrs and Rev. S. H. Kennedy to our congregations, the interest in the Foreign Mission has increased to a point never before reached. Besides, the convener was able to make the welcome announcement of increased liberality to the General Fund, and the further reduction of the debt by £200. We had with us Mrs and Rev. S. H. Kennedy, who were both looking well notwithstanding their long, weary journeys and many meetings on behalf of the cause to which they are so devoted. Synod had the privilege of again hearing Mr Kennedy presenting in his forceful way the urgent claims of North Syria, and the responsibility that rests upon the Reformed Presbyterian Synods of Scotland and Ireland to go in and take possession of this land for Christ.

It was a great pleasure to Synod to congratulate Mr Kennedy on his having had the honorary degree of Doctor of Divinity conferred upon him by the Board of Geneva College, U.S.A. They who are acquainted with the life, character, and work of Dr Kennedy know that he well deserves and will worthily wear this honour.

On Thursday morning we had the report on the Congregational Aid Fund, presented by Rev. S. Kennedy. This fund, so vital to the well-being of the whole Church, was never so generously supported as last year, yet the convener warned the Synod of the probable failure of the fund this year to meet all the grants, and reasonably asked that more earnest efforts should be made to maintain the fund by increased annual givings and a more united effort on the part of the whole Church to increase the invested capital.

The Colonial Mission report, read by Rev. S. Ferguson, indicated that Rev. H. K. Mack was maintaining, if not largely extending, the cause of the Covenant in that Australian land which is so far distant in miles, but so near in kinship.

There were many other reports before the Synod concerning which we would like to write, but space will not permit us to do more than mention some of these. There was the Ministers' Widows' and Orphans' Fund report, presented by Rev. J. A. Lyons; the Instruction of the Young report, by Rev. J. R. Wright; the Twentieth Century Fund report, by Rev. W. M'Cullough; the report on the State of Religion and Sabbath Observance, by Rev. W. M'Knight; reports on the *Covenanter*, on Covenant Renovation, on Temperance and Statistics, all of them interesting and important, and all of them evidencing earnestness and fidelity and, we believe, progress in the work of the Kingdom of our Lord and Saviour Jesus Christ.

Synod rose on Friday evening, to assemble again in adjourned meeting on the 5th October, to complete several items of business left unfinished. The Moderator adjourned the Synod by pronouncing the benediction, and the members departed from Cullybackey after a most happy meeting, and, we believe, a season of spiritual refreshing.

1911

The Minutes of the Special Meeting

OF THE

Reformed Presbyterian Synod of Ireland,

HELD IN COLLEGE STREET SOUTH, BELFAST,

FOR THE RENEWING OF THE COVENANTS, AND FOR THE EFFECTIVE PUBLICATION OF OUR DISTINCTIVE PRINCIPLES.

SESSION I

AT COLLEGE STREET SOUTH, BELFAST, 3rd OF OCTOBER, 1911, 12 O'CLOCK NOON

The Synod of the Reformed Presbyterian Church of Ireland met, as specially appointed, and was, by the Moderator, Rev. S. R. M'Neilly, B.A., constituted with praise and prayer.

On Wednesday, 20 June 1990, at the Synod of the Reformed Presbyterian Church, held at Creevagh RP Church, Ballybay, Co Monaghan, there was held a Service of Covenant Renewal. This was followed by Covenant Renewal services in the congregations of our denomination throughout the past year. It is appropriate, therefore, that we turn to a sermon preached by the Rev RJ McIlmoyle at the Covenant Renovation in 1911, although the sermon was not printed in *The Covenanter* until October 1916.

Covenant-Renovation.

LET US ARISE, AND GO UP TO BETHEL—Genesis 35 : 3.*

These were words addressed by Jacob, on one occasion, to "his household, and to all that were with him." God had come to Jacob with the exhortation, "Arise, go up to Bethel, and dwell there : and make there an altar unto God, that appeared unto thee when thou fleddest from the face of Esau thy brother." In obedience to this Divine call Jacob prepared himself and called upon his household to go to Bethel. He had been there before. At that place he had

*A sermon preached by Rev. R. J. M'Ilmoyle, in connection with the Synod's Renovation of The Covenants, on 3rd October, 1911.

had a wonderful manifestation of God's love and tender care. At that place he had covenanted with the Eternal. But Bethel was also the scene of vows which had been partially neglected and forgotten. God had abundantly blessed Jacob when friendless and alone; and Jacob, rising to a high pitch of enthusiasm, vowed to the Lord. He went on his way, but by and by forgot his vow.

Just thus have we all acted time and again. But God remembers the promises we make, the promises we fail to keep. He in love reminds His people of their forgotten mercies, of their broken vows. These bonds were not for Jacob's day only. They are for all time. And to-day they come to us in all the fulness of their meaning. As a Church we are met for the Renovation of the Covenants. We are about to engage in what we consider a solemn duty. We are obeying what we believe to be God's call. We are saying one to another, "Let us arise and go up to Bethel."

Jacob's conduct in the carrying out of his resolve may speak to us wisely and well as we take this solemn step.

As we look forward to the work to which we have set our hands we say, first of all—The duty is a solemn one. For mortal man to come and, with uplifted hand, swear to the living God—that surely is solemn work. The position is such that human flesh and blood unaided by Divine grace might well shrink back. That the position is a responsible one, that the duty is solemn, will be readily admitted. How solemn! "Thou shalt swear in truth, in judgment, and in righteousness." Again, "Ponder the path of thy feet." And again, "Keep thy feet when thou enterest into the house of God." Let us consider with Whom we have to do—a God so great, so holy. Let us consider, too, how poor, how sinful we are. And, considering these things, let us remember where our strength and sufficiency is, so that we may enter into this engagement with God in a fit and becoming manner. Great is the distance between a king and a beggar, between a prince and a peasant. But between God and man, between the Creator and His created ones the distance is beyond computation. God humbleth Himself to behold the things that are in heaven. That is condescension. How great, then, yea, infinite is His condescension in beholding the sinful things that are on earth! Let us, therefore, have grace whereby we may serve God acceptably, with reverence and godly fear. The duty is a solemn one.

We ask in the next place, What are we to infer from this fact? And, first of all, we are to infer that notwithstanding the solemnity and notwithstanding the responsibility our duty is to go forward.

Some may say, the step is so solemn we fear to take it. Take the case of Christ's people obeying His dying command to commemorate His death. That, too, is a solemn step to take, so solemn that Christ says, in reference to it, "Let a man examine himself." But this examination is not with a view to finding reasons for staying away, but with a view to coming, as Christ would have His people come.

Again, take the case of parents dedicating their child to God in baptism. It is a tremendous responsibility, parents standing up and in the presence of angels and men dedicating their child to God, and promising to discharge towards it parental duties faithfully and well. But what is implied in their so dedicatng their child? They are not thereby creating a new relationship either between themselves and God or between themselves and their child. These relationships exist already, and the parents in presenting their child for baptism are simply acknowledging the relationships. God by giving them their babe has laid them under obligation to train it for Him. And in receiving the ordinance of baptism for their child and taking the vows implied therein, they are simply acknowledging that obligation. It is a solemn thing to come and acknowledge the responsibility, but more solemn still would it be to stay away under the circumstances.

Just so here. The Covenants sworn to by our forefathers we regard as our own. The matter of them we believe to be Scriptural. The vows contained in them are not supererogatory. They speak of the claims that God has upon His people—of the relationship He requires them to stand in to Him. In covenanting and in renewing the Covenants, we are simply acknowledging the claims of God upon us. Responsible as it is to come, it were more responsible still to stay away under a feeling that the responsibility constituted a barrier.

In the second place, we are to infer that so solemn and responsible is the step it becomes us to ask, WHEREWITH SHALL WE TAKE IT?

Jacob, in view of the solemn step he was about to take, said unto his household and to all that were with him, "Put away the strange gods that are among you, and be clean, and change your garments." Idols had got into the home of Jacob. They are in the best of homes—worshipped by the best of families. Whatever takes the place of God in the heart is a strange god and an idol. "Covetousness," we read, "which is idolatry." When Jacob in obedience to the Divine call, determines to go to Bethel, he feels the need for self-examination, for searching of heart, for reformation.

Wherewith, then, shall we take this step? Only in humble dependence on Divine grace. May our prayer be that if God go not with us He will carry us not up hence. May our prayer be that God will go before, that God will lead the way.

But if God will lead, we must follow. Successful leading always implies faithful following. Often in the Bible are God's people represented as following their great Leader. You try to follow a friend by a way you know not, say, through a crowded thoroughfare in one of our large cities. So long as you keep near to your leader, it is a comparatively easy thing to follow. But by and by you lag behind, and then it becomes more difficult. The distance between you and your friend becomes greater, other objects come in between, and they come in because you make room for them, and ere long your friend is lost to sight, or you only get a glimpse of him occasionally.

So with us. We allow earthly objects to take the place of Christ in the heart. These are our idols, strange gods. They mar our vision of the Divine Leader. They make following Christ more difficult. If God would lead, we are to follow, and in order to our following the Psalmist's prayer should be ours, "Search me, O God, and know my heart: try me, and know my thoughts: and see if there be any wicked way in me, and lead me in the way everlasting." This is a rare request taken in all its comprehensiveness. It is not natural for man to desire that which would wound his pride or hurt his vanity. Yet such must be the result of the answering of this prayer. The man who truly prays this prayer is a man anxious that God would bring his sin to light, a man anxious to know the evils of his nature—in short, a man desirous of making progress in the Divine life. Look at the range of this examination—"Search me, and know my heart." Another translation reads, "O Jehovah, Thou hast explored me and Thou knowest me." The Psalmist knows very little of his own nature, of his own real self; but he knows enough of himself to distrust himself. "Man, know thyself," is a maxim all-important but difficult of realization. A great philosopher on one occasion wandered into the Royal Gardens at Berlin, and when an officer enquired of him, "Who are you, sir?" he replied, "I don't know, I shall be glad if you can tell me." The officer reported him for a lunatic. But he was'nt that. However it may be from the philosopher's point of view, from the Christian standpoint we must see ourselves with other than natural eyes to know ourselves aright.

If God is to search us and so to lead us, there is necessary on our part confession and repentance.

Confession, what is that ? An acknowledgment of sin, some will say. Yes, but more than that. Confession is a thing that is naturally repugnant to man. And it is so, just because man is apt to limit its meaning. If our confession is to mean anything, it will be the unveiling of our hearts before God, and the acknowledging of our sin. But if it is to mean anything, it will also be something more. The Psalmist confessed when he said, " 'Gainst Thee, Thee only, have I sinned." But Peter also confessed when he said, "Thou art the Christ the Son of the living God."

The schoolboy may come and acknowledge his wrong-doing only to get punished for it. The person who has offended against the law may come and acknowledge his fault only to be brought under the punishment such a breach of the law entails. But with the sinner it is difficult. With shame and confusion of face we say we are guilty, we have sinned. But we are able also to say, "If we confess our sins, He is faithful and just to forgive them." And we hear Him, the Judge of all the earth, saying, "Deliver from going down into the pit, I have found a ransom."

Let us come, then, and acknowledge our sins. This acknowledgment, however, must not only be general, it must also be particular. Let us be ready to join with others and say, "All have sinned and come short of the glory of God." "All we like sheep have gone astray." We are not better than others. Whatever has been our parentage, whatever our upbringing, all have sinned.

But, then, there is a tendency, a strong temptation, to rest in generalities. We are apt to entertain the thought that if we are no better than others, we are at least not any worse. If we are not all we might be, others are as bad. There is in true acknowledgment of sin a feeling of separateness, a feeling of loneliness, a realisation that in the matter of sinning we stand where no one else has ever stood. In God's creation there are no duplicates. No two things are exactly alike. No two men have exactly the same privileges, the same opportunities, the same responsibilities. Each one has to answer for his own privileges, opportunities, and responsibilities. And each one has failed in his duty in respect to all of these. It follows, then, that while there is a brotherhood as it were embracing all men with regard to sin in general no two men sin exactly alike. We must get down to particulars and realize that our sin is different from the sin of others.

A true acknowledgment of sin leads to a fuller knowledge of our own selves. For the right discharge of any duty we need Divine grace. God gives grace, and more grace. It is not how little we can ask, but how much we can use. The more use we make of the grace we have, the more grace we shall get. The more work we do for God, instead of our resources becoming exhausted thereby, the more we shall be able to do. Confession is a duty. The more we discharge that duty, the better qualified are we for the further discharge of it. The more we examine ourselves, the better qualified are we for such examination, the better shall we know ourselves.

We are all liable to be deceived, especially to be deceived concerning ourselves. The mariner who navigates his vessel amidst hidden rocks, and currents, and whirlpool, throws out his line and examines his charts. The traveller as he journeys on an unknown path and in the darkness of the night takes heed to his footsteps. So the believer surrounded by dangers unknown should prove his own self.

You begin to rid a store room of its contents. As you proceed with your work you will come upon this thing and the other thing you expected to find ; but you will also come upon other things you are surprised to find. Some of these you yourself had put there at one time, but you had forgotten about it. Others are there without your special permission or knowledge. At the presence of those you are surprised. Just so with regard to these sinful hearts of ours. Self-examination reveals many things to us. It brings to light many hidden sins. It reveals sins we were perhaps not altogether unconscious of, but also many sins we never thought we were guilty of.

Another thing that militates against the right discharge of the duty of confession is Satan's temptation to make an excuse for our sin. Often sin is discovered, sin so apparent, so open, so flagrant that we cannot deny it, and Satan knows that he need not suggest our denying it. Then he tempts us to do what he no doubt considers the next best thing—to make an excuse for our sin. Adam sinned in the garden, sinned in such a way that he could not deny his sinning. But immediately he proceeds to make an excuse for his sin ; and not only so, but seems to roll the blame upon God. "The woman," he said, "The woman whom Thou gavest to be with me, she gave me. . . and I did eat."

Repentance is also necessary. We cannot be entirely free from sin, but if we are truly repentant we will not permit sin to reign in the life. Christ is the Son of the Living God. Of Him it is said, "Thou hast, O Lord, most glorious, ascended up on high, and in triumph victorious led captive captivity." Sin is a bondage, a captivity, that holds men bound, that leads them captive at its will. But its reigning power has been broken by Christ. He has taken the captivity, the bondage and made it a captive. His people through Him do the same. Sin does not reign over them. They reign. Sin no longer leads them captives. They trample it underfoot, and make it a captive.

In repentance we offer no apologies for the existence of sin. Iniquity may not be regarded in the heart and yet sometimes appear in the life. A man may be overtaken in a fault, and yet not an habitual wrongdoer. Temptation comes to all, and a Christian may be overcome of evil. But he makes no apologies. Neither does he try to hide his sin. In sorrow he repents, and in humble dependence on Divine grace he turns from his sin. The penitent soul evinces a desire to obtain the sanctifying influences of the Spirit of God, and He neglects not to apply to the throne of heavenly grace. He wrestles with God. He exercises faith in the blood of the covenant. He comes with confidence, yet withal reverently to Him Who is able to save to the uttermost.

But some will say, What has all this to do with the special work in connection with which we are met ? Well, "If I regard iniquity in my heart the Lord will not hear me." He will not hear us when we pray. He will not hear us when we covenant. He will not hear us when we renew our Covenants. Our Covenanterism is not something tacked on, as it were, to our ordinary religion. We do not regard ourselves as Christians plus Covenanters. As we have said, the vows contained in the Covenants we are about to renew are not supererogatory. They are enjoined in God's Word. They are such as Christians should take. For the renewing of the Covenants, then, we need the preparation that is necessary for the performance of every Christian duty.

We need confession and repentance as individuals and as a Church. We have adopted a high standard. We have espoused great principles. Have we been faithful ? At such a time as this we should remember what we have vowed. We should remember, too, what our fathers achieved. And as we think of our vows and our own forgetfulness to pay, let us remember not only our fathers' deeds, but our fathers' God. As we read the account of the heroism and bravery of those who in their day occupied the high places of the field, our experience and our language should be that of the Psalmist, "O God, we have heard with our ears, our fathers have told us what work Thou didst in their day, even in the days of old."

The shepherd to himself would say,
"The winds are now devising work for me!"
And truly, at all times, the storm that drives
The traveller to a shelter summoned him
Up to the mountains: he had been alone
Amid the heart of many thousand mists
That came to him and left him in the heights.
—*Wordsworth's "Michael."*

February, 1910 One Halfpenny

The Morning Watch

Vol. XXIII. *Edited by Rev. J. P. Struthers, M.A., Greenock.* No. 2.

A Shepherd's Life.

A FEW weeks ago I had a talk with an elderly shepherd, now resting from his calling, but still abounding in good deeds. His eye, his voice, his step—I wish I could reproduce them to you—all made me feel how fittingly the two words "Gentle Shepherd" go together.

The sky had the leaden look that tells of coming snow, and we fell a-talking about storms.

"I once found three sheep," he said, "that had been in a snow wreath sixteen days. I was probing here and there in the likely places with a long ten-foot pole, and came on them that way. One of them was dead; the others had trampled on it. I carried the living ones into a small field close by. They weren't good at walking at first, but they soon came round all right. I left them to feed themselves, and one of them nursed a lamb the April after. That was an unusual storm. The wind was so fierce that a herd was lifted off his feet and carried as he guessed about 30 yards, so he said, and his leg was broken about the knee. He never herded any more, but he is in his grave now. We lost more than twenty sheep that year. Every place was filled up with snow, then the burn was dammed, and the sheep were smothered and drowned, all in one night's time. In a time like that a shepherd can't do much at night, for he can't see.

"In a storm sheep are driven before the blast. In moderate fine weather they face the wind, but they go further after it when it comes from the east; they are fonder of that wind than of any other. There must be something very bracing and refreshing about it."

"That explains," I remarked, "what Job says about the wild ass snuffing up the east wind," whereupon the shepherd gave me a look that made me wonder at the time how he could be ignorant of such a well known verse as that, but a look, at the same time, that haunted me, and made me turn up my Concordance, ten days afterwards, to make sure that I had not misquoted a passage familiar to me from my boyhood. And then I saw the meaning of that look! Jeremiah speaks in two places, chs. 2, 24, and 14, 6, about wild asses snuffing up the wind, and Hosea describes Ephraim as following after the east wind, and Habakkuk says the faces of the Chaldeans shall sup up as the east wind, or, as the Revisers put it, "are set eagerly as the east wind." But though Job speaks several times about wild asses, it is not they, but wise men about whom the question is asked, "Should he fill his belly with the east wind?" I must verify my references more frequently, I see, specially when I talk with shepherds!

"They would be pleased when you dug them out. Were they very grateful?"

"Na, na. You can't tell whether a sheep's grateful or no. It says nothing, and makes no sign."

"But do the sheep not come running to welcome the shepherd every day when they see him coming?"

"Na, na. When they see you, they begin to move away. They don't like to be disturbed. None that are reared on the hill will come to you of their own accord. If they are fond of you, it is guess work, for there's no speech. A pet lamb, one that had been brought up in the house, might fondle you for a little. Pet lambs go through a lot of manœuvres, but they are very mischievous."

"Does a shepherd know many of his sheep?"

"Some shepherds know faces much better than others. But few of them would know more than the half, and some wouldn't know the tenth part of them."

"You might tell me how you used to spend your day, say in summer."

"We ettled to get up about 4 o'clock as a rule."

"And then took breakfast?"

"Na, na. The first thing I did I went to the top of the hill. There was a glen with a range of hills from 700 to 1600 ft high on both sides of it, and I had the one side of one of these hills to look after. The sheep would be near the top of the hill in the morning."

"What would they be doing all night?"

"Lying resting. They eat nothing through the night, till the back end of the year, when the nights are long, and then they rise for an hour or two for a little refreshment.

"When I got to the top of the hill, I would go along the ridge till I got a complete view of our ground, and saw that there were no stragglers. Then home for breakfast about 8 or 8.30, and rest for a couple of hours. If all was right, of course one got quicker on."

"Did you get your meals regularly, as a rule?"

"Na, na. I might be on the hills all day. But if things were all right, I would come home, and start about ten to go round a second time, this time taking the centre of the ground. The sheep would now be in the bottom at the foot of the hills, and one hadn't so far to go.

"I would start on my third round about two or three. The sheep begin to go up the hill then, and the shepherd goes up the bottom and stirs them up, and then they scatter themselves. If all was right I would get home about 6 or 7, and would be done with them for the day."

"Then did you count them once or twice, or how often, every day?"

"Na, na. We often gave a rough guess, but we counted them *pointedly* only twice a year when they were clipped in June or July, and again when they were "keiled," that is when they get their winter mark in November. Besides this winter mark of brown or red which you can see at a glance, every man has his own private mark for his sheep, generally two nips in the near or left lug, cut out with an iron like the things they mark railway tickets with. They used to brand them on the face with a hot iron long ago."

"You said you got home early, 'if everything was right.' What might be wrong?"

It is noteworthy that no less a person than the Rev JP Struthers should express thanks to our Irish representatives. Principal James Denny, in paying tribute to Struthers after his death in January 1915, said that he was the only man of genius with whom he was ever intimately acquainted. Rev John Paterson Struthers MA was born in Glasgow and his university career was of the highest distinction. His first ministerial charge was Whithorn, where he laboured for three years, before being inducted in Greenock in 1882, in succession to the late Rev Dr James Kerr. The genius of Struthers became widely known through his children's magazine, *The Morning Watch*. Struthers could write on any subject and the coverage given to the shepherd and the sheep in the February 1910 magazine no doubt had interest for the Irish Moderator.

20 THE MORNING WATCH.

"We might have to examine one of the hefts, for example, to see that there were no maggots in any of the sheep. There is a fly that lays its eggs in the wool, then a maggot grows in the skin, and in warm close weather the sheep might die in a few days. If we find a maggot we have a solution that we put on, and we rub the place and the maggot falls out.

"We had to see, too, that none of the sheep were coupit, or lying on their backs. Days and even weeks might pass without a case of this, for much depends on the nature of the ground. Steep hill sides are not so bad, neither is marshy ground, but on level ground, specially when it fairs after rain and there's a blink of sun, sheep are very kittle to coup. They lean over to rub themselves, and fall. They enjoy lying on their backs for a little, but they soon begin to swell, and they can't get up. Death comes in an hour or two, but I knew of a herd on the Water of Ken, who, on his way to church one Sabbath, saw a sheep coup, and he took off his boots to cross a burn to lift it, and when he got to the place it was dead."

"You said something about a heft. What's that?"

"The 700 or 800 sheep that a shepherd has care of are made up of four or five or more companies, and each of these is called a heft. Hefts differ in size, just like Presbyteries — some big, some little. Three score is a small heft, nine score would be a big one. And each heft keeps by itself, though they belong to one flock. They mix with their neighbours at the bottom during the day, but as they go up the hill, if the night's good, they each go, as the Bible says of the disciples, 'to their own company.' And the hefts all know the boundaries beyond which they must not go."

"And how is that?"

"The sheep are born on the place, and every year some of the lambs are drafted away and sold, and some of the old mothers, five or six years old, are sent away to the low country to be fed on the turnips for the market, but others of the younger ewes are kept, and their young ones take the place of those that are sent away. So there is always a generation that knows the place, and they teach the younger ones; but if one brought a lot of young sheep from Falkirk, the shepherd would have to herd them very closely for a time, till they learn the walk. But once they learn it, you will see a whole herd moved, and not one of them will pass the boundary line, even where there is no fence."

These and many other things—stories of the clipping time, and the fights of the black faced horned rams, how two of them would go back 30 yards, and then run at each other head on—I wish I could repeat exactly as he told me.

But here is an exercise your fathers or mothers might give you some Sabbath evening: In what ways is a man better than a sheep, and in what ways is he worse? and why is it that Jesus Christ calls Himself The Good Shepherd?

REV. J. P. STRUTHERS, M.A.

Born 1851—Died 1915.

1912

The Covenanter

Dervock.—This congregation has just presented its minister with a new rubber-tyred driving trap. This is the fourth presentation Mr. M'Ilmoyle has received from his loyal and spirited congregation since he came amongst them a little over seven years ago. On three other occasions he received a cow, a purse of sovereigns, and a cheque, respectively; and now his congregation has testified afresh to the good will and harmony existing between pastor and people. Mr. M'Ilmoyle at the same time received a driving rug, presented by the Messrs. Carson Bros.

A Notable Prize.—Miss Tillie Carson, daughter of Mr. Robert Carson, Elder in Dervock Congregation, and a pupil of the Ballymoney Intermediate School, has taken First Place in Ulster and won a Gold Medal for an Essay sent in to the Ulster Association for the Prevention of Cruelty to Animals. In all, there were 2 218 candidates, which makes Miss Carson's success unusually well worth recording. It reflects the highest credit on herself and the school.

1913 John McIlmoyle, cousin of the Rev RJ, was ordained to the Gospel ministry in Creevagh, Co Monaghan, and installed to the pastorate there on 16 September.

1916

Presentations by Dervock Congregation.—A deputation from Dervock Congregation waited on the Minister on the evening of September 8th. Mr. Robert Clarke presided, and stated that the object of their visit was to make a presentation to their Minister in token of the high esteem in which both he and Mrs. M'Ilmoyle were held by the Congregation. Mr. Robert Nevin handed Mr. M'Ilmoyle a cheque for a substantial amount. Members of the deputation having spoken, and, amongst other things, having referred to the fact that Mr. M'Ilmoyle had had more than one opportunity of leaving the Congregation for other fields of labour, but had elected to remain in Dervock, Mr. M'Ilmoyle suitably replied. At the same time Messrs. Robert Carson and David Taggart were each presented with a gold watch. Messrs. Carson and Taggart have led the praise service of the Congregation gratuitously for forty years. During all this time they have scarcely, if ever, been absent from their places even for a single day, and these presentations are indicative of the respect and esteem in which they are held by the Congregation. The company were hospitably entertained by Mrs. M'Ilmoyle.

1917

Northern Presbytery.—Annual Conference at Ballymoney.—The date fixed for the Conference is July 24, and the general discussions will be on 'War Problems.' The Rev. R. J. McIlmoyle will preside. There will be five Papers—The Sabbath Question, the Drink Question (Social Problems), the Religious Problem, the Political Problem, and the Christ and the Crisis, by—Mr. W. Lytle, B.A.; Revs. J. Ramsey, LL.B., J. R. Wright, B.A., A. Holmes, and J. McC. Cromie, B.D., respectively. All of the problems mentioned, and many more, are still pressing for solution. The outlook is still exceptionally grave

As a Church we have publicly declared that National rebellion and other National sins have imperilled victory. In this we have been supported by Admiral Beatty, and other eminent Christians in public services and the religious Press—but, alas! the number is small.

The aims of the Conference will have been realized if it should prove the means of mobilising the moral and religious resources of the Covenanter Church, so that she shall be in a position to organize and carry to a successful issue a fresh campaign on behalf of National Righteousness.

It is to be hoped that all the families within the bounds of the Presbytery will make a special effort to be present. We shall be greatly delighted and encouraged by the presence of as many members as possible from the other Presbyteries of the Church.

All are heartily invited to come and make the meeting a success.

R. Holmes,
Convener of Conference Committee.

Obituary

The following Minute has been put upon the Records of the Dervock Session:—The Session of Dervock Congregation desires to put on record its deep sense of loss sustained by the death of Mr. John Fleming, of Croagh, one of its oldest members.

The late Mr. Fleming was well versed in the Scriptures, understood, believed in, and acted upon the principles of the Covenanting Church, and was both willing and able to defend her position when occasion demanded.

For some years, owing to failing health, he was not privileged to wait on God in the ordinances of the sanctuary, but up to the last he took a lively and intelligent interest in the welfare of Zion.

In his home life he was a beloved and godly husband and father, training his children in the way of God. As the head of the household, he was diligent in attending to religious duties. His home was truly one of the dwellings of Jacob. Not only was family worship observed, but the male members of the family were accustomed during the father's lifetime to lead in devotional exercises at the family altar.

He answered well to the Scriptural representation of what an elder ought to be.

1918-1919

Obituary

Mrs. Mary Nevin, wife of Dr. J. L. Nevin, died at Ballymoney on 5th October, 1918. Her old home at Carnaff offered a warm welcome and generous hospitality to the preachers of a past and passing generation when Dervock was without a fixed pastor. In Ballymoney for over 30 years with the utmost gentleness and meekness, her interest in the Church and its ministers, and in her own Congregation in particular, was unceasing. Her hand was in every good work. Her sympathy was with every one who needed it. She had the esteem and love of all who knew her. She had the many friends of one who showed herself friendly, and the presence of a Friend who " sticketh closer than a brother."

Presentation.—On Wednesday evening, February 19th, 1919, a deputation of the ladies of the R. P. Congregation, Dervock, met at the residence of Mr. and Mrs. Getty, Dervock, and presented them with a Barometer, in solid oak frame, and a Silver Teapot and Stand, as an appreciation of their valuable services to the above Congregation.

1920 The name of the Rev RJ McIlmoyle as a prizewinner for his pedigree Border Leicester Sheep appears again and again at the agricultural shows throughout the Province. We have selected (see later) the Border Leicester results from some of the shows over forty-three years, for he was exhibiting and still winning in 1963. But which year he began is uncertain. Possibly the year after he joined the Society of Border Leicester Breeders in 1915 and when he acquired sufficient stock? Rev RJ's flock number was BL435 and the actual metal ear marker is in the proud possession of his great friend and rival in the latter years, Mr Samuel Black, Coleraine Road, Portstewart.

At the Coleraine Agricultural Show, as reported in the *Coleraine Chronicle* on 5 June 1920: **Border Leicester Sheep**: *Ram any age*: 1 Rev RJ McIlmoyle, Dervock; 2 Robert Morrow, Carncullagh, Stranocum

---

1921 In September *The Covenanter* reported:

–A pleasant surprise in the form of a presentation from the ladies of the Carnaff Congregation was given recently to Mrs. M'Ilmoyle at the Manse, Dervock. After tea, provided by the ladies, the presentation of a very handsome Tea Set, with Silver Tea Kettle on stand, and Silver Spoons, was made, the address being read by one of the ladies. The recipient responded, thanking all the kind donors for their beautiful gifts.

Service is the rent you pay for the space you occupy.

THE COLERAINE CHRONICLE, JUNE 26

NORTH ANTRIM SHOW

SPLENDID DISPLAY

ANOTHER BALLYMONEY TRIUMPH.

In the annual Show held at Ballymoney on Tuesday the North Antrim Agricultural Association recorded another triumph. Eighteen years have rolled by since Ballymoney had its first Show; and within the intervening period the enterprising Association has gone from success to success until the exhibition is now one of the best and most popular in the country. Right in the centre of a fertile and prosperous agricultural district, which has long ago been famed for the quality of live stock produced and kept, the Route capital has an ideal situation, and the steadily growing success of its annual exhibition is but to be expected. "Show-day" is looked upon by the people of two counties as the chief event of the year. It is a great social occasion on which old acquaintanceships are renewed and new friendships formed.

The Association is fortunate in many respects · above all in the possession of an excellently-equipped and beautifully-situated show-ground, the vista from which extends past the County Antrim boundary and into County Derry, the line of demarcation being provided by the Bann "as it runs through the plain." Since last year various improvements have been carried out in the grounds. A new grand stand has been planned, the old one having been cleared away, and it would have been ready for this year's Show but for unavoidable delay in the delivery of necessary materials for its construction.

By road and rail crowds of people flocked into the town on Tuesday, and the scene inside the grounds was one of gaiety and animation. A frowning sky in the morning did not promise well, but it was well on in the afternoon before rain made its unwelcome appearance, causing those amongst the crowd who had come without coats or umbrellas to scurry to the marquees and horse and cattle sheds for shelter. However, the rain was not continuous, and save for another brief but heavy shower about an hour later the weather conditions were not altogether unfavourable.

Since its inception the Association has rendered an indisputably valuable service to agricultural interests; and it is gratifying to find that the Show continues to be so loyally supported by the residents over a wide surrounding district. Exhibits were present in large numbers not only from all over Counties Antrim and Derry but from distant parts of the Province as well.

SHEEP.

Border Leicester ram, any age—1, Rev. R. J. M'Ilmoyle, Dervock; 2, Robert Morrow, Carncullagh, Stranocum.

Border Leicester ewe, having produced lambs prior to 1920—1 and 2, Rev. R. J. M'Ilmoyle; 3, Robert Morrow.

Border Leicester shearling ewe—1, Robert Morrow; 2, Rev. R. J. M'Ilmoyle.

Border Leicester ram lamb—1 and 3, Robert Morrow; 2, Rev. R. J. M'Ilmoyle.

Border Leicester ewe lamb—1, Rev. R. J. M'Ilmoyle; 2, Robert Morrow; 3, Hill Smith, Glenbank, Ballycastle.

Ewe, other than pedigree, having reared lambs in 1920—1, Robert Morrison, Carncullagh, Dervock; 2, Hill Smith, Glenbank, Ballycastle; 3, Samuel M'Clure, Glennylough, Ballymoney.

Best lamb, other than pedigree—1, Hill Smith; 2, Thomas Henry, Ballycraigagh, Stranocum; 3, Robert Morrison.

Black-faced ram, any age—1 and 2, Robt. Smith, Glenbank, Ballycastle.

Black-faced ewe, having produced lambs during 1920—1, 2, and 3, Robert Smith.

SPECIALS.

The M'Clure silver cup, presented by Mr. Wallace M'Clure, Linenhall Street, Ballymoney—Won by Rev. R. J. M'Ilmoyle.

Border Leicester silver medal, presented by the Society of Border Leicester Sheep-breeders—Won by Rev. R. J. M'Ilmoyle.

SWINE.

Boar, farrowed previous to 1st November, 1919—1, Richard W. Lusk, Knockahollett; 2, David J. M'Conaghie, Liscolman, Dervock; 3, Peter P. Gray, Dirraw, Finvoy.

Boar, farrowed on or after 1st November, 1919—1, Peter P. Gray.

Sow, farrowed previous to 1st November 1919, in pig, or having a litter within 6 months preceding the show—1. Wm. Finlay, Ballytaggart, Kilraughts; 2, James M'Queston, Friary, Pharos.

Sow, farrowed on or after 1st November, 1919—1 and 2, Thomas Cummins, Bottom, Ballymena; 3, Wm. Finlay.

Litter of pigs—1, James M'Queston.

From the **Coleraine Chronicle**, 10 July 1920

DERVOCK WAR MEMORIAL INSTITUTE
A SUCCESSFUL BAZAAR

Dervock and district sent forth their full quota of fat, sturdy lads for the great game in the world arena of war. They placed everything, even to life itself, at their country's service, and it is a gratifying fact that such a splendid spirit of self-sacrifice has not been forgotten. The good folk of the Dervock district remember those who sprang into the breach; and while expressing in a practical manner their appreciation of the service of those who have returned they have raised a fitting monument to the gallant dead. The Dervock War Memorial Institute, the first, perhaps, to be erected in Ireland, is almost completed. It comprises a main hall, with seating accommodation for upwards of 400 persons, together with large reading and recreation-rooms, and a splendid kitchen. The cost incurred in building was £2,000, the site being placed free at the disposal of the Building Committee by Captain CG Macartney, Lissanoure Castle. The committee, of which Dr RC Miller was chairman, and Mr Samuel Killen CPS, hon secretary, is to be congratulated on the success of the project in which they had generous and spontaneous support.

On Monday the Institute opened its doors to the public, the occasion being a bazaar, the object of which was to raise £800 to cover the balance of the contract price and to furnish and equip the building in a style worthy of its splendid architecture. The Institute was decorated gaily with bunting and the bazaar opened auspiciously. The various stalls were laden with beautiful and valuable articles, claiming a host of ready purchasers. Fine weather prevailed and there was a large attendance present when Dr RC Miller called upon Captain CG Macartney to preside at the opening ceremony, which was gracefully performed by Mrs SJ Lyle, Ballycastle. Captain Macartney said it afforded him particular pleasure in accepting their invitation to preside over that day's proceedings. He was certain, and sorry also, that there were some present to whom that would be a sad occasion, bringing remembrance of loved ones lost. To those they extended heartfelt sympathy. What a wonderful and noble part their womankind had played in the late war in spite of awful troubles and sorrows that could not be conceived. The lady upon whom he would presently call to open the bazaar was a striking example of the noble, glorious women he had so inadequately tried to portray. They were sorry that her gallant husband could not be present that day (Applause). Undoubtedly there were many ex-soldiers present and he would like to say a word for them. He wanted to put the soldier's case before them as well as possible. Everyone knew and would admit that there was no one better loved than the gallant soldier-boy (Laughter and applause). He really thought that it was quite possible that there were some who thought that the soldier was different from the ordinary civilian. In his own experience, he had found the boys just as human and as sympathetic as any ordinary person. It was everyone's duty to help the soldier, and to see that he had a chance to be happy. He hoped that these remarks would be interpreted in the spirit in which they were presented, merely and solely to further cement the esteem, regard and brotherly love which he hoped would continue to exist between all classes in the Dervock district (Applause). As he had said, the soldier was human, and liable to err. What he did not like was to be ostracised for ever for any little mistake. The soldier wished to be led firmly and justly, but he despised and hated to be led by weak, vacillating people in authority who said one thing and did the opposite. While the primary object of their war memorial was to perpetuate the memory of their gallant dead, it was also for the soldier who had been spared to come home. He trusted that the Institute would always offer a whole-hearted welcome to any soldier who wished to participate in the entertainment it afforded. He appealed to the men to do their best for the interests of the community at large. He took them back to the days when they were part of the "good old D Company" of the 12th RIR. If they retained the old spirit of D Company he was certain that Dervock would be the most prosperous, peaceable and contented little spot in the North of Ireland (Applause). If they all pulled together, it would surely be a simple, manly, additional respect to the memory of those brave, heroic comrades no longer with them. He had great pleasure in calling upon Mrs Lyle to declare the bazaar open.

Mrs Lyle said she felt greatly honoured in being asked to declare the bazaar open. She was especially interested in the welfare of the men of "good old D Company". She was glad that the memorial to those who had fought to make their homes secure had taken that original and practical form. Those gallant men had stood between them and ruin. They were only average men perhaps, but the divine spark had sent them out knights errant. They were thankful for those men who had died at the highest standard of manhood, and left them richer by their memory. They were now doing what they could to perpetuate the memory of those who had fallen, but a responsibility remained. They must see that the parents, wives and children had their rights, and that the men who came home were looked after (Applause). Many of these had suffered in health, and care should be taken that nothing was left undone for their comfort. Let them think of the black days of 1914, when nothing was considered too good for their fighting-men and let them remember how their own home-bred country boys went back time and again into that hideous hell in France (Applause). She hoped that the Institute would be of great usefulness to men who came back as well as a fitting memorial to their dead (Applause). A beautiful bouquet was handed to Mrs

Lyle by Miss Minnie Patrick, the little daughter of Mr and Mrs J Patrick, Dervock. A vote of thanks to Mrs Lyle and Captain Macartney was passed on the motion of Rev WN Maxwell BA, seconded by Rev Samuel Barnhill. Sales proceeded, and within the hall and in the immediate vicinity a scene of activity was witnessed which augured well for the complete success of the bazaar. We append a list of stall-holders and those in charge of games and competitions.

Work and Fancy Stall: Mrs Macartney (Lissanoure), Mrs Montgomery, Mrs McIlmoyle, Mrs J Patrick, Mrs D Patrick, Mrs Killen, Mrs Green, Mrs TJ Patrick, Miss D Quin, Miss Kennedy, Miss E Quin, Miss A Carson, Miss G Gault and Miss E McIlmoyle; **Cake Stall**: Miss Stuart, Miss McNeill, Miss M Miller, Miss Carson, Miss Mitchell, Miss K McNeill, Miss M Mitchell; **Refreshment Stall**: Mrs Miller, Mrs Crothers, Mrs Warnock, Mrs Davidson, Mrs Nicholl, Mrs Maxwell, Mrs Kennedy, Mrs Wilson, Miss Clarke, Miss Lilley, Miss Matthews, Misses Huey, Miss I Morrison, Miss Pinkerton, Miss Connolly, Miss Peden, Misses Miller, Miss Hamilton, Miss J Huey, Miss Kirkpatrick, Miss S Huey and Miss Morrison; **Farm Produce Stall**: Mrs Thomson, Mrs Barnhill, Mrs Warnock, Miss Martin, Miss A Morrison, Miss Gilmour and Misses Warnock; **Bagatelle**: Messrs John McGrotty and Thos Chestnutt; **Nail-driving**: Mr Robert J McCaw; **Shooting**: Rev RJ McIlmoyle, Messrs John Norris, John Johnston, David McAlister, Daniel Carson, Alex Carson, Wm Bellingham and F Simpson; **"Sherlock Holmes" Competition**: Rev Francis Davidson, Messrs A McAlister and J McGrotty; **Bean-Bags**: Mr D Carson; **Quoits**: Mr J Simpson. The following contributed to the half-hour concerts held during the afternoon: Mrs Montgomery, Mrs Leslie, Miss A McAlister, Miss Marjorie Orr, Miss Denny, Miss E Miller, Miss Barnhill, Mr McKaig, Mr Shannon, Mr Fred Barnhill and Rev WN Maxwell.

At the re-opening ceremony on Wednesday, on the motion of Dr Miller the chair was taken by Mr L Denny, The Whins, who after a few appropriate remarks called upon Mrs Stuart, Glenmanus House, Portrush, to open the second day's proceedings. This task Mrs Stuart performed in graceful fashion and was presented with a bouquet of flowers by Miss Eleanor Davison. A vote of thanks to the Chairman and to Mrs Stuart was proposed by Major JA Montgomery, seconded by Rev RJ McIlmoyle and cordially passed.

Only a memorial monument now (1991) stands in the space behind the first tree on the left.

Photographs of modern Dervock: Archie McKeeman & Ronnie Perry

January 1924

THE MINISTERS' SICK BENEFIT FUND.

At its Annual Meeting in June of last year, Synod decided to inaugurate a Fund to be known as the Ministers' Sick Benefit Fund. A set of Rules in connection with the administration of the scheme was drawn up and a Committee appointed to take charge of the matter.

The need for such a Fund has been apparent for some time. Our ministers are none too well paid for their services. It takes a good deal of economy in the manse to make ends meet as regards ordinary expenses, not to speak of the cost of educating a family. Should the head of the home be laid aside through illness the outlook is dark indeed.

The object of the Fund is to make provision for such a contingency. The Committee are empowered to make such grants to ministers temporarily laid aside as the circumstances of the case require, and the state of the funds permit.

Synod is not making any general appeal for funds to the members of the Church, all ministers of the Church in actual service being required to make an annual contribution of £1.

Some time ago, however, Mr. Alexander Parkhill, a member of Session of Bready Congregation, called at the Dervock Manse, and left two one-hundred pound notes—one hundred from himself, and one hundred from his sister Miss Parkhill, to be invested for the benefit of the Fund, the interest accruing each year to be used at the discretion of the Committee. The Committee gratefully acknowledge the generosity of Mr. and Miss Parkhill in this matter, and thank them for the example they have set and the help they have given.

God has blessed other members of the Church with a goodly portion of this world's goods. Who will follow a noble and inspiring example?

This is one way of using a God-given talent, of lifting a heavy burden from many a manse home, and of encouraging young men of ability to give themselves to the work of the ministry.

Still another donation has come to hand from Mr. David Park, a member of Milford Congregation, who sends, through Rev. James Blair, a cheque for £5.

Again the Committee would say, Thank You.

Copies of the Rules and any information regarding the scheme may be had from Rev. R. J. M'Ilmoyle, Dervock, Co. Antrim, Convener of Synod's Committee.

Dervock.—A Social evening was organised by this Society and held on December 18th. About 130 were present, including many representatives from the neighbouring Societies of Ballyclabber, Ballymoney and Kilraughts. After tea, Rev. R. J. M'Ilmoyle presided and delivered a helpful address, which was followed by a varied programme consisting of brief addresses and musical items contributed by a number of the members and friends present.

NORTH ANTRIM AGRICULTURAL ASSOCIATION LTD

***From the Coleraine Chronicle* of February 1924**

The annual meeting of the North Antrim Agricultural Association, Ltd, was held in the Town Hall, Ballymoney, the President, Senator JG Leslie DL, in the chair. The balance sheet for the past year was submitted by Mr J Pettigrew, Secretary. In proposing the adoption of the balance sheet, Mr JG Best JP, said the two points which stood out most prominently were the fact that they were due the bank £1,428 and that they had made a loss of £99 on the year's working. Subscriptions had fallen off by £58, which, with a falling-off in entry fees, admissions to Show and guarantees, amounted to £148. A good deal of that was due to the Show getting a wet day, and, if the day had turned out favourably, he held that the result of the Show would have been £50 in their favour. More interest and more entries would have to be obtained; otherwise they could not work the Show. The present year would be a test one, and, on this, he thought, the future of their Show would largely depend. Last year the Secretary had promised to reduce the wages bill by half, and he had accomplished more than this. £130 in the year for printing seemed very stiff. He moved the adoption of the balance sheet. The Rev RJ McIlmoyle, in seconding, said the Executive Committee had discussed the balance sheet and, on the whole, were satisfied with it. The one thing they had got to settle was how they were going to revive interest in the Show. It would be an awful pity if, in a progressive place like North Antrim, the Show would go down. The following officials were re-appointed: President, Senator JG Leslie DL; Vice-President, Mr J McElderry JP; Treasurer Mr RB Thomson, Secretary Mr J Pettigrew, Assistant Secretary Mr W Beckett. The following Executive Committee was appointed: Mr M Cunningham, Rev RJ McIlmoyle, Messrs JG Best JP, JT Burnside, HC Wilson, WWB Keers CoC, William Stuart JP, RD Pinkerton JP, Thomas Macafee JP, Hugh Gray, Andrew Keers JP and James McKinney. It was decided to hold a spring meeting on the 8th April and the summer meeting on the 4th June. The following members of the Executive Committee were appointed to form sectional committees by adding two other members, with power to add to their number, each sectional committee to be responsible for all entries and the working of the section, subject to the approval of the Executive Committee: horses, Mr Hugh Gray; cattle, Mr J McKinney; sheep, swine and goats, Rev RJ McIlmoyle; poultry and home industries, Mr A Keers JP; and dogs Mr HC Wilson. The Rev RJ M'Ilmoyle referred to the prevalence of sheep worrying and asked if it was a fact that if the County Council did not put into operation the law that all dogs should be tied up from sunset to sunrise, the police had no control over dogs. Mr WWB Keers said something should be done. A neighbour of his had lost seven sheep through being worried by dogs and on the other side of the road a man had lost three. Sheep owners were compelled to take their sheep in at night, which was a great grievance. It was agreed that the Chairman and Mr Keers should go into the matter with a view to taking action at the County Council meetings.

Tom Hanna

1924 I can recall that when I was a theological student, and even after I had entered the ministry in 1956, the Rev RJ McIlmoyle, in speaking to me, would usually ask "Are you related to the late Rev Tom Hanna of Bready [1919-24], for I knew him well?" My reply would invariably have been "Yes, he was a brother of my father, John Hanna of Corkey, and a brother of Sam Hanna of Lavin". Alas, Tom was an uncle whom I never knew, for he was dead before my time, but I was often told the full story of his call to and preparation for the ministry and not least from his mother, my grandmother Hanna. This made a very great impression on me and was one of the factors which, by God's Spirit, led me to Christ at the time of her death, on 14 January 1946, in her 85th year. As the Rev James Blair expressed it in the obituary, "one of the greatest sorrows of her life was the seemingly untimely death [on 5 February 1924, aged 37 years] of her son Rev Thomas Hanna BA". My grandfather Hanna, after whom I am named, died before my time, on 13 June 1925, at the age of 85 years. Incidentally, his birthday, like that of the Rev RJ McIlmoyle, fell on 10 April, but he was born 35 years earlier, in 1840. **RH**

1925 The March issue of *The Covenanter* reported that calls from Knockbracken, Cregagh Road, Belfast and Botanic Avenue, Belfast, had been made out to the Rev RJ McIlmoyle of Dervock. He later stayed proceedings.

1925

Limavady—Mr. John M. Crawford, of Parkersburg, West Virginia, U.S.A., whose father, the late Mr. Joseph Crawford, of Limavady, was a member of Limavady R.P. congregation and acted for some time as its precentor, recently visited his relatives and friends in Limavady and district. During his stay he attended public worship in this Church and generously contributed £20 to the congregational funds.

See also **1957**. The office-bearers in the year 1926 were:

PASTOR—REV. R. J. M'ILMOYLE.

Session—Robert Carson, David Taggart, John M'Fall, Alexander Carson, Robert Clarke (Clerk).

Committee Archibald M'Keeman, Jas. Fleming, Robert M'Fall, John Chestnut, Robert M'Conaghy, James Lyons, Wm. J. Boyd, Hugh M'Quigg, Daniel L. Carson, John Getty, Robert J. Campbell, Charles Millar, Samuel Killen, Daniel Carson, jun., David Hunter, Thomas Pollock, Samuel Barr, W. G. Finlay, Robert Patterson.

Stipend due 1st February, May, August and November.

Committee meets Second Wednesday of February, May, August and Nov.

Women's Missionary Association—President, Mrs. M'Ilmoyle ; Vice-President, Mrs. Clarke ; Treasurer, Miss Clarke.

Young Women's Missionary Association—President, Miss Taggart ; Treasurer, Miss A. L. Millar ; Secretary, Miss A. E. Carson.

C.Y.P.U.—President, Miss A. E. Carson ; Vice-President, Mr. R. J. Carson ; Treasurer, Mr. V. M'Ilmoyle ; Secretary, Miss R. Killen.

The Bible Class and Sabbath Schools opens at 11 o'clock, a.m. Public Worship at 12 o'clock, noon.

Agents for Periodicals—"Covenanter," John Getty ; "Witness," Robt. Clarke.

1926 In January *The Covenanter* reported that "Newtownards and Killinchy have united in calling Rev RJ McIlmoyle, Dervock". He later stayed proceedings.

The Rev RJ was often invited to conduct special services in many of our congregations, as several recent congregational histories bear testimony. For example, during the ministry (1908-1923) of the Rev William Warnock BA in Dromara, the Rev RJ was frequently preaching at Communion seasons. Later, under the ministry of the Rev Alexander Gilmour MA, the Rev RJ conducted special services in Dromara on Sabbath, 4 June 1926. Special collections were taken up on behalf of the renovation fund, the gallery of the Dromara Church having been transformed into a Lecture Hall.

1927

.—The Committee of Dervock Congregation waited on Mr. Robert Carson, at his home at Conagher, not long ago, and presented him with a solid oak writing desk.

Mr. Carson has been treasurer of Dervock Congregation for many years. Just recently he made a trip to the United States on a visit to his relatives there.

His brother, Mr. James Carson, head of the Carson Crockery Co. in Denver, is well known in the home country, being at business in Ballymoney in his early days, and having made repeated trips across in recent years.

In recognition of his services, and as a welcome home, the Committee expressed in a tangible way their feelings towards Mr. Carson.

Mr. W. Finlay made the presentation.

Mr. Carson made a neat reply, and afterwards entertained the Committee to tea.

1927 Stranraer called the Rev McIlmoyle of Dervock. He stayed proceedings.

1928 At the close of the Pre-Communion service in Kellswater, on Friday 8 June, during the ministry of the Rev John McIlmoyle, Messrs Samuel Wasson, Samuel Rock and Samuel Moffett were ordained to the office of ruling elder. Rev RJ McIlmoyle, Dervock, who had conducted the service, also addressed the newly-ordained elders and people. Rev SW Lynas, Cullybackey, and Mr Robert Gault (Mrs John McIlmoyle's father), Limavady, were also associated with the minister and Session in the Act of Ordination. On 1 August the Northern Presbytery visited Dervock congregation. The commendations in the finding were as follows:

> "Presbytery is gratified with the attendance of the people on the Public Ordinances and with their liberality towards the schemes of the Church We further note with pleasure the strength of Temperance sentiment in the Congregation, the respect shown for the Sabbath, and the interest taken by all in the welfare of Religion.
>
> The minister occupies a high place in the affections of the people. Presbytery notes with gratitude the testimony borne to his worth and work in making known the Way of Life, and bearing witness to the distinctive principles of the Reformed Presbyterian Church. His pastoral work also deserves high appreciation.
>
> Recent additions having been made to the Session there is now a large and efficient band of elders, and Presbytery rejoices in the testimony borne to their faithfulness in the discharge of their duties in the oversight of the flock.
>
> The temporal affairs of the Congregation are capably looked after by the Committee, which is composed of men of business ability who possess the entire confidence of all the members. The beautiful state of the Church buildings is a matter for hearty congratulation, and the fact that they have been recently renovated and are debt-free is proof of the loyal co-operation and support given to the Committee by all the members of the Congregation.

The following minute was adopted by Limavady Session on 17th October, 1928:

Session desires to put on record its sense of the great loss suffered by the Limavady congregation by the death of **Mr. Robert McIlmoyle** on 24th September, 1928. He had reached the great age of 92 years and was in years very much the senior elder and one of the senior members in office in the Session. He was ordained to the office of the eldership on February 13, 1890, and for 38 years was zealous in the discharge of his duties and in seeking the spiritual good of the congregation. In 1908 he was appointed Clerk of Session on the death of Mr. W. S. Wilson. Though he was unable for the last few years to attend the meetings of session, or serve at the communion table, he was ever interested in the welfare of the congregation, and earnest to advise younger and inexperienced office-bearers. He was most regular in the performance of every religious duty, and manifested his pleasure at being privileged to be present at public worship so frequently in old age. Towards the end, he rejoiced that he had not deferred until then the making of his peace with God. He was respected in the community for integrity and uprightness. In the home, he was a wise and diligent father, and the results of his training are seen in his family, of whom one son is minister of Dervock congregation, and one is an elder, and one an elder elect in Limavady.

To the sorrowing widow and children and friends we tender our sincere sympathy, praying that the God of all consolation may comfort them in their grief with His Own grace and peace.

—R.B.L.

Rev RJ McIlmoyle's father

AT COLERAINE SHOW

Coleraine Chronicle, 15 June 1929

Border Leicester ram any age 1 John Browne, Elagh House, Derry; 2 David N Browne, Lenamore, Muff, Co Donegal; 3 Samuel Craig, Castlecatt, Bushmills **Border Leicester ewe** registered or eligible rearing lambs, 1929 1 & 2 Rev RJ McIlmoyle; 3 K & W Moore, Ballynacannon, Macosquin **Border Leicester ewe** now ear-marked, rearing lambs, 1929 1 & 3 John H Crowe, Letterloan, 2 James McF Young **Crossbred ewe** (BL or BF cross), rearing lamb or lambs, confined to a radius of 10 miles 1 James Bailey, Dundarg, Macosquin; 2 Wm A Campbell, Ballylagan; 3 JS Blair, Ballinteer **Pure bred ram** running with an unregistered flock 1 David N Browne; 2 John H Crowe; 3 R Dunlop, Ballyversal. **Border Leicester shearling ewe** 1 & 3 Rev RJ McIlmoyle; 2 John Browne. **Border Leicester ram lamb** 1 Rev RJ McIlmoyle, 2 & 3 John Browne; **Border Leicester ewe lamb** 1 & 3 Rev RJ McIlmoyle, 2 John Browne; Black-faced horned mountain ram, any age, shown in wool 1 & 2 David Gibson, Rathsherry, Broughshane; 3 William Jackson, Coleraine **Black-faced horned mountain ewe, shorn or unshorn, rearing lamb or lambs** 1 & 2 David Gibson; 3 W Jackson. **Black-faced horned mountain year-old ewe, shorn or unshorn** 1 & 2 David Gibson; 3 William Jackson. **Suffolk ram or ram lamb** 1 Isaac Hill, Cloughan, Cloyfin; 2 R Dunlop; 3 John R Dunlop, Ballyversal **Suffolk ewe or ewe lamb** 1, 2 & 3 Isaac Hill. **Ewe or ram lamb, other than pure-bred, the progeny of a county premium ram** 1 Samuel McCandless, Ballinteer; 2 SJ Hanson, Macleary; 3 John Maybin, Billy, Bushmills

Special prizes for sheep Silver Cup presented by an admirer of the breed, for the best BL shearling ewe: Rev RJ McIlmoyle. **McIlmoyle Silver cup** for the best sheep in the show: Rev RJ McIlmoyle; cup presented by Mr William M Crowe, "Wynnefield", Philadephia, for best Border Leicester ewe, not earmarked, rearing lambs in 1929: J H Crowe. Silver medal presented by the Society of Border Leicester Sheep Breeders for the best exhibit in BL section, champion certificate for the best Border Leicester sheep in the show: Rev RJ McIlmoyle.

Goats (under rules of Ulster Goat Society) **Best pure-bred goat, female** 1 Miss K McIlmoyle, Dervock, Rosary; 2 Rev RJ McIlmoyle, Dervock, Snowdrop. **Best cross-bred goat in milk** 1 James Dunlop, Carnabuoy; 2 William Taggart, Newbuildings, Ballymoney; 3 Frank Telford, Church's Walk, Coleraine. **Best old Irish goat in milk** 1 Frank Telford. **Best kid**, any variety; born 1929, 1 Maria Keely, Railway Cottages, Coleraine, Lily; 2 Jack Getty, Kilmoyle, Ballymoney, Bonzo; 3 William Taggart, Beauty

---

ULSTER FARMERS' UNION

Year Book

AND ANNUAL REPORT

1964

U.F.U. Branch honours secretary

The residenct' of Mr. R. W. M'Fall, Ballygobbin, Ballymoney, was the venue for a private function on Monday, March 11, 1974, when the chairman and vice-chairman of Carnmoon branch of the Ulster Farmers' Union presented Mr. M'Fall with a gift from the branch in recognition of his long service as honorary secretary.

The minutes of the first meeting were read as follows: —

"A meeting was held in Carnmoon School on February 12, 1932, and was addressed by Rev. R. J. M'Ilmoyle on the working of the Ulster Farmers' Union and farming difficulties in general. At this meeting it was decided to form a branch of the Ulster Farmers' Union in Carnmoon. Mr. M'Ilmoyle then asked the assembly to elect their office-bearers for the coming year. The office-bearers elected were: — President, John M'Fall; vice-president, James Stewart; treasurer, John Moore; secretary, R. W. M'Fall.

"The president's election was proposed by T. M'Conachie and seconded by J. Moore; vice-president, by J. M'Fall, seconded by J. M'Laughlin; secretary, by T. M'Caonaghie, seconded by James Stewart; treasurer, by T. M'Conachie, seconded by Mr. Cochrane.

"The committee elected was as follows: — Carnmoon — John M'Laughlin, Alex. Hill; Magherintendry — Tom M'Conachie, William Getty; Straidbilly — William Hayes, John Steele; Cosey — William Colvin, John M'Alister; Craigpark — John Anderson, James Johnston; Ballyoglagh — W. J. M'Kaigue, Bob M'Keeman, W. Campbell; Islandranny — John Hill, James Thompson; Croagh — James Fleming, John Hill; Turfahun — John Rankin, S. Cochrane; Carnan — John Chestnutt, James Moore.

"Delegates to headquarters — John M'Fall, Thomas M'Conachie."

Mr. M'Fall has served as honorary branch secretary ever since, and the U.F.U. in general, and Carnmoon branch in particular, are deeply indebted to him for his services over such a long period. It is hoped that both he and Mrs. M'Fall will be long spared to enjoy the Branchs' gift

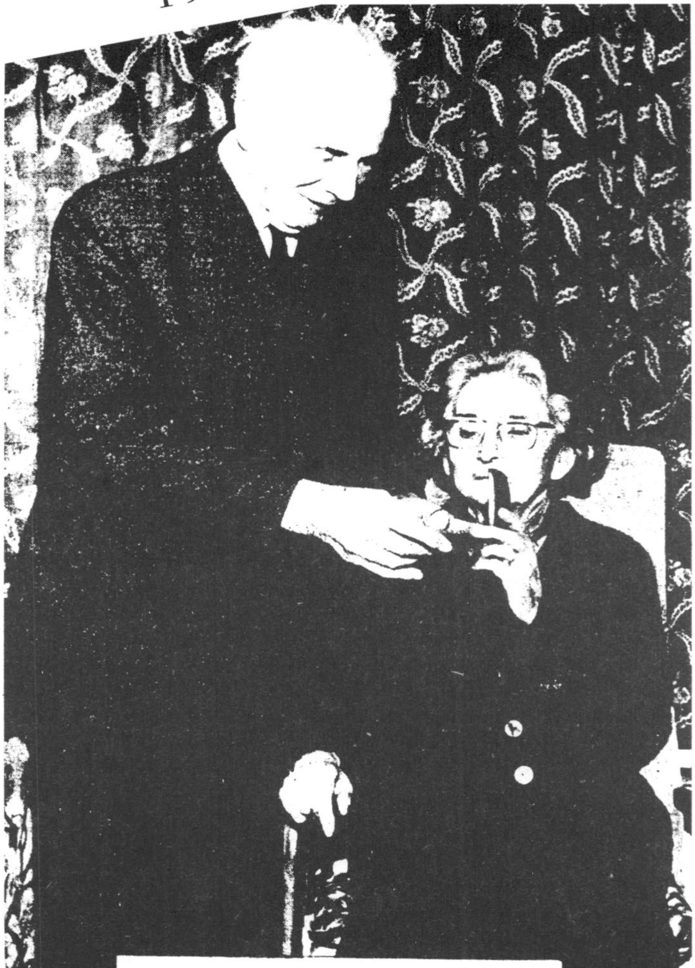

Mr. Robert McFaul and his wife admire the Gold Watch presented to Mr. McFaul by the Carnmoon Branch of The Ulster Farmers' Union to mark his services as Honary Secretary to the Branch since it's formation in 1932

CAUSES OF HUMILIATION, 1932

1. We humble ourselves because of the lack of true religion in the world. Many fail to profess Christ; while of those who do, many lack whole-hearted consecration. A spirit of utter selfishness holds men back from service, and God is hindered thereby.

2. We humble ourselves because of the modernistic tendencies of the times in the world and in the church. Men depart more and more from the good old paths, and ever hanker after something new.

3. We humble ourselves because of the pleasure-seeking tendencies of the times. Men are lovers of pleasure more than lovers of God. The gambling spirit grows apace, and the young especially refuse to take life seriously.

4. We humble ourselves because the nations still refuse to own Christ as King, and to accept His Word as the guide in all legislative action. Men are daily and hourly forgetting the fact that the nation that will not serve God shall perish.

CAUSES OF THANKSGIVING, 1932

1. We thank God for His great love manifested in the person of Christ.

2. We thank God for the written Word, and the privilege of reading and studying it without fear.

3. We thank God for the heritage we have received, and for the privilege we enjoy in that we may add thereto, and leave the world better than we found it.

4. We thank God for the healthy temperance sentiment abroad, and for the fact that sobriety is steadily making progress.

5. We thank God that at home and in the foreign field there are evidences of true spiritual life and growth, an earnest of the gathering in of the full harvest.

Respectfully submitted,

R. J. M'ILMOYLE, Convener.

On Wednesday, 20th January, the R.P. Literary Society met in Grosvenor Road Lecture Hall. Rev. R. J. M'Ilmoyle gave an instructive and entertaining address on "The Art of Public Speaking," which was characterised by a high sense of humour. It was decided to discontinue the meetings of this Society owing to lack of interest on the part of the city congregations. Rev. R. N. Lyons brought the meeting to a close by engaging in prayer. K.B.

After the ordination of Samuel McKay Calderwood to the Gospel ministry, and his installation as minister of Kellswater congregation, on 14 December 1932, invited guests, who included ministers and their wives, were entertained to luncheon in Whiteside's Hotel, Ballymena. On behalf of all the guests Rev RJ McIlmoyle proposed a vote of thanks to Kellswater congregation and this was seconded by the Rev SW Lynas BA, Cullybackey.

1933

At the Annual Social Meeting, held some time ago, Mr. Daniel Carson was presented with a piece of furniture as a token of good-will on the occasion of his marriage to Miss Nan Biggart, Druckendult, the congregation at the same time extending a hearty welcome to the bride. Mr. Carson is Treasurer of the congregation, a position held for many years by his late father, Mr. Robert Carson. He is also, as his father had been, Superintendent of the Sabbath School. He had been ordained an Elder while still young in years and is an enthusiastic member of the Young People's Society.

On the same evening a presentation was made to Mrs. Patterson, who, for a number of years, had led the Choir in the Praise Service of the congregation. Reference was made to the fact of the good attendance she was able to make since her appointment to that position.

The members of the Dervock C.Y.P.S. held the annual business meeting of the Society at the home of Mr. and Mrs. Daniel Carson, Druckendult. On their arrival the company were entertained to tea, after which Rev. R. J. M'Ilmoyle, in a short speech, introduced a special feature of the evening, which was a presentation of a beautifully inscribed Bible to Mr. Carson on the occasion of his marriage. The presentation was made by the youngest member of the Society, Master Craig Millar. Mr. Carson suitably replied, thanking the members for their beautiful gift and good wishes. A number of games were then indulged in until a late hour, when supper was served, and the singing of "Auld Lang Syne" brought a pleasant evening to a close.

COVENANTER YOUNG PEOPLE'S UNION SECRETARIES, 1933

Ballenon—Miss A. E. Macartney, Searse, Jerretzpass.

Ballyclare—Miss E. M. Armour, Burnbank, Ballyclare.

Ballyclabber—Miss L. McCollum, Lisnablaugh, Coleraine.

Ballylaggan—Miss B. Creelman, Hillview, Camus, Coleraine.

Ballymena—Miss Warwick, Warden Street, Ballymena.

Ballymoney—Miss M. McKay, Eastermede Gdns., Ballymoney.

Dublin Road—Miss E. Douglas, 5 Wellington Park Terrace, Belfast.

Grosvenor Road—Miss D. Macauley, 17 Landscape Terrace, Belfast.

Trinity Street—Miss E. Holmes, 33 Thorndale Ave., Belfast.

Creevagh—Miss J. Crawford, Springfield House, Ballybay.

Cullybackey—Miss E. M. Gardner, Kirkinroila, Ballymena.

Dervock—Miss S. Finlay, Langfield, Armoy.

Faughan—Miss V. Laird, Ardmore, Drumahoe, Londonderry.

Glasgow—Miss E. H. Gilfillan, 74 Middleton St., Ibrox, Glasgow

Kellswater—Miss L. Gaston, Slatt, Ballymena.

Kilraughts—Miss B. Young, Drumdollagh, Stranocum.

Knockbracken—Mrs. G. Archer, Lissabreeny, Near Belfast.

Larne—Miss M. Blair, Carndhu, Carnduff, Larne.

Limavady—Miss E. McIlmoyle, 90 Main Street, Limavady.

Londonderry—Miss N. S. Macdonald, 12 Collon Terrace, Londonderry.

Milford—Miss E. Warnock, The Manse, Milford.

Newry—Miss J. L. Martin, c/o. Miss Graham, Talbot Street, Newry.

Rathfriland—Miss M. Cromie, Grallagh, Rathfriland.

ALL THE WAY FROM AUSTRALIA, May 1991 My memories [per Robert Simpson, Ballee, Ballymena] of 'RJ' go back to the 1930s, when he entertained us at the Farmers' Union Annual General Meetings. In later years, when he became much older, the local branch of the Farmers' Union made certain that, if he was going a long distance to a meeting, someone would accompany him. I did this on one occasion. On our way there we called at an hotel for an evening meal. After the meal he produced a packet of cigarettes and smoked one, explaining that he only smoked this one cigarette a day. Then, out came a little black note-book. He looked up when he had last spoken at this particular branch of the Farmers' Union and then made a list of the stories to tell that night. He said he never told the same story twice at the same place. He used a letter of shorthand for each story. He then dated a new page and put the name of the branch and put a row of shorthand down the side of this page. He filled in between stories with reminiscences which were quite extempore and it just came out of him naturally, like the 'juice out of a ripe orange'.

After all these years, I can only remember two of his stories; at best the bare bones of them, without his embellishments. They went something like this. (1) This clergyman was going up Shipquay Street in Derry when he overtook this woman pushing a pram; so he gave her a helping hand up the street. When they got to the Diamond, the woman was most profuse with her thanks for his help. The clergyman said that was all right, but maybe he could have a peep at the baby. To this the woman replied: "Oh it's not a baby, I was just down the street getting a dozen bottles of stout for my old man". (2) These two ministers were in neighbouring churches and they decided to combine to visit members of their respective congregations in out-of-the-way parts of the country. They called at this home and the lady of the house asked them if they would like something to eat. They said they would, as young ministers were always hungry. By good fortune, the good lady had cooked two young chickens, which she had killed that morning. When they had eaten, one of the ministers remarked on the fuss a large rooster was making at the kitchen door, adding that he appeared to be a very proud bird. The lady said, "And why not? He has just seen two of his sons go into the ministry today." My most vivid recollection of RJ McIlmoyle was seeing him driving his sheep about a mile from the village of Dervock to his farm, every morning and evening, and wheeling his bicycle, so that he could ride the other way. After his death, I bought his farm from his family and farmed it along with my other land at the Urbal, until I came to Western Australia at the beginning of 1970. My father, the late Robert Erskine of Dunaverney, was a great friend of 'RJ', as they both shared a great interest in sheep.

James W Erskine, Box 214, Mount Barker,Western Australia, 6324

MISSIONARY ORDAINED.—GROUP OF MINISTERS AT REFORMED PRESBYTERIAN CHURCH, KILRAUGHTS, NEAR BALLYMONEY, FOR THE ORDINATION OF MR. ARCHIBALD GUTHRIE, B.A. (CENTRE FRONT ROW), MISSIONARY-DESIGNATE TO SYRIA

Back (left): Rev John McIlmoyle MA, Faughan; Rev John Watters BA, Bailiesmills & Knockbracken; Mr Thomas J McKee, Colporteur; Rev JW Calderwood, Bready; Rev Prof J Ramsay LLB, Ballymoney; **middle**: Rev SM Calderwood MA, Kellswater; Rev James Campbell BA, Convoy & Stranorlar; Rev JR Wright BA, Ballyclabber; Rev WGM Martin BA, Portrush; Rev JH McGladdery BA, Ballyclare; Rev RJ McIlmoyle, Dervock; Rev SW Lynas BA, Cullybackey; Rev JTM Blair BA, Stranraer; Rev RB Lyons BA, Limavady; Rev S Kennedy BA, Rathfriland; Rev James Blair, Kilraughts; Rev JK Dickey BA, Londonderry; **front**: Rev AC Gregg BA, Greenock; Rev Joseph McEwen (retired); Rev Archibald Guthrie BA (missionary); Rev Prof William Russell, Trinity Street, Belfast; Rev James A Lyons BA, Dublin Road, Belfast

12 September 1934

OFFICE-BEARERS OF THE W.M.U. FOR 1933-34.

President: Mrs. Evans, The Beeches, Cullybackey.

Vice-President: Mrs. Teaz, Elville, Larne.

Treasurer: Mrs. J. A. Lyons, 86 Eglantine Av., Belfast.

Secretaries: Mrs. J. M'Ilmoyle, Victoria Park, Londonderry; Miss E. S. Mathers, Bogslea, Londonderry.

Committee: Mrs. M'Farlane, Rockview Manse, Newry; Mrs. Macaulay, 17 Landscape Terrace, Belfast; Mrs. Wright, R.P. Manse, Coleraine.

———⊙———

ORDINATION OF OUR NEW MISSIONARY.

The ordination of Mr. Arch. Guthrie, B.A., will (D.V.) take place at Kilraughts R.P. Church, Wednesday, 12th September, at 12 o'clock.

We understand the following arrangements for Mr. Guthrie's Ordination were made by the Northern Presbytery at its last meeting:—The opening exercises, Prof. Ramsey; the Sermon, Rev. A. C. Gregg, B.D.; the Narrative, Rev. James A. Lyons, B.A.; Questions to be put by the Moderator of Presbytery (Rev. W. M'Cullough, B.A.); Ordination Prayer, Rev. James Blair; the Charge to Newly-Ordained Missionary, Prof. Russell; the Address to the People, Rev. W. J. Moffett, B.A.; the Closing Exercises, Rev. J. W. Calderwood (the Moderator of Synod).

We trust a large company of friends of our Mission will be present on this very important occasion, and we ask for the earnest prayers and good wishes of all the members and adherents of the Church on behalf of our young missionary, as he sets his face toward the field to which, we believe, the Lord has called him in His wonderful grace.

"They 'mong the heathen said: The Lord
Great things for them hath wrought.
The Lord hath done great things for us,
Whence joy to us is brought."
The Lord be praised for evermore!

—J.A.L.

At the 1935 Synod of the Reformed Presbyterian Church of Ireland the roll of the Northern Presbytery read as follows

NORTHERN PRESBYTERY.

MINISTERS.	ELDERS.	CONGREGATIONS.
S. H. Kennedy, B.A., D.D.*	....	Alexandretta & Idlib, [Syria.
William Lytle, B.A.*......	....	Antioch and Suadea, [Syria.
Archibald Guthrie, B.A.*	....	Missionary to Syria.
James R. Wright, B.A....	John McDowell, *alt.* D. J. McCollum*.........................	Ballyclabber.
Alex. R. Wright, B.A. ...	James Smyth, *alt.* John Kelly*...	Ballylaggan.
Prof. John Ramsey, LL.B.	Samuel L. Lyons....................	Ballymoney.
Samuel W. Lynas, B.A....	H.W. Reid, *alt.* W. B. McKelvey	Cullybackey.
R.J. McIlmoyle, G.A., M.C.†	Wm. G. Finlay........................	Dervock.
Wm. McCullough, B.A....	John Holmes..........................	Drimbolg.
....	....	Garvagh.
S. M. Calderwood, M.A....	Alex. Wilson, *alt.* Samuel Rock	Kellswater.
James Blair, G.A., M.C....	Wm. J. Pinkerton, *alt.* Thomas Loughridge*	Kilraughts.
W. G. M. Martin, B.A....	J. R. McKee, *alt.* Robert Holmes	Portrush.
....	....	Ringrash.

*Not present at any of the Sessions.
†Graduate in Arts, McCrea-Magee College, Londonderry.

Death of the Rev John McIlmoyles' father

Limavady congregation mourns the death, on 23rd November, 1935, of **John M'Ilmoyle,** senior elder of the congregation, a man greatly respected by the community for piety and good works. He had almost completed his 82nd year, and though in frail health for some years, he yet made the effort to come to public worship as often as possible. Truly, he was glad to go up to the house of his Lord ; and this not merely in his declining years but through his whole life. He gave willingly and fully of his strength and talent to serve his Master in the work of the congregation. For many years he led the praise service ; first singly, and then in conjunction with others. For a long time, too, he had a class of senior boys in the Sabbath School ; his teaching and example left their impress upon the lives of many who are now men. Having been for many years a member of Committee, he was chosen and ordained to the eldership on November 5th, 1908. and brought to that office the same high ideals, zeal, diligence and wisdom. A welcome visitor by the sick bed, a true leader in the district prayer-meeting, he was found faithful in all the duties of his office. Ever a staunch friend and valued counsellor of his pastor, he delighted to converse of things eternal. There was no fear as he came to the valley of the shadow ; and no feeling of hopeless sorrow but rather of joyful remembrance in those who remain. His family rise up and call him blessed. He leaves behind a widow and a family of three daughters and two sons—one of whom follows in his steps as an elder in the home congregation and the other is minister of Faughan and senior editor of this magazine. We commend them to the love of the Heavenly Father, the comforts of the gospel of Christ and the hope in the promises of God.

R. B. L.

BALLYMENA SHOW

BIG ENTRY AND FINE ATTENDANCE

A SPLENDID EXHIBITION

Ballymena Show, the thirty-sixth event organised by the County Antrim Agricultural Society, was held on Wednesday, and attracted a gratifying attendance. For the 320 classes there was an entry of 2,628 exhibits, and in all sections the high quality of previous years was maintained.

The well-filled shorthorn classes were notable, and the many famous herds which were represented included those at Castledawson, Broughshane, and Cloughmills. The female champion of the show was the famous daughter of a famous dam, "Castledawson White Lupin," bred by the exhibitor, Mrs. Chichester-Clark from the great "Augusta Lupin."

The section for sheep attracted many well-known exhibitors, Rev. R. J. M'Ilmoyle, Dervock, with Border-Leicesters figuring prominently in the awards.

The attractiveness of the horse-jumping programme was enhanced by a military display, and this section proved popular with the vast crowd of spectators. In the championship wall jump a notable win was secured by Mrs. E. E. Morrison, Wigmore, Aghadowey, with "Snowball."

The more spectacular events of the afternoon were somewhat marred by heavy rain.

Among the prize-winners were the following:—

BRITISH FRIESIANS

Bull, born in or before 1934—3, E. B. Gage, Moyarget, Ballycastle—Summer Island Guardsmanest.

Cow or heifer, in calf or in milk, three years old or over—3, E. B. Gage—Summer Island Lovely.

SHEEP

"M'Cay" Cup, for the best one-shear Border-Leicester ewe, bred and owned by a County Antrim farmer—Won by Rev. R. J. M'Ilmoyle, Dervock; res., H. C. Smith, Armoy.

Champion certificate for the best exhibit in the Border-Leicester sheep classes—Won by Rev. R. J. M'Ilmoyle; also reserve.

Special prize by the Society of Border-Leicester Sheep Breeders, for the best exhibit in the Border-Leicester section—Won by Rev. R. J. M'Ilmoyle; also reserve.

BLACKFACE (Open)

Ram, one year old—2, F. & J. M'Leod, Ballybogie, Clough.

Ram, over one year old—2, F. & J. M'Leod.

Ewe, one year old—1, F. & J. M'Leod.

Ewe, over one year old, suckling blackface lamb or lambs—2, F. & J. M'Leod.

Ewe lamb, dropped in 1935—3, F. & J. M'Leod.

Ram lamb, dropped in 1935—3, F. & J. M'Leod.

BLACKFACE (Confined)

Ram, one year old—1 and 3, F. & J. M'Leod.

Ram, two years old and upwards, used by the owner with his ewes on his hill grazings during the previous season—1, F. & J. M'Leod; 3, James Sayers, Corkey, Cloughmills.

BORDER-LEICESTER (Open)

Ram, any age—1, Rev. R. J. M'Ilmoyle, Dervock—Lanook; 3, Hill C. Smith, Ballybregagh, Armoy.

Ewe, one year old—1 and 2, Rev. R. J. M'Ilmoyle.

Ewe, over one year old, suckling lamb or lambs—2, Rev. R. J. M'Ilmoyle.

Ewe lamb, dropped in 1935—1 and 2, Rev. R. J. M'Ilmoyle.

Ram lamb, dropped in 1935—1, Hill C. Smith; 2, Rev. R. J. M'Ilmoyle.

SWINE

Boar, Large White, farrowed on or after 1st June, 1934, and on or before 31st December, 1934—2, Peter P. Gray, Dirraw, Finvoy—Kirkmoyle Captain.

Boar, Large White, farrowed in 1935—1 and 2, Peter P. Gray—Drumlee Captain and Finvoy Captain.

Gilt, Large White, farrowed in 1935—1 and 2, Hugh Gray, Ballymoney.

GOATS

Challenge Certificate, presented by the Ulster Goat Society, for the best goat in the show that has not won a similar award in 1935—Reserve, John G. Barbour, The Manse, Cloughmills—Ravenhill Evangeline.

Male goat of any breed, calculated to improve the local stock—2, John G. Barbour—Ravenhill Barney.

Gotling, i.e., she goat, any variety, over one and not exceeding two years, that has not borne a kid—1, John G. Barbour.

Male or female kid, dropped in 1935—2, Miss M. M'Ilmoyle, Dervock.

1935

15/6/1935

ANTRIM SHOW.

BALLYMONEY EXHIBITOR'S SUCCESS

At Antrim Show on Wednesday the Henderson Cup for the best farm horse (non-pedigree), two years old or over, the property of a bona-fide farmer, was won by Daniel Carson, Ballymoney, with "Druckendult Defender." The same animal was also first in its class.

In the class for cobs, 15 hands and under, shown in saddle, first prize went to "Reliance," owned by Mrs. H. R. Morrison, Wigmore, Aghadowey, who also secured second place in the class for hunter, mare or gelding, five years old and upwards, over 13.7, shown in saddle.

Rev. R. J. M'Ilmoyle, Dervock, won first prize with "Lanark" in the class for Border Leicester rams. He was also a prize-winner in other classes.

First prize for male goats was secured by J. G. Barbour, Cloughmills.

In the open jumping competition Mrs. H. R. Morrison's "Reliance" secured second place. First prize in the stone wall jump was taken by Mrs. Morrison's "Snowball."

FROM 'THE LADY ON THE BUS' (*see Introduction*) In my youth there were three entertainments in the year, the Sunday School Social, the Church soiree, and the Farmers' Union Social, but the last of these was *the* night of the year, because one of the speakers was the Rev RJ McIlmoyle, the Sheep King. Tickets, probably one shilling each, were bought immediately the date was known. If my memory serves me right, the evening began with Grace. Then came the tea and various speeches on how to fatten pigs or produce more milk, but I did not care about these. I had come for one man only and when he rose to his feet we could relax. I thought he had a lugubrious face and that probably added to the effect of his stories. It's the way he told them! He would begin very seriously, but somehow he introduced a funny story and we were all convulsed with laughter. Stories such as these. (1) "A minister was visiting his congregation. He called with an old lady who lived alone in a thatched cottage. After some time she made tea and served it in bowls at the fireside. The minister was intrigued by a pet pig which sat looking up at him. At last he mentioned this to his hostess. "Och", says she, "it knows its own wee bowl."

(2) A new minister had announced beforehand the families whom he would visit in the next week; so they were prepared. Mrs Brown had cooked some small chickens, and asked her guest if he could eat one? He said yes. Then her husband joined in and said, "Could he eat two"? Again the answer was yes. The minister ate heartily, nearly too heartily for his hosts, sampling everything on the table. When the meal was finished, he sat on talking. A large rooster appeared on the fence outside and began to crow triumphantly. "That is a magnificent bird you have", said the minister. "He is very proud." Mr Brown could stand it no longer. "Not much wonder", he said, "he has two sons in the ministry." (3) Another story about a minister: again a woman on her own; again she entertained him to tea. This lady suggested a boiled egg. He agreed, delighted. She suggested two. "Certainly", said he. When the meal was finished, a large cat jumped in over the half-door. "Is that your cat?", asked his Reverence. "No", says she, "all hungry gorbs call here." (4) A countryman took a short cut through a graveyard, three nights a week, on his way to see his girlfriend. A playboy thought he would perpetrate a trick on him; so he dug a deep hole in the path, covered himself with a sheet and hid behind a headstone. Everything went according to plan and the next time the man went through the graveyard he fell into the hole. His tormentor appeared, looked down at him and said, "What are you doing in my grave?" The countryman, undismayed, looked up and said "What are you doing out of it?"

When my Ballymoney friend was being driven to work in Bushmills on cold winter mornings in the late Forties, she would have seen Mr McIlmoyle walking along the road with his crook. Her companion remarked, "There is the good shepherd tending his flock". Her aunt in Ballymoney knew who was in the garage office when the request came for tea and two slices of fruit loaf, buttered. The said visitor always had time to stay and talk, no matter how busy he was. When in hospital during his last illness he was in a bed with high sides to keep him safe. But at night he would jump out and go up one side of the ward and down the other, looking at every patient, and would then go back to bed quite happily, evidently re-assured that all was well in the fold. The nurses were very upset when he died. I have heard from two different sources that [in one sense] he had no sense of humour; also that he never told his age.

Jane Megaw, Markstown, Cullybackey

AT JOHN RAMSEY'S MINISTERIAL JUBILEE, 1936

(This token of esteem for a wise and faithful Presbyter is presented to Rev. Prof. JOHN RAMSEY, LL.B., on the occasion of his Jubilee as Pastor of Ballymoney Congregation by his Ministerial Brethren of the Northern Presbytery).

Back (left): Rev SM Calderwood MA (Kellswater); Rev AR Wright BA, Ballylaggan; Rev WGM Martin BA, Portrush; Rev SW Lynas BA, Cullybackey; Rev J Blair GAMC, Kilraughts; **front**; Rev W Lytle BA, Missionary to Antioch and Suadea, Syria; Rev W McCullough BA, Drimbolg; Rev Prof J Ramsey LLB, Ballymoney; Rev JR Wright BA, Ballyclabber; Rev RJ McIlmoyle GAMC, Dervock

1936

Presentation to Prof. Ramsey. Immediately after the February Meeting of the Northern Presbytery, the ministers adjourned to the Criterion Cafe, Ballymoney, for lunch, the function having been arranged in honour of Prof. Ramsey. After luncheon Rev. William M'Cullough, acting as chairman, made reference to the unique position occupied by the guest of honour. He reminded the brethren that Prof. Ramsey was brought up within the bounds of the Presbytery, became a student under its care, received from it his licence to preach, and was subsequently ordained by it to the pastorate of the Ballymoney Congregation, which he had served during the past 50 years.

Rev. R. J. M'Ilmoyle then presented to Prof. Ramsey a little memento of the occasion in the form of an enlarged and framed photograph of the ministers of the Presbytery, suitably inscribed and autographed. Rev. J. R. Wright then spoke of the character and worth of Prof. Ramsey as a co-presbyter and friend.

Prof. Ramsey, in reply, expressed his appreciation of the action of his brethren, and stated in the course of his speech that at the present time there were more ministers in the Presbytery than at any other period within his memory.

Revs. James Blair, William Lytle, S. W. Lynas, S. M. Calderwood, W. G. M. Martin, and A. R. Wright having spoken their congratulations to the guest, the meeting closed with the Benediction.

(A copy of the photo is presented with this issue of the "Covenanter.")

Kellswater—The Congregation and many people of the surrounding district had a time of quickening and spiritual uplift through Special Evangelistic Meetings held in the Church from Sabbath 1st March till Friday, 6th March. The speakers were Revs. Alexander Gilmour, M.A., R. J. M'Ilmoyle, William M'Cullough, B.A., and S. R. Archer, B.A. On the opening night the attendance was augmented by the neighbourly act of closing the United (Kells and Connor) Evening Service. Still throughout the week the attendances were very good, reaching high water mark on Friday when the House was packed. On the last evening many, in one way or another, gave evidence of having been blessed during the week and stated that they were sorry the meetings were not continuing another week

1937 The Rev AC Gregg concluded thus his address as a delegate from the Scottish Synod to the Irish Synod on 22 June:

> I am delighted to be here amongst you, and I hope all of you who are here and many more from Ireland will be able to come over to Scotland next year, and join in the commemoration of the noble Covenant of 300 years ago. The occasion will, I believe, be an uplifting and memorable one. and the younger ministers, to whom the Covenanter Convention of 1896 is unknown unless by hearsay, should do their best to attend the Convention of 1938.

ROYAL ULSTER SHOW BALMORAL

***Coleraine Chronicle*, 29 May 1937**

Border Leicester: *Ram two shear and upwards*: 1 Rev RJ McIlmoyle, Dervock, Co Antrim - Lanark; *Shearling ram*: 2 Rev RJ McIlmoyle - Annan Majestic; *Border Leicester Ewe, having reared a lamb or lambs in 1937*: Rev RJ McIlmoyle; *Ram lamb*: **1&3** Rev RJ McIlmoyle;

***Coleraine Chronicle*, 19 June 1937**

Champion certificate for best exhibit in the Border Leicester sheep classes: Rev RJ McIlmoyle special prize of £3 presented by the Society of Border Leicester Sheep Breeders for the best exhibit in the Border Leicester Section: Rev RJ McIlmoyle; Cup for the best one-shear Border Leicester ewe, bred and owned by a County Antrim farmer: Rev RJ McIlmoyle

---

QUALITY SHEEP AND SWINE

Splendid success from every point of view attended the North Antrim Agricultural Association's thirty-fifth annual show at Ballymoney on Tuesday last.

The exhibitors represented all parts of Ulster, and the entries constituted a record, while the attendance of the general public was most encouraging to the promoters of an exhibition which has long enjoyed a big measure of deserved popularity. Not only were the entries more numerous than ever before, but there was an all-round improvement in the standard of quality, and competition generally was exceptionally keen.

There was a notably good section of heavy horses, yearlings of marked quality being particularly prominent. Here, as also in the cattle section, which, too, was remarkably good, there were animals that had won at Ballymena, Coleraine and other Northern shows.

Sheep and swine made up an excellent display and, collectively viewed, the show was one of the best yet held in the Route capital which, as is well-known, is the hub of one of the most progressive agricultural districts in the Province.

The judge was very favourably impressed by the fine array of Border-Leicester sheep, and he experienced not a little difficulty in placing them in order of merit. An outstanding ram was shown by the Rev. R. J. M'Ilmoyle, one of the principal exhibitors in the section.

SHEEP. 26/6/1937

Border-Leicester ram, any age—1, **Rev.** R. J. M'Ilmoyle, Dervock; 2, J. B. Kirkpatrick, Boardmills, Lisburn; 3, Hill C. Smith, Ballybregagh, Armoy.

Border-Leicester ewe, having reared lambs in 1937—1 and 3, Rev. R. J. M'Ilmoyle; 2, Hill C. Smith.

Border-Leicester ram lamb—1, and 3, R. J. M'Ilmoyle; 2, J. B. Kirkpatrick.

Lamb, bred off Border-Leicester premium ram, located in County Antrim—1, J. & R. Dunlop, Ballyversal, Cloyfin, Coleraine; 2 and 3, Samuel Craig, Castlecatt, Bushmills.

Non-pedigree ewe, having reared lambs in 1937—1, 2 and 3, Fred M'Curdy, Camus, Coleraine.

Ram, from a non-registered flock—1, J. & R. Dunlop; 2, Wilfred Tweed, Ballymacwilliam, Ballymoney; 3, Wm. Erskine, Ballymoney.

Non-pedigree ram lamb—1, Bobbie Glass, Monaghan, Ballymena; 2, J. & R. Dunlop; 3, T. & A. Scally, Magheracastle, Ballycastle.

Non-pedigree ewe lamb—1 and 3, Samuel Craig; 2, T. & A. Scally.

SWINE

Large white Ulster boar, any age—1, Andrew Hynds, Finkiltagh, Portglenone—Finkiltagh Duke 2nd; 2, Peter P. Gray, Dirraw, Finvoy—Ballywoollen Tiger; 3, Andrew Hynds—Finkiltagh Duke

---

BLACK SHEEP AT BALMORAL

Mrs Lucy McKinstry, 2 Mosside Road, Dunmurry, Belfast: "I do well remember RJ, as he was affectionately known, back sixty years ago, coming to Hillsborough Young Farmers' Club socials, to tell his wonderful stories. The hall was packed and he got such a reception. I also remember him showing his Border Leicester Sheep at Balmoral over sixty years ago and he was such a dapper little figure in the show ring. In those days the owners of cattle and sheep slept near their animals in the stalls. One of the cattle owners played a trick on RJ when he was asleep, for he dyed one of his show sheep black. That caused trouble the next morning. Are there any Reformed Presbyterians or others who remember that incident at Balmoral over sixty years ago?"

WHEN THEY ALL GET A DRINK ...

From Mrs Rita M McCollum, "Glasgort", 2 Kirkmoyle View, Ballymoney: I remember, around 1938, being at the annual Church Social, or 'swaree' as it was then called, at Macosquin Presbyterian Church, where my parents were members and indeed my father had been an elder for about 30 years until his death. In those times the Social was held in the Church and the late Rev WS McClelland was the minister. On the particular evening to which I refer it was the late Rev RJ McIlmoyle who was the guest speaker. The Chairman introduced him and, as the Rev McIlmoyle came forward on to the platform, a good many of the younger boys (who might not even have been members of the Church, but were sitting in the back pews) commenced to bleet, imitating sheep, because the late Rev McIlmoyle was known far and wide because of his interest in Border Leicester sheep and had won many trophies & cups. Anyway, between clapping and bleeting, it was a very noisy few minutes. Mr McClelland tried to quieten them by using his hands desperately, by way of telling them to stop, but it only got worse. However RJ just turned to the Chairman and said, "It is all right, Mr McClelland. When they all get a drink, they will all settle down and keep quiet". Then as he commenced to speak, suddenly there was quietness. Lots of laughter followed as he proceeded to tell his stories.

SOLDIER'S MOVING FAREWELL

From the *Ballymena Observer* of 4 October 1940: "A Social for members of the Tully Branch of the Ulster Farmers' Union took place in Tully Schoolroom. Rev RJ McIlmoyle occupied the chair and also told stories." **Mr John McKillen, 57 Rankinstown Road, Ballymena**, a member of Kellswater RP Church, recalls a party piece which the Rev RJ performed in Tully School, entitled "A Soldier's Farewell to His Aunt". Another artiste or someone from the audience, was chosen to act the part of the aunt and the Rev RJ's moving "farewell" has remained vividly ever since in the memory of John McKillen.

Why are we called Covenanters?

Who we are

Covenanters are the successors of those faithful people who, when the progress of Reformation was threatened in Scotland, pledged themselves in Covenant to maintain a pure Gospel and a Scriptural form of worship and to promote national righteousness and civil and religious freedom under Christ.

During the persecution of the Scottish Church between 1660 and 1688, it is estimated that 18,000 Covenanters suffered death, destitution, torture or banishment to slavery rather than compromise their allegiance to Jesus Christ, rather than forsake their testimony for the Crown Rights of Jesus Christ as the sole Head of Church and State.

In 1690, when the nation and the Church in general set aside the National Covenant of Scotland of 1638 and the Solemn League and Covenant of 1643, a steadfast minority determined to retain them as the basis for a continuing distinctive testimony.

However the basis for Covenanting is not only historical - it's true origin is in biblical theology, being founded upon the Covenant of Grace by which God freely offers to sinners life and salvation by Jesus Christ, requiring of them faith in him, that they may be saved; and promising to give to all those that are ordained unto life His Holy Spirit, to make them willing and able to believe.

We are Presbyterian in Church Government and because of strict adherence to the principles of reformation promoted in Scotland in the sixteenth and seventeenth centuries, have adopted the formal title, Reformed Presbyterian.

We are found in many parts of the world today having spread from Scotland to Ireland and later to the United States and Canada, to Australia, Cyprus and Japan also with missionaries in France.

In anticipating the Tercentenary Convention in 1938, Mr Robert Holmes, Ballymoney, was in reminiscent mood:

> As we recall the 1896 Convention, so rich in delightful experiences of social and spiritual fellowship between the delegates of the three Covenanting Churches, we should be inspired with new determination to make the forthcoming Convention an unqualified success.
>
> This is eminently an occasion which calls us to join together, heart and soul, not only to revive the memory of our Covenanting forefathers and their splendid achievement on behalf of civil and religious liberty, but also to confirm one another in our devotion, by word and deed, to the imperishable principles for which they lived and died.

The Tercentenary of the National Covenant of Scotland was celebrated from Tuesday, 28 June, to Friday, 1 July 1938. Convention meetings were held in Hope Street Free Church, Glasgow, and in Greyfriars Church, Edinburgh. On the previous Sabbath, 26 June, Tercentenary services were held also at places associated either with the death of martyrs or with some other memorable event in the history of the Scottish Covenanters. It is to be noted that in the handbook setting out the programme for that Sabbath at Moniaive the preacher expected was Rev RJ McIlmoyle, but in the memorial volume of the Convention it was the Rev TM Slater DD, Montclair, USA, who preached the sermon at James Renwick's birth-place in Dumfriesshire. Possibly the Dervock minister had not travelled to Scotland until the Monday; the handbook, of course, was published some months before the date of the Convention and, as its preface explains, "change may require to be made in some points when the actual business is reached".

Greyfriars Church, Edinburgh

SOCIETY OF BORDER LEICESTER SHEEP BREEDERS

President.

ROBERT S. FORREST, Thornhome, Carluke, Lanarkshire.

Vice-President.

HARRY B. MOYES, Kilmux, Leven, Fife.

Council.

D. H. SANDERSON, The Birks, Stamfordham, Northumberland.
JOHN F. GRANT, South Kingennie, Kingennie, Angus.
R. C. CAMERON, Greenlawdean, Greenlaw, Berwickshire.
C. M. BAXTER, Clanmurray, Dromore, Co. Down.
WILLIAM MACDONALD, Estate Office, Rock, Alnwick.
THOMAS G. FORSYTH, New Smailholm, Kelso.
REV. R. J. M'ILMOYLE, Dervock, Co. Antrim.
NIVEN M. PATERSON, Bank House, Turriff, Aberdeenshire.
JOHN YOUNG, 12 Kay Park Terrace, Kilmarnock.
HARRY FINDLAY, Myreton, Dundee.
WILLIAM G. GROSSART, Dunjarg, Castle Douglas.
ROBIN G. MURRAY, Waulkmill, Biggar.
JAMES L. WHYTE, Hayston, Glamis, Angus.
JOHN FORDYCE, Balfarg, Markinch, Fife.
JOHN JEFFREY, Deuchrie, Dunbar.
JOHN C. NOBLE, Loanfoot, Skirling, Biggar.
JAMES FINDLAY, Bogardo, Forfar.
DONALD CROSS, Knockdon, Maybole.
WILLIAM M. MILNE, Balbinny, Forfar.
DAVID S. MINTO, Ardmore, Udny, Aberdeenshire.

WINNERS OF MEDALS AND PRIZES OFFERED BY THE SOCIETY OF BORDER LEICESTER SHEEP BREEDERS AT VARIOUS SHOWS IN 1938.

ROYAL AGRICULTURAL SOCIETY, CARDIFF—*60-Guinea Silver Cup and Gold Medal*—W. Gilchrist Macbeth, Dunira, with Ram, (11770), Waulkmill Lynn.

ROYAL ULSTER AGRICULTURAL SOCIETY, BELFAST—*£5 Prize*—Rev. R. J. M'Ilmoyle, Dervock, with Ewe, B L 255, M 39, by (10872), Sandyknowe Topsman.

NORTH-WEST OF IRELAND AGRICULTURAL SOCIETY—*£3 Prize*—Rev. R. J. M'Ilmoyle, Dervock, with Ram Lamb, B L 435, O 1, by (10994), Annan Majestic.

THE ROYAL AGRICULTURAL SOCIETY OF VICTORIA—*Gold Medal*—

CO. ANTRIM AGRICULTURAL ASSOCIATION—*Silver Medal*—Rev. R. J. M'Ilmoyle, Dervock, with Ram Lamb, B L 435, O 1, by (10994), Annan Majestic.

CO. ARMAGH AGRICULTURAL SOCIETY—*Silver Medal*—Rev. R. J. M'Ilmoyle, Dervock, with Ewe, B L 255, M 39, by (10872), Sandyknowe Topsman.

FLOCK 82E.

Vincent H. M'Ilmoyle, 17 Causeway Street, Portrush, Co. Antrim.

RAM.

Ram used in 1938.	Sire.	Dam.
(11334), Temple Bar	(10355), Headline	(B L 842), H 14

EWE.

Ewe.	Sire.	Dam.
N 1	(9991), Lanark	(B L 858), J 7

FLOCK 435.

Rev. R. J. M'Ilmoyle, Dervock, Co. Antrim.

RAMS.

Rams used in 1938.	Sire.	Dam.
(11334), Temple Bar	(10355), Headline	(B L 842), H 14
(11457), Bogardo, £200	(11181), Howie's £160	(B L 52), K 19A
(11762), Top Castle	(11342), Tiptop	(B L 16B), L 1

EWE.

Ewe.	Sire.	Dam.
(B L 42E), N 6	(11588), Greylad	(B L 33B), K 10

(11809) BALLOO BARON. B L 44B. Lambed 1938.
Breeder and Owner—John C. Stewart, Balloo.
Sire—(11094), Dervock Pullover; *breeder*—Rev. R. J. M'Ilmoyle.
Dam—B L 393, K 15.
S.D.—(9924), Fruithill Baron; *breeder*—Robert W. Bell.
S.G.D.—(6360), Morrow's Square Measure; *breeder*—James Morrow, Junr.
S.G.G.D.—(5672), Culloden Footprint; *breeder*—William R. Ross.

(11810) BALLYMACREELY PULLOVER. B L 652. Lambed 1938.
Breeder—William D. S. Minnis, Ballymacreely. *Owner*—William J. Barr, Burren.
Sire—(11094), Dervock Pullover; *breeder*—Rev. R. J. M'Ilmoyle.
Dam—B L 79c, K 1.
S.D.—(8362), Journey's End; *breeder*—Robert Magill.
S.G.D.—(8903), Saucy Sam; *breeder*—Samuel Stokes.
S.G.G.D.—(7152), Ballymecashon Favourite; *breeder*—Joseph Minnis.

(11866) COMBER RECORD. B L 925. Lambed 1938.
Breeder—William J. Horner, Glassmoss. *Owners*—Meeke Brothers, Fedney.
Sire—(11278), Pretts Mill Advertiser; *breeder*—Alexander Clarkson.
Dam—B L 453, M 1.
S.D.—(10281), Dervock R. J.; *breeder*—Rev. R. J. M'Ilmoyle.
S.G.D.—(8113), Test Match; *breeder*—James Howie, Junr.
S.G.G.D.—(6943), Hillend Willie; *breeder*—Hugh Hamilton.

(11867) CONTACT II. B L 83c. Lambed 1938.
Breeder—Arthur McCoubrey, Grovehill. *Owners*—Murphy & Stanfield, Ballymackilreiney.
Sire—(11499), Clanmurray Mist; *breeder*—C. M. Baxter.
Dam—B L 725, J 2.
S.D.—(9485), Double Option; *breeder*—George Ervine.
S.G.D.—(7944), Fruithill Sailor King; *breeder*—Robert W. Bell.
S.G.G.D.—(6992), Lyonston Mascot; *breeder*—William Wallace.

(11883) DERVOCK LEADER. B L 67D. Lambed 1938.
Breeder—Rev. R. J. M'Ilmoyle, Dervock. *Owner*—The Earl of Leitrim, Mulroy.
Sire—(10994), Annan Majestic; *breeder*—Richard Temple.
Dam—B L 255, M 18.
S.D.—(10610), Banker's New Deal; *breeder*—Niven M. Paterson.
S.G.D.—(9690), Sandyknowe Ringleader; *breeders*—T. & M. Templeton.
S.G.G.D.—(6514), Border Masterpiece; *breeder*—John Young.

As War Clouds Gathered

TWO-SHEAR EWE, B L 255, M 39. Sire, (10872), Sandyknowe Topsman ; Dam, B L 255, I 22, by (7382), Sandyknowe Supreme.
Winner of £5 Special Prize given by The Society of Border Leicester Sheep Breeders for Champion Exhibit in the Border Leicester Section at The Royal Ulster Agricultural Society Show, Belfast, 1938.
Bred by Messrs. J. & W. Young, Skerrington Mains, Hurlford, Ayrshire. Owned and Exhibited by Rev. R. J. M'Ilmoyle, Dervock, Co. Antrim.

1939

Dervock.—ORDINATION OF ELDERS.—In spite of heavy rain the Church Building at Dervock was well filled with an eager and attentive Congregation on Sabbath, 15th October, when at the conclusion of the ordinary service, Messrs. N. Fleming, R. Patterson, R. M'Fall and R. J. Campbell were ordained to the office of the Eldership. The Pastor, Rev. R. J. M'Ilmoyle, was assisted on the occasion by Rev. J. M'Ilmoyle, Faughan, who preached the sermon and delivered an address to the newly ordained Elders, and to the people. Messrs. A. Carson, W. G. Finlay and J. Lyons, members of Session also took part in the Ordination.

1940

Bready—On the last Sabbath of September, a special evening service was held in Bready, this service was conducted by Rev. R. J. McIlmoyle, Dervock. A collection was taken to help to provide wool for the ladies who are knitting for H. M. Forces.

1941

Dervock—Rev. Nevin Lyons of Grosvenor Road, Belfast, has just presented Dervock Congregation with a Clock for use in the Church building. Speaking to the Congregation ; Mr. Lyons spoke of the influence of his early home training on his life, referring specially to the influence his mother's training had had on him. He asked the Congregation to accept of the Clock as his gift in memory of their mother.

Rev. R. J. McIlmoyle, on behalf of the Congregation, thanked Mr. Lyons for the gift. He said that once upon a time the name Nevin was a household word in the Congregation, and that now the name Lyons is a household word in the Church—three ministers in our small Church bearing that name.

This clock still faithfully tells the time in Dervock Covenanting Meeting-house.

BORDER LEICESTER FLOCK BOOK

VOLUME XLIV. (1942)

FLOCK 435.

Rev. R. J. M'Ilmoyle, Dervock, Co. Antrim.

RAMS.

Rams used in 1941.	Sire.	Dam.
(11560), Fruithill Highspot	(11369), Young Beechhill	(B L 171), J 4
(12279), Dual Control	(10683). Duplicator	(B L 182), H 76
(12447), Silver Gleam	(11933), Golden Gleam	(B L 171), L 5

RAMS—*Continued.*

Rams used in 1941.	Sire.	Dam.
(12938), Mac's Glory, R 1	(11560), Fruithill Highspot	(B L 1B), P 2
(13029), Whitehill Highspot, R 4A	Do.	(B L 435), O 8

EWES.

Ewes.	Sire.	Dam.
Q 4	(12447), Silver Gloom	O 8
(B L 1B), P 20	(11995), Lawson's Glory	M 39

(12937) LYALL'S FAVOURITE. B L 95E. Lambed 1940.

Breeder—Andrew Scott, West Moneylaws. *Owner*—Andrew Scott, Panama.

Sire—(11657), Millern ; *breeder*—James Lyall.

Dam—B L 1B, O 76.

S.D.—(11501), Coming Event ; *breeder*—J. Ian Cumming.

S.G.D.—(8101), Stockmark ; *breeders*—T. & M. Templeton.

S.G.G.D.—(8457), Sandyknowe Sonny Boy ; *breeders*—T. & M. Templeton.

(12938) MAC'S GLORY. B L 66C. Lambed 1941.

Breeder—Rev. R. J. M'Ilmoyle, Dervock. *Owner*—William M. Glenn, Drumbarnett.

Sire—(11560), Fruithill Highspot ; *breeder*—Robert W. Bell.

Dam—B L 1B, P 2.

S.D.—(11995), Lawson's Glory ; *breeder*—John Lawson.

S.G.D.—(10859), Renmure Silver Jubilee ; *breeder*—James C. Moyes.

S.G.G.D.—(9881), Dunjarg Favourite ; *breeder*—William G. Grossart.

(12939) MACOSQUIN ROVER. B L 748. Lambed 1936.

Breeder and Owner—William Moore, Ballynacannon.

Sire—(10096), Snowfall ; *breeder*—Samuel Bell.

Dam—B L 645, G 5.

S.D.—(7014), Morrow's Square Balance ; *breeder*—James Morrow, Junr.

S.G.D.—(7179), Conqueror Yet ; *breeder*—William J. McKee.

S.G.G.D.—(6379), Ormonde ; *breeder*—James O'Hare.

(12844) DAVY PERFECTION. B L 441. Lambed 1941.

Breeder—David Smith, Kilmaurs Mains. *Owner*—Robert Wilson, Dockrayrigg.

Sire—(12354), Lawson's Perfection ; *breeder*—John Lawson.

Dam—B L 87D, O 2.

S.D.—(11113), Eshott Bold Boy ; *breeder*—A. B. Howie.

S.G.D.—(10070), Sandyknowe Investment ; *breeders*—T. & M. Templeton.

S.G.G.D.—(8899), Sandyknowe Rising Sun ; *breeders*—T. & M. Templeton.

(12845) DERVOCK HIGHSPOT. B L 703. Lambed 1941.

Breeder—Rev. R. J. M'Ilmoyle, Dervock. *Owner*—Andrew Alexander, Clogher.

Sire—(11560), Fruithill Highspot ; *breeder*—Robert W. Bell.

Dam—B L 435, O 8.

S.D.—(10994), Annan Majestic ; *breeder*—Richard Temple.

S.G.D.—(10610), Banker's New Deal ; *breeder*—Niven M. Paterson.

S.G.G.D.—(9690), Sandyknowe Ringleader ; *breeders*—T. & M. Templeton.

(12846) DERVOCK'S DANDY. B L 69F. Lambed 1941.

Breeder—Rev. R. J. M'Ilmoyle, Dervock. *Owner*—John Huston, Ballyportery.

Sire—(12447), Silver Gleam ; *breeder*—Robert W. Bell.

Dam—B L 435, P 8.

S.D.—(11457), Bogardo, £200 ; *breeder*—James Findlay.

S.G.D.—(10872), Sandyknowe Topsman ; *breeders*—T. & M. Templeton.

S.G.G.D.—(7382), Sandyknowe Supreme ; *breeders*—T. & M. Templeton.

(13027) WESTFIELD DEPUTY. B L 231. Lambed 1941.

Breeder—Harry Franks, Westfield. *Owner*—Timothy O'Sullivan, Cloughduv.

Sire—(11559), Fruithill Ever Ready ; *breeder*—Robert W. Bell.

Dam—B L 188, N 66.

S.D.—(11251), Parvenu ; *breeder*—Col. Balfour.

S.G.D.—(9963), Highland Boy ; *breeder*—John Fordyce.

S.G.G.D.—(7182), Cootehill ; *breeder*—Louis Bowden.

(13028) WHITECAIRNS GENERAL. B L 29A. Lambed 1941.

Breeder—John A. Rose, Whitecairns. *Owner*—William Watt, Rogiehill.

Sire—(12331), Heather Blossom ; *breeders*—S. J. & T. Cardno.

Dam—B L 831, P 2.

S.D.—(11218), Mosstown Monarch ; *breeder*—Robert L. Watt.

S.G.D.—(10248), Bullion ; *breeder*—Niven M. Paterson.

S.G.G.D.—(9575), Jack Johnstone ; *breeder*—Harry G. Johnstone.

(13029) WHITEHILL HIGHSPOT. B L 435. Lambed 1941.

Breeder and Owner—Rev. R. J. M'Ilmoyle, Dervock.

Sire—(11560), Fruithill Highspot ; *breeder*—Robert W. Bell.

Dam—B L 435, O 8.

S.D.—(10994), Annan Majestic ; *breeder*—Richard Temple.

S.G.D.—(10610), Banker's New Deal ; *breeder*—Niven M. Paterson.

S.G.G.D.—(9690), Sandyknowe Ringleader ; *breeders*—T. & M. Templeton.

Mr Robert Bell, Portstewart, writes: My late father, RW Bell JP, Fruithill, Hillsborough, Co Down, was one of a dozen farmers who introduced Border Leicester sheep to Ireland in 1899. I remember my father telling me that at an agricultural show he got into conversation with a young clergyman who was standing by and admiring one of my father's sheep which had won the Border Leicester Sheep Championship. The young clergyman was the Rev RJ McIlmoyle, who in the course of conversation requested and was given the necessary information as to how to become a member of the Border Leicester Sheep Breeders Society and also the owner of suitable foundation sheepstock. I remember Mr McIlmoyle himself telling me how he had travelled to Hillsborough to see how sheep were prepared for shows. I look forward to reading the book on his Reverence, as he and my father became great friends.

Miss Maye Long, Aghadowey, recalls: Fifty years ago, as a teenager with my aunt Amy Hanna, I accompanied RJ McIlmoyle on his visit to Farmers' Union meetings and concerts from Dervock to Islandmagee. He called here at Aghadowey and collected us, plus two more talented folk singers, Tommy Jamieson and John Ramsey. In the months of January and February, when weather conditions were not good, we would set off, sometimes going to two places in the one night. I remember going to Finvoy, then later to Glenwherry, and we did our party pieces. RJ was not a good driver and if he backed into a lamp post, even at the City Hall at 1 am, or bumped into a ditch somewhere in the country, he just asked "Is anyone hurt?" and drove on. When you heard his stories, maybe twice on the same night, these were engraven in your mind and I as a teenager used to act his speech! It is difficult to recall everything, after all these years .... he always concluded by striking a serious note. His story I best remember was about the train driver who had negotiated a difficult journey. A passenger went to him, shook his hand and said, "A good run, a very good run". He hoped that when we came to life's end, the Master would take us by the hand and say "A good run, a very good run". I feel sure that was what was said to him!

CRASH References have been made by several to the fact that the Rev RJ was not the best driver of a car. Perhaps that was due to failing eyesight. He was involved in an accident with his car and trailer, an Austin 10 HP, registration HMG 726, at 8.30 am on 22 May 1946 at the Roddenfoot Railway Bridge (known locally as the Cow Bridge), Ballymoney. A drain across the road was partly filled in, so that traffic could use the left-hand side, heading out of the town. Two cyclists, James McIlreavy and Archie Stewart, were crossing the bridge at the same time as the Rev RJ and in the same direction ... when Archie came off and later was taken to the Route Hospital. He was not badly injured. The Rev RJ was later convicted of careless driving under the Road Traffic Act and the same reported in the local press. One of the two RUC constables dealing with the above case has written, "I remember RJ well, a man slightly bent forward, wearing thick glasses with little or no frames. I was never speaking to him again, but I remember him on the platform at a social in Drumreagh Presbyterian Church Hall. I also remember seeing him in the fields attached to the RP Manse on the Bushmills Road, Dervock. He was working with his sheep which were all a lovely honey colour from the dip which he used."

BIOGRAPHICAL SKETCH.

Robert Nevin was born at Carnaff, near Dervock, October 21st, 1817. The Nevin family came originally from Scotland, and settled first at Kilmoyle, about five miles from Ballymoney. Robert's father and mother bore a striking likeness to each other, and this likeness, mental and physical, was largely transmitted to their children. They were gifted with a bright intelligence and a sparkling humour, suppressed somewhat by a refined natural modesty and gentleness of demeanour, but quickened and mellowed by the inner fire of a deep and irrepressible piety. James Nevin made a comfortable and prosperous home for his family in Carnaff, and was a tower of strength to the cause of religion and temperance in the congregation and district.

MISUNDERSTOOD SCRIPTURES.

A CRITICAL EXAMINATION OF SOME PASSAGES IN THE INSPIRED WORD, RESPECTING THE IMPORT OF WHICH THERE HAS BEEN MUCH DISCUSSION AND DIFFERENCE OF OPINION; WITH A VIEW TO ESTABLISH THE REAL MEANING.

BY THE

REV. ROBERT NEVIN, D.D.,

AUTHOR OF "STUDIES IN PROPHECY."

MEMORIAL VOLUME,

CONTAINING BIOGRAPHICAL SKETCH BY REV. PROF. CHANCELLOR, D.D., AND FUNERAL SERMON BY REV. PROF. DICK, M.A.

Londonderry:

JAMES MONTGOMERY, CARLISLE ROAD.

MDCCCXCIII.

PSALM XXIII.—A NEW VERSION.

[By the Rev. ROBERT NEVIN, D.D. Written years ago on the fly-leaf of his pocket Bible.]

Rendered as closely to the original as possible.

1. Jehovah's my Shepherd; my wants He'll supply;
2. In pastures of verdure He'll make me to lie;
   By streams of repose He will lead me along;
3. My soul in its weakness He'll cause to be strong.

   In right paths He'll lead me, for His own name's sake;
4. And when through death's valley my journey I take,
   No evil I'll fear, for Thou with me wilt be;
   Thy rod and Thy staff they will still comfort me.

5. My table Thou'lt spread in the presence of foes;
   My head Thou anointedst, my cup overflows.
6. Pure goodness and mercy shall still follow me,
   And God's house my dwelling for ever shall be.

The above is identical, in several points, with the version in the New Psalter adopted by our Church in America, and, on the whole, will bear comparison with the best versions that have been published.

1942

Dr. James L. Nevin died in the Route General Hospital on March 20th, 1942, at the age of 88 years. His father, John Nevin of Carnaff, was a much respected member of Dervock Congregation, and brother of the late Rev. Robert Nevin, D.D., of Londonderry. One of his sisters was the wife of the late Rev. A. S. Lyons of Newry, and mother of Revs. Jas. A. and R. N. Lyons. A graduate of Royal College of Physicians, Edinburgh, he began practice in Ballymoney in 1883, and for almost half-a-century kindly and gently ministered to his patients. A student of good literature, with the tastes of an antiquarian and naturalist, he was frequently called on to lecture and teach, and was a fluent and well-informed speaker. He was interested practically in the down-trodden and the unfortunate.

Independent in his thinking, he was courageous enough to stand up for an unpopular cause when convinced of its rightness. Inheriting his father's generous disposition, in cases of hardship he looked for no fees, and even refused them when offered. He was a trusty and loyal friend, and was held in high esteem by the Congregation. Twice he was nominated for the eldership but declined the office. For years he was Secretary of the Missionary and Temperance Association. The interests of the Congregation were ever before him. On his retirement from practice, and going to visit a niece in Australia, he placed in the Treasurer's hands a cheque to cover his stipend for ten years. His place at public worship was seldom, if ever, vacant. And when the burden of years grew heavy, and strength of limbs failed, he came tottering on the arm of his son or of his nurse to the Sabbath services and to the Lord's table. He was a warm friend of his minister, and resented reproach cast on any in the calling. In his weakness he was ever cheerful, kindly and thoughtful, and attracted the esteem and affection of all who waited on him. He leaves one son, Jas. C. Nevin, Cashier in the Northern Bank, Bangor, who showed true filial care and attention to his father in his years of infirmity.

Faughan—A most enjoyable entertainment was held in the Victoria Hall, on Thursday, 2nd April, under the chairmanship of Rev. R. J. McIlmoyle, Dervock. The hall was well filled and a varied programme was submitted by talented artistes from Ballymoney, Limavady and Londonderry districts. At the close the hearty thanks of the audience and of the Congregation were accorded to all who had taken part.

Congregational Aid Fund—The Committee met on Tuesday, 14th July, under the Chairmanship of the Moderator of Synod, Rev. R. B. Lyons. All the ten members were present except one. The main business was the allocation of the special or additional grants for 1941.

A discussion took place as to how best to deepen the interest of the Church in the C.A. Fund, and the question of the augmentation of Ministers' salaries generally and Mr. Robert Holmes was requested to write a special article for an early issue of "The Covenanter" on the subject, and Rev. R. J. McIlmoyle (Rev. S. W. Lynas, alternate), was requested to bring the whole matter of increased ministerial support before Synod at its adjourned meeting. Both members acceded to the request.

The Northern Presbytery, in its report to the 1943 meeting of Synod, gave the information that

> Presbytery has made arrangements to celebrate the bi-centenary of the formation of the Reformed Presbytery, also the tercentenary of the Solemn League and Covenant, at Ballymoney on 27th July.
>
> Mr. M. Young, B.A., licentiate, is still on war work.
>
> Respectfully submitted,
>
> J. R. WRIGHT, JUN., Moderator.
> R. J. MCILMOYLE, Clerk.

The

Solemn League

and

Covenant,

1643

Addresses Delivered

at the

Tercentenary Celebration,

Belfast, 1943

DAVID IRVINE, LTD., PRINTERS, LONDONDERRY.

THE KING'S CALL TO PRAYER

JUNE 6, 1944

The King's Call to Prayer

FOUR YEARS AGO our nation and Empire stood alone against an overwhelming enemy, with our backs to the wall.

Tested as never before in our history, in God's providence we survived that test; the spirit of the people, resolute, dedicated, burned like a bright flame, lit surely from those unseen fires which nothing can quench.

Now once more a supreme test has to be faced. This time the challenge is not to fight to survive, but to fight to win the final victory for the good cause. Once again what is demanded from us all is something more than courage and endurance. We need a revival of spirit, a new unconquerable resolve.

After nearly five years of toil and suffering, we must renew that crusading impulse on which we entered the war and met its darkest hour.

We and our Allies are sure that our fight is against evil and for a world in which goodness and honour may be the foundation of the life of men in every land.

That we may be worthily matched with this new summons of destiny, I desire solemnly to call my people to prayer and dedication.

We are not unmindful of our own shortcomings, past and present. We shall not ask that God may do our will, but that we may be enabled to do the will of God, and we dare to believe that God has used our nation and Empire as an instrument for fulfilling His high purpose.

I hope that throughout the present crisis of the liberation of Europe, there may be offered up earnest and continuous and widespread prayer.

We who remain in this land can most effectively enter into the sufferings of subjugated Europe by prayer, whereby we can fortify the determination of our sailors, soldiers, and airmen who go forth to set the captives free.

The Queen joins with me in sending you this message. She well understands the anxieties and cares of our womenfolk at this time, and she knows that many of them will find, as she does herself, fresh strength and comfort in such waiting upon God. She feels that many women will be glad in this way to keep vigil with their menfolk as they man the ships, storm the beaches, and fill the skies.

At this historic moment, surely not one of us is too busy, too young, or too old to play their part in a nation-wide, perchance a world-wide, vigil of prayer as the great crusade sets forth.

If, from every place of worship, from home and factory, from men and women of all ages and many races and occupations, our intercessions rise, then, please God, both now and in future not remote, the predictions of an ancient psalm may be fulfilled:

> *"The Lord will give strength unto His people; the Lord will give His people the blessing of peace."*

H. R. H. King George VI

NORTH ANTRIM YOUNG FARMERS

Successful Ballymoney Show

STRONG DISPLAY OF LIVESTOCK

1944

THE progressive spirit which animates North Antrim young farmers was strikingly exemplified in the agricultural show held at Ballymoney on Tuesday under the auspices of Finvoy, Kilraughts and Moycraig Young Farmers' Clubs. There were over 400 entries in the livestock sections, including poultry, and 360 in the home industries section.

For a first attempt the show was a magnificent success. Quality in the classes devoted to horses and cattle reached that high standard for which the district extending over wide areas of Counties Antrim and Derry has long enjoyed an enviable reputation. All other sections were also well filled, and the display collectively viewed, was an outstanding one.

A demonstration of silage filling was given by the County Antrim Committee of Agriculture, and there was an attractive display of agricultural machinery.

Ideal conditions favoured the exhibition and the attendance of the public was of the large dimensions associated with pre-war Ballymoney shows. The crowd reached its highest peak by the afternoon, when horse-jumping and other equestrian competitions were the big attraction, and the enclosure presented a scene of animation, a pleasing touch of colour being imparted by the bright attire of the womenfolk.

To sum up, it was a splendid show, excellently organised and carried through, and all concerned merit hearty congratulations, especially the very courteous and obliging young hon. secretary, Mr. James Pollock, whose multitudinous duties were performed efficiently and well.

SHEEP

Pedigree B.L. Ram Lamb—1, Rev. R. J. M'Ilmoyle, Dervock; 2, James Campbell, Bushmills; 3, W. L. Moore, Priestland. Pedigree B.L. Aged Ram—1, Rev. R. J. M'Ilmoyle; 2, W. L. Moore. Pedigree B.L. Ewe Lamb—1, Rev. R. J. M'Ilmoyle; 2, W. L. Moore; 3, J. Smith, Ballybregagh. Pedigree B.L. Gimmer—1 and 3, Rev. R. J. M'Ilmoyle; 2, W. L. Moore. Pedigree B.L. Ewe, with lamb or lambs at foot—1, Rev. R. J. M'Ilmoyle. Non-Pedigree B.L. Ram Lamb—1, James Smith; 2, C. Hill, Croagh, Bushmills; 3, R. O. Stewart, Dunloy. Non-Pedigree B.L. Ewe Lamb—1, J. M. Lees, Cloyfin; 2 and 3, R. O. Stewart. Non-Pedigree B.L. Ewe, with lamb or lambs at foot—1 and 3, R. Chestnutt, Ballytaggart; 2, C. Hill. Special Prize of 15s (presented by Mr. John M'Conaghy, Ballytaggart), for best cross-bred Sheep, the property of a member of Finvoy, Kilraughts, or Moycraig Y.F. Clubs—J. B. G. Kirkpatrick, Kilraughts. Cross-bred Ewe, any age, with lamb or lambs at foot—1 and 2, J. B. G. Kirkpatrick; 3, C. Hill. Special Prize of 15s (presented by Mr. John McConaghy), for best Sheep in this class, the property of a member of Finvoy, Kilraughts, or Moycraig Y.F. Clubs—J. B. G. Kirkpatrick. Best in Show—Rev. R. J. M'Ilmoyle; reserve, J. M. Wilson. Suffolk Ewe Lamb—1, Isaac Hill, Cloyfin; 2, R. A. M'Clintock, Ballymena; 3, J. Marshall Wilson. Suffolk Ram Lamb—1 (and special) and 3, J. M. Wilson 2, W. A. Dunlop. Suffolk Ewe, any age, with lamb or lambs at foot, or having produced a lamb in 1944—1, J. M. Wilson; 2, Miss J. R. Long, Garvagh; 3, R. A. M'Clintock. Suffolk Ram, any age—1, J. M. Wilson; 2, R. A. M'Clintock; 3, W. Campbell. Special Prize of 15s (presented by Mr. John M'Conaghy), for best animal the property of a member of Finvoy, Kilraughts or Moycraig Y.F. Clubs—W. A. Dunlop; reserve, W. Campbell

LIMAVADY YOUNG FARMERS

COLERAINE CHRONICLE, 1944

Successful Revival of Annual Show

ALL PREVIOUS RECORDS ECLIPSED

THE PHENOMENAL SUCCESS which attended the revival on Saturday last of the Limavady Young Farmers' Club's annual show, which had been in abeyance owing to the war situation since 1939, must be attributed in large measure to the introduction of a number of equestrian events.

The show, which was held at Rathbreadymore, on the outskirts of the town, in a field kindly granted by Mr. J. B. M'Nickle, Main Street, Limavady, broke all records both for entries and the number of spectators, the crowd being estimated at almost 6,000. As for the entries, the grand total was 1,200, of which 390 were in the livestock section; while in the equestrian events alone, there were over 150 entries, drawn from many parts of the North of Ireland. The exhibits, both in the livestock and home industries sections, were all of an exceptionally high standard.

Following the judging, there was a parade of prize-winners and turn-outs, after which came the great attraction of the day, the horse jumping, riding, and driving competitions—a novel feature for Limavady where it was the first event of the kind—and the various competitions were watched with great interest and enthusiasm by the huge crowd.

The show was admirably organised by the officials of the Club, all of whom are to be congratulated on the outstanding success which attended the fixture.

During the day the results were announced, and a running commentary made, over a public address system.

SHEEP (Open)

Pure-bred Border-Leicester ewe, any age—1, Rev. R. J. M'Ilmoyle, Dervock; 2, J. Whyte, Mulkeeragh, Limavady; 3, W. J. Hyndman, Gortmure, Newbuildings, Derry.

Pure-bred Border-Leicester ram, any age—1, Rev. R. J. M'Ilmoyle; 2, W. L. Moore, Priestland, County Antrim; 3, J. Neill, Whitehill.

Pen of two pure-bred Border-Leicester lambs—1, Rev. R. J. M'Ilmoyle; 2, W. J. Hyndman; 3, John Neill; 4, J. Whyte.

Pure-bred Suffolk ram, any age—1, M. Drennan, Castlelecky, Magilligan; 2, A. S. Clyde, Main Street, Garvagh; 3, M. Gault, Ballyquelin, Limavady.

Pure-bred Suffolk ewe, any age—1, M. Drennan; 2, J. M. Mark; 3, H. Irwin.

Pen of two pure-bred Suffolk lambs—1, Miss Long, Rose Lodge, Garvagh; 2, M. Drennan; R. Loughrey, Gortnarney, Limavady.

Pen of two Suffolk cross lambs—1, H. Irwin; R. Oliver, Lislane, Drumsurn.

Pen of three cross-bred ewes—1, J. Purcell, also awarded special prize for best exhibit the property of a member of a Young Farmers' Club; 2, J. M'Cloy; 3, A. Smyth, Littlederry, Limavady.

Pen of two cross-bred lambs—1, J. Loughery, Drumagosker; 2, A. Smyth; 3, Mrs. Thompson-M'Causland, Drenagh.

Black-face horned ram, any age—1, Mrs. Thompson-M'Causland.

Pen of three black-faced horned ewes—1, W. Loughery, Aughansillagh, Limavady, also awarded the Millar Challenge Cup (presented by Mr. T. D Millar) for best exhibit; 2, S. H. Barr; 3, T. C. M'Cracken.

1944 Annual Meeting of Synod
extracts from the Minutes of Monday 26 June 1944
(Outgoing Moderator: Rev RB Cupples)

---

6. The Moderator addressed the Synod, and called upon the members to appoint his successor.

7. Rev. Wm. McCullough moved, That Rev. Alexander Reid Wright, B.A., minister of Ballylaggan congregation, be appointed Moderator of Synod for the ensuing year. The motion was seconded by Rev. R. J. McIlmoyle, and passed unanimously.

8. Mr. Wright took the chair, and addressed the Synod.

SESSION II.

Tuesday Morning, 27th June, 10 till 12.30 o'clock.

Synod resumed. The Moderator in the chair.

Rev. S. Kennedy conducted devotional exercises.

The minutes of the previous sederunt were read and confirmed.

14. An apology was received from Rev. R. B. Lyons for absence from the opening meeting of Synod.

15. The following were appointed to draw up a minute on the death of Rev. Wm. Warnock:—Revs. R. B. Lyons and J. W. Calderwood.

16. Professor McFarlane proposed, and Rev. R. J. McIlmoyle seconded, and it was cordially passed, That the following message be sent to the King:—

"We, the Synod of the Reformed Presbyterian Church in Ireland, met in Belfast, would humbly express to your Majesty our heartfelt appreciation of your action in calling the nation to prayer, of our thankfulness for the successes which the Lord the Governor of the nation has granted to your armies and those allied with them, and we would assure your Majesty of our wholehearted support in this crusade against evil, and of our united, earnest, and continued supplications for an early and complete victory over the forces of oppression";

17. To which the King replied as follows:—

Buckingham Palace.

Clerk of Synod,
Reformed Presbyterian Church,
Grosvenor Road, Belfast.

"Please convey to Synod of the Reformed Presbyterian Church in Ireland assembled at Belfast, the sincere thanks of the King for their kind and loyal message, which His Majesty greatly appreciated."

PRIVATE SECRETARY.

DERVOCK

BORDER LEICESTER FLOCK

No. B.L. 435

OWNER:

REV. R. J. M'ILMOYLE, DERVOCK,
CO. ANTRIM

BORDER LEICESTER EWE

Sire, Sandyknowe Topsman (10872); dam by Sandyknowe Supreme (7382). Bred at Skerrington Mains, she has an unbeaten showyard record, including the Championship at the Royal Ulster Show, Belfast, on two occasions.

Flock has won over 80 show awards in each of four consecutive seasons.

STOCK RAMS IN USE IN 1944:—

MAC'S GLORY (12938)

and

ELSRICKLE TRIPLET (12582)

FULL BROTHER TO LAWSON'S GLORY (11995).

INQUIRIES INVITED.

YOUNG FARMERS' CLUB SHOW.

1/7/1944

1,500 ENTRIES AT CULLY-BACKEY.

Entries totalling 1,500 were received for the annual show held by Cullybackey Young Farmers' Club on Saturday. There was also an enjoyable horse-jumping and driving programme.

Cup winners in livestock sections included the following:—**Horses** (best agricultural animal in show), W. W. Brown, Ballinaloob, Dunloy, and T. Buchanan, Clough. **Sheep**, Rev. R. J. M'Ilmoyle, Dervock.

The following were cup winners (home industries)—Miss Ethel Paul, Cullybackey; Miss Mamie Montgomery, Ballyclug. Agricultural section—Robert King, Laymore; W. Herbison, Clougher; Rev. R. J. M'Ilmoyle, Dervock; W. J. Hill, Gloonan, Ahoghill; Maurice Knowles, Fenagh.

First prize-winners were:—**Horses**—James Parke, Carnlea, Ballymena; A. and J. M'Ilveen, Connor, Kells; W. W. Brown, Ballinaloob, Dunloy; William Campbell, Finvoy, Ballymoney; Huston Dunlop, Mullinsallagh, Portglenone; Francis Smith, Killyflue, Ballymena; Robert Kennedy, Ballee, Ballymena; James Kenny, jun., Drumrankin, Cullybackey; John H. M'Millan, Carnlea; Thomas G. Buchanan, Clough; David Gibson, Desertderrin, Ballymoney.

Cattle—James G. Simpson, Fenaghy, Gracehill; William Sands, Ballyconnelly, Cullybackey; James Rock, Carnbeg, Clough; Robert Herbison, Clougher, Ballymena; W. W. Brown; Sam Blair, Glenhue, Cullybackey; James Martin, Ballyclose, Cullybackey; Frank Black, Carninney, Ballymena; Samuel Watson, Glenhue, Cullybackey; W. Adams, Killylodge, Glarryford; G. W. Wilson, Ballygarvey, Ballymena; James Lusk, Carntall, Carnmoney; J. H. Kissack, Bellaghy, Killagan; Robert King, Laymore, Ballymena.

Sheep—Rev. R. J. M'Ilmoyle; David Simpson, Diamond, Cullybackey; John M'Grath, Tullygrawley, Glarryford; John Dale, Ballygarvey, Ballymena; John M'Master, Ballycloughan, Ballymena; James H. Coleman, Dromore, Glarryford; David Rock, Lislunnan, Kells; Henry Speedy, Drummaul, Randalstown; Master S. S. M'Burney, Knockboy, Broughshane; John C. M'Clure, Ballyminstra, Ahoghill; R. A. M'Clintock, Laymore, Ballymena.

Goats—Nora Thompson, Lisnafillan, Gracehill.

Poultry—Mrs. C. Gardiner, Ballycraigy, Ballymena; Margaret M'Alister, Lisnamurrican, Broughshane; Tom Adams, Carncoagh, Rathkenny; George Davison, Redcliffe, Cullybackey; Neil Reid, Hillmount, Cullybackey; James Hamill, Oldstone, Muckamore; George Whiteside, Eglish, Rathkenny; Mr. Milliken, Ballycloughan, Ballymena; J. S. Henry, Portstewart.

COLERAINE CHRONICLE, SATURDAY, JUNE 16, 1945

BALLYMONEY SHOW

YOUNG FARMERS CLUBS' ENTERPRISE

BIG CROWD ENJOYS EXCELLENT EXHIBITION

PRIZE LIST

THE VICTORY SHOW of the Ballymoney District Young Farmers' Clubs, comprising Finvoy, Kilraughts, and Moycraig, on Tuesday, proved a success from every point of view. The relaxation of the petrol restrictions gave an uplift to the attendance, hundreds of motor vehicles being closely parked in all the roads adjoining the Showground. The young farmers by their enterprise, excellent organisation, and enthusiasm well deserved to see their efforts reach such wonderful fruition, the entries in the aggregate constituting a record. The entries in the horse section showed a slight increase, with a more marked increase in the cattle section, especially the dual-purpose and dairy classes. In the horse and cattle classes the exhibits were of a very high standard, and competition was exceptionally keen. Sheep, goats, swine, poultry, butter and eggs, home industries, and honey all made good classes.

Although the weather was unpromising in the morning, it improved as the day wore on, and the Show and the equestrian events in the afternoon were greatly enjoyed by a crowd of about five thousand.

The "Pride of Ulster" Pipe Band, under Pipe-Major Wm. M'Erlain, provided a musical programme.

The officials of the Show, particularly the excellent hon. secretary (Mr. James Pollock), are to be cordially congratulated

BORDER LEICESTER SHEEP - JUDGE

Border-Leicester and C.B. Sheep:—Judge—Mr. W. A. Bell, Fruit Hill, Hillsborough; chief steward, Mr. Austin Sayers, Larchfield, Kilraughts. **Suffolk Sheep:**—Judge—Mr. Thomas A. Galbraith, Derry; chief steward—Mr. James M'Laughlin, Carolelis, Mosside. **Goats:**—Judge—Rev. R. J. M'Ilmoyle, B.A., Dervock; chief steward—Mr. Norman Morrison, Finvoy. **Swine:**—Judge—Mr. W. J. M'Elroy, Rossdowney House, Derry; chief steward—Mr. James R. M'Clure, Church View, Kilraughts. **Poultry:**—Judge—Mr. W. J. Robinson; chief steward—Miss Ena Hill, Edarone, Stranocum. **Butter and Eggs:**—Judges—Miss M. E. Dick, Poultry Instructress, Antrim, and Miss M. Reid, Poultry Instructress, Antrim; chief steward—Miss Annie Torrens, Finvoy. **Home Industries:**—Judges:—Miss Miller (Ballymena), Mrs. Carson (Ballymena), Miss Bamber (Farm Lodge, Ballymena), and Mrs. Pinkerton (Ballymena); chief stewards:—Handwork Section—Miss Annie Campbell, Mullan House, Finvoy; Cookery Section—Miss Jean Dinsmore, Ballyportery, Culcrum. **Honey:**—Judge:—Rev. R. J. M'Dermott, B.A., The Manse, Glarryford; chief steward—Mr. George Cochrane, Moycraig. **Gate Stewards**—Mr. James Laughlin, Culmore House, Kilrea, and Mr. Wilson Pettigrew, Legacurry

SHEEP

Pedigree B.L. Ram Lamb—1, Robert Smith, 15 Golf Terrace, Portrush; 2, J. P. Camac, M.R.C.V.S., Derrykeighan, Dervock; 3, A. M'Curdy, The Haw, Bushmills.

Pedigree B.L. Aged Ram—1, J. P. Camac; 2, Rev. R. J. M'Ilmoyle, Dervock; 3, James H. Coleman, Glarryford, Co. Antrim.

Pedigree B.L. Ewe Lamb—1, 2 and 3, Rev. R. J. M'Ilmoyle.

Pedigree B.L. Gimmer—1 and 2, Rev. R. J. M'Ilmoyle.

Pedigree B.L. Ewe, with lamb or lambs at foot—1 and 2, and special prize, Rev. R. J. M'Ilmoyle.

Non-pedigree B.L. Ram Lamb—1, James Smith, Ballybregagh, Armoy.

Non-pedigree B.L. Ewe Lamb—1, Robert Chestnutt, Ballytaggart, Kilraughts.

Non-pedigree B.L. Ewe, with lamb or lambs at foot—1, Robert Chestnutt.

Cross-bred Ewe, any age, with lamb or lambs at foot—1, Robert Chestnutt.

Cross-bred Ewe, any age, with lamb or lambs at foot—1, 2 and 3 and Champion Rosette—J. B. G. Kirkpatrick, Ballynagashel, Kilraughts.

Suffolk Ewe Lamb—1, William A. Dunlop; 2, J. Marshall Wilson; 3, R. A. M'Clintock, Laymore, Ballymena.

Suffolk Ram Lamb—1, R. A. M'Clintock; 2, William A. Dunlop; 3, J. Marshall Wilson.

Pair of Suffolk Lambs (1 ewe and 1 ram)—1, W. A. Dunlop; 2, R. A. M'Clintock.

Suffolk Ewe, any age, with lamb or lambs at foot, or having produced a lamb in 1945—1 and special, J. Marshall Wilson; 2, R. A. M'Clintock; 3, J. C. M'Clure, Hill View, Ahoghill.

Suffolk Shearling Ewe—1 and 3, R. A. M'Clintock; 2, J. C. M'Clure.

Suffolk Ram, any age—1, J. Marshall Wilson; 2, William A. Dunlop; 3, John C. M'Clure.

GOATS.

Goat, in milk—1, Thomas Dickson, Gate End, Ballymoney; 2, Robert Dunlop, Charlotte Street, Ballymoney; 3, Thomas Dickson.

COLERAINE CHRONICLE, SATURDAY, JUNE 23, 1945

YOUNG FARMERS' CLUB SHOW

Successful Coleraine Venture

SPLENDID ALL-ROUND DISPLAY

CONGRATULATIONS are due to the Coleraine Young Farmers' Club on the great success of their first agricultural show venture, held at the Showgrounds, Coleraine, on Saturday last. All sections were splendidly filled, those for horses and cattle particularly so, and the display, regarded as a whole, was a remarkably good one. The crowning touch was imparted by the excellent weather which favoured the exhibition, and when the equestrian events —promoted for the Club by the Route Hunt—were got under way in the afternoon the crowd of spectators had reached most encouraging dimensions.

As the judging of the horses and cattle proceeded and so, too, with the sports later on, the results were announced by Mr. J. F. Hunter, J.P., to all parts of the ground by means of a public address system installed by Mr. R. H. Adams, Portrush, and this added distinctly to the interest and enjoyment of the spectators.

The secretarial arrangements for the show were ably and efficiently carried out by Mr. W. O. Harper, M.R.C.V.S., with Miss Dora Archibald as assistant, and Mr. J. R. Jackson, M.R.C.V.S. (President of the Young Farmers' Club) rendered similarly good service as secretary of the sports section. Many other members of the club executive co-operated with energy and enthusiasm, and the net result of their combined efforts was an excellently run and very good show which should encourage them to essay further triumphs in years to come. The entire proceeds of the exhibition were in aid of the Red Cross Agriculture Fund.

OFFICE-BEARERS AND OFFICIALS.

President—Mr. J. R. Jackson, M.R.C.V.S.; Vice-Presidents—Rev. Rt. Hon R. Moore, Captain H. R. Morrison, D.L., Major J. L. Baxter, Messrs. John Black, James Dalzell, John Hart, S. J. Henry, J.P., S. S. Henry, J.P., J. F. Hunter, J.P., W. Jackson, J.P., H. Maxwell, J. W. Morrow, M.R.C.V.S., and J. W. Stewart; Show Committee—Miss M. Lyons, Miss E. M'Ilmoye, Messrs. Harold Adams, Hugh Campbell, Wm. Crowe, Jim Glenn, Thomas Glenn, James Hemphill, Jack Henry, Thomas Linton, Daniel M'Powell, Nevin Smyth, Jim Reid, and Kenneth Taylor; Hon. treasurer—Mr. Jack A. Craig; Hon. Secretary—Mr. Wm. O. Harper, M.R.C.V.S.; Assistant Hon. Secretary—Miss Dora Archibald; Hon. Veterinary Surgeons—Messrs. D. Reid Marshall, M.R.C.V.S., J. W. Morrow, M.R.C.V.S., and J. H. Morrow, M.R.C.V.S.

JUDGES.

Clydesdale and Draught Horses—Mr. A. C. B. Montgomery, Lochfergus, Kirkcudbright, Scotland. **Young Hunters**—Mr. John Barron, M.H., Mallusk, Glengormley. **Shorthorn and Crossbred Cattle**—Mr. W. J. Morrison, Andraid, Randalstown. **Ayrshire and Variety Cattle**—Mr. Robert King, Laymore, Ballymena. **Sheep**—Rev. R. J. M'Ilmoyle, Dervock, and Mr. James Ellison, Ballydrain, Comber. **Poultry, Butter and Eggs**—Miss R. E. Dick, Antrim. **Pigeons**—Mr. W. Stinson, Ballymoney. **Home Industries (Baking)**—Mr. H. J. Black, Portstewart. **Horse-jumping and Riding**—Messrs. John Barron and J. Alfred Jackson, Derrydorragh.

LIMAVADY SHOW SCORES BIG SUCCESS

Over Fifteen Hundred Entries

SPLENDID EQUESTRIAN PROGRAMME

The fourth annual show held under the auspices of the Limavady Young Farmers' Club, at Rathbreadymore, on the outskirts of the town, on Thursday, reflected the progressive spirit and enthusiasm of the members who spared no effort to bring the event into the forefront of all similar undertakings and make it the biggest and best held this year in the Province. In this they were entirely successful, new records being set up for the number of entries received in all departments, and making a grand total of 1,611. The widespread interest taken in the event was shown by the very big crowd it attracted from all over Co. Derry and many other parts of the North-West. The weather was ideal.

Following the phenomenal success of the show on its revival last year, the officials decided to enlarge the excellent showgrounds, and widen the scope of the show by including additional classes and features, and their enterprise was splendidly rewarded by the support they received. In addition to the livestock section, in which the exhibits were of outstanding quality, there was a splendid show of home industries, fruit, flowers, and vegetables which was staged in marquees in the grounds, and reached the dimensions of a very considerable show on its own account. The exhibits in this department were generally of a high standard and made a most interesting display.

THE JUDGES.

The judges were:—Horses—Mr. W. Wilson, Barrhead, Glasgow. Cattle—Mr. Victor Love, Bready, Co. Tyrone. Sheep and Goats—(Border-Leicester) Mr. Jacob Horner, Comber; (Black-face) Mr. Hamilton, Belfast. Pigs—Mr. G. Lowe, Hillsborough. Poultry—Miss R. E. Dick, Church Street, Antrim. Game Poultry—Messrs. W. Turner, Gorticloughan, Garvagh, and J. R. Jackson, M.R.C.V.S., Coleraine. Eggs and Butter—Miss A. A. Park, Craigmore, Maghera. Jam—Mrs. M. I. Smith, Castlederg. Cookery—Mrs. Suffern, Crumlin. Fruit, Flowers and Vegetables—Mr. and Mrs. Hamilton, Malone Nurseries, Belfast. Flax—Mr. J. Bankhead, Belfast. Potatoes—Mr. S. Smith, Kilkeel. Needlework — Mrs. Brown, Enniskillen.

The equestrian events were judged by Messrs. G. Nugent, D. Hall Christie, J. C. Drennan and W. Wilson; and the other officials were:—Judges' stewards, —Messrs. P. Fitzpatrick and J. F. Hunter, J.P.; call stewards—Messrs. J. Shannon and M. Drennan; paddock stewards—Messrs. H. Gough, B.A., and Boyd Love; hon. veterinary surgeon—Mr. S. Forgie, M.R.C.V.S.

In the novelty dog show the judges were —Mr. and Mrs. J. R. Jackson, Group-Captain Turner, Limavady, and Group-Captain Bett, Ballykelly.

SHEEP.

Special Prizes.

Best exhibit, the property of a member of a Young Farmers' Club —Fred Purcell, Carrick House, Limavady.

Cup, presented by Mr. T. Millar, Limavady, for best group of three black-faced sheep, the property of the same exhibitor —James Harkin, Knockaneil, Swateragh.

Prize, presented by Mr. R. Glenn, Campsie, for best Border-Leicester gimmer—Rev. R. J. M'Ilmoyle, Dervock.

Pure-bred Border-Leicester ram—1, James Gallagher, Carrigans, Co. Donegal; 2, J. Whyte, Mulkeeragh (South), Limavady; 3, Rev. R. J. M'Ilmoyle, Dervock.

Pure-bred Border-Leicester ewe—1 and 2, Rev. R. J. M'Ilmoyle; 3, Jack M'Elroy, Rossdowney.

Pure-bred Border-Leicester ram lamb—1, Rev. R. J. M'Ilmoyle; 2, James Gallagher; 3, Jack M'Elroy.

Pure-bred Border-Leicester ewe lamb—1 and 2, Rev. R. J. M'Ilmoyle; 3, James Gallagher.

Pure-bred Suffolk ram—1, Mat. Drennan, Castle Lecky, Magilligan; 2, Joseph Nutt, Magheramore, Limavady; 3, John M'Cloy, Tullyarmon, Limavady.

Pure-bred Suffolk ewe—1, Wm. M. Crowe, Letterloan, Coleraine; 2, Mat. Drennan.

Pure-bred Suffolk ram lamb—1, Mat. Drennan; 2, John Loughery, Drumagosker, Limavady.

Pure-bred Suffolk ewe lamb—1, Wm. M. Crowe; 2, Mat. Drennan; 3, John Loughery.

Black-faced horned ram—1, James Harkin; 2, James Semple, Glassakerin, Slaughtmanus; 3, Allison Barr, Ballykelly.

Black-faced horned ewe—1, W. Loughery, Aughansillagh, Limavady; 2, James Harkin; 3, T. M'Cracken, Drummonds, Magilligan.

Black-faced horned ram lamb—1, Joseph Gibson, Derrychrier P.O., Co. Derry; 2, T. M'Cracken; 3, James Semple.

Black-faced horned ewe lamb—1, T. M'Cracken; 2, James Harkin; 3, James Semple.

Pen of two cross-bred ewe lambs (B.L. x B.F.)—1, Fred Purcell; 2, Alex. Smyth, Littlederry, Limavady; 3, James Purcell.

Pen of two cross-bred ewe lambs (BL. x BF.)—1 and 3, John Loughrey; 2, Alex Smyth

1945

Limavady—At the close of the pre-communion service, Rev. R. B. Lyons, B.A., pastor, expressed the good wishes of the Congregation to Mr. J. A. Cresswell Blair, B.A., on the eve of his departure to become minister of the Congregation of Creevagh, and on behalf of the Congregation presented him with an envelope of banknotes as a parting gift and token of their esteem. Mr. Blair thanked the Congregation for their generous and kindly thought. Mr. Blair is the fifth minister of the Church in active service who was brought up in Limavady Congregation.

Rev JAC Blair BA was a nephew of the Rev RJ McIlmoyle

Ordination of Mr. J. A. C. Blair, B.A.

The Southern Presytery met in Creevagh Church building on Thursday, 8th November, 1945, to ordain Mr. Joseph Alexander Cresswell Blair, B.A., licentiate of the Western Presbytery, to the gospel ministry, and to induct him to the pastoral oversight of the Congregation of Creevagh. The opening exercises were taken by Rev. S. Kennedy, B.A., who had baptized Mr. Blair. Rev. Charles Presho, B.A. Loughbrickland, gave a sermon on I. Cor. i. 21. The principles of Reformed Presbyterianism were expounded and defended by Rev. Wm. Dodds, B.A., Ballenon. A full and interesting history of the Congregation was given by Rev. Prof. McFarlane, B.A., Clerk of Presbytery, who also put the prescribed queries to the minister-elect and Congregation. Rev. R. B. Lyons, B.A., led in the ordination prayer. Rev. R. B. Cupples, B.A., Fairview, gave the charge to the new minister, and Rev. W. H. Pollock, B.A., addressed the Congregation. Rev. S. R. Archer, B.A., Rathfriland, conducted the closing exercises.

After the assembled Congregation, for whom some seating had to be placed in the aisles, had had an opportunity to greet the new minister, almost the entire company assembled again and the ladies of the Congregation dispensed a tasty and bountiful tea ; and were assisted by efficient stewards. Rev. R. B. Cupples, B.A., who had been interim-Moderator of Session during the vacancy, presided at the subsequent meeting. Mr. T. J. Moffett welcomed the new minister on behalf of the Congregation. Rev. Mr. Blair, who was heartily received, paid tribute to the many friends who had helped him along life's journey to that day, and spoke of his ideals for his ministry.

Addresses of congratulation and good wishes were delivered by Revs. R. N. Lyons, R. J. McIlmoyle, R. B. Lyons, S. Kennedy, Prof. J. McIlmoyle, C. Presho and J. Barkley (Presbyterian), by Miss M. L. Dunlop and by Messrs. McCune and Paisley, Theological Students. On the motion of Rev. Hugh Wright, seconded by Rev. T. Semple, a hearty vote of thanks was passed to the ladies of the Congregation for their hospitality. On behalf of the Congregation, Mr. Adam Moffett presented Mr. Cupples with a cheque in recognition of his services during the vacancy.

1946

Death of the mother of the Rev Prof John McIlmoyle MA, Faughan

———————————— **Mrs. John McIlmoyle,** a senior member of Limavady Congregation, widow of an elder, and one of the mothers of Ministers, passed away on 15th February at the age of 91. During her long connection with the Congregation, she always showed a deep interest in its well-being, was a loyal supporter of its organisations, and was ever exemplary in attendance on public and private ordinances. She was able to attend public worship until a little over a year before her death, and rejoiced in the prayer meetings which were held periodically in her home. She loved her Lord and Saviour, and delighted in the things unseen and eternal. Blessed with good health and surrounded with loving care, she continued interested in the affairs of the Church, even in the last few weeks of weakness. " The memory of the just is blessed."

1947

To the 1947 annual meeting of Synod, the Northern Presbytery reported that

At the meeting of Presbytery on 17th June, 1947, Rev. R. J. McIlmoyle, who had been Clerk of the Presbytery for thirty-seven years, intimated his resignation from this office. This resignation was accepted with deep regret, and tribute was paid to Mr. McIlmoyle's great efficency as Clerk for so many years.

Rev. J. T. Moffett Blair was appointed Clerk in succession to Mr. McIlmoyle.

Presbytery has decided to hold the next statutory meeting at Portrush.

Respectfully submitted,

W. J. Gilmour, *Moderator.*
J. T. Moffett Blair, *Clerk.*

Rev. W. J. Gilmour

[Mr Gilmour died on 8 September 1991]

THE COVENANTER.

Dervock Congregation has just lost one of its oldest members by the death of **Mr. Alexander Carson,** lately of Conagher. Mr. Carson had attained the ripe old age of 92 years. He possessed the rare quality of ever trying to keep abreast of the times and yet remaining true to the old school of orthodoxy. He had a deep rooted loyalty to the church of his fathers, and as long as health permitted was never absent from the services of the sanctuary. Of a cheery disposition, he ever had a word of encouragement for all with whom he came in contact. He was the last surviving member of a large family of brothers and sisters, all born and brought up at Conagher. He is survived by two daughters, Mrs. A. F. McIlmoyle of Grosvenor Road, Belfast, and Mrs. McFall of Dervock. Mr. R. J. Carson, Treasurer of Dervock Congregation is a nephew. To all who feel the poorer for his going we tender sincere sympathy.

Death of the Rev RJ McIlmoyle's mother

Mrs. Robert McIlmoyle of Limavady Congregation passed away on 13th August, 1947, at the venerable age of 95. Blessed with good health, she was able to attend public worship until a very few years before her death. From her marriage she identified herself devotedly with the life and work of the Congregation. She cared greatly for spiritual things, and ever sought the peace and prosperity of Zion. Wife of an elder, she was a true mother in Israel, and her piety descends to her family. Three sons (one minister and two elders), three daughters and many grand-children survive her, and many of them are members and office-bearers in different Congregations.

Northern Presbytery's Tribute.

After the Meeting of the Northern Presbytery on 5th November, the Members of Presbytery and their wives met for lunch in Ballymoney. The purpose of this function was to pay tribute to the work and worth of Rev. R. J. McIlmoyle, who had recently resigned from the Clerkship of the Presbytery, after having served in this capacity for over 37 years. Revs. W. J. Gilmour (Moderator of Presbytery), Prof. J. Ramsey, Wm. McCullough, J. R. Wright, A. R. Wright, J. T. Moffett Blair (who has succeeded Mr. McIlmoyle as Clerk of Presbytery), and Mr. Peter Findlay spoke of the efficiency with which Mr. McIlmoyle carried out his duties, and of the esteem in which both Mr. and Mrs. McIlmoyle are held by all who know them. Rev. A. R. Wright gave some interesting facts regarding the Clerks of the Northern Presbytery. In 136 years there had been only five ministers who held this office. They were :— Rev. W. J. Stavely, minister of the united charge of Kilraughts, Dervock and Ballymoney, 36 years ; Rev. Thomas Houston, minister of Knockbracken (which was then under the Northern Presbytery), 11 years ; Rev. Wm. Toland, minister of Kilraughts, 19 years ; Rev. Prof. J. D. Houston, minister of Ballyclabber, 33 years ; nd Rev. R. J. McIlmoyle, minister of Dervock, 37 years.

It could be of interest to some to count the number of ordination and installation services at which the Rev RJ McIlmoyle, as clerk of the Northern Presbytery from 1910 to 1947, would have had the responsibility of delivering the congregational historical narrative or of reading the Formula of Subscription to the Westminster Standards, Confession of Faith and Catechisms etc. He took up those duties at Rev Alex Gilmour's ordination in Drimbolg on 14 March 1911 and at Rev JR Wright's installation in Ballyclabber on 25 April 1911.

—On the evening of 4th November, the manse at Dervock had a pleasant surprise in the form of a cheque from the members of the congregation, given as a token of kindness after Mrs. McIlmoyle's accident.

MINUTES

OF THE

Proceedings of the Reformed Presbyterian Synod of Ireland

ANNUAL MEETING, 1950

in the Reformed Presbyterian Church

Grosvenor Road, Belfast

SESSION II.

Tuesday Morning, 20th June, 10 till 12.30 o'clock.

27. The Clerk tendered to Synod his resignation of the Clerkship of Synod.

28. Rev. R. J. McIlmoyle moved, Professor McFarlane seconded, and it was passed—That Synod accepts with regret the resignation of the Clerk, Rev. Wm. Dodds, and thanks him for the valued services he has rendered the Church in this capacity since his appointment thirteen years ago, and for the diligent, conscientious, and faithful way in which he has always discharged the duties of the office.

29. Rev. R. J. McIlmoyle nominated Rev. Adam Loughridge of Portrush for the Clerkship of Synod. Rev. James Blair seconded the nomination; supported by Rev. J. Renwick Wright, and passed unanimously.

30. Mr. Loughridge intimated his acceptance of the appointment, and thanked Synod.

Presbytery Visitation in 1950 and the following is an excerpt from the Finding:

-The Northern Presbytery met at Dervock on 2nd August for the visitation of the Congregation. Representatives who answered the prescribed questions were Messrs. Robert McFall and Neil Fleming for the Session; David Miller and Robert Blakeley for the Committee; James Kerr and Archie McKeeman (jun.) for the Congregation. Rev. J. R. Wright, B.A., put the questions, and on the basis of the answers given a favourable finding prepared by a Committee consisting of Rev. W. J. Gilmour, Mr. W. M. Aiken and Rev. W. McCullough (Convener), was adopted by Presbytery. In this finding the following items were emphasised :—" Presbytery is satisfied that the Minister, Session and Committee are diligent and faithful in their respective spheres and receive the co-operation and confidence of the whole congregation. We congratulate Mr. McIlmoyle on his long years of fruitful service, during which time, while many have entered on their rest, the level of the membership remains high, and we rejoice that in his pulpit and pastoral ministrations he retains the freshness and force of earlier years.

Presbytery commends the congregation, because by increased liberality towards ministerial support and the various schemes of Synod, it has adapted itself to the economic changes of the time. We praise you for this. It gives us much pleasure, that, as a people you seek to uphold the testimony of the Reformed Presbyterian Church, and to extend the Kingdom of our Lord and Saviour Jesus Christ.

At the close of the meeting the Congregation entertained the Presbytery to lunch in the High Street Cafe, Ballymoney. A vote of thanks was moved by Rev. A. Loughridge, seconded by Rev. S. M. Calderwood. Mr. R. J. Carson replied for the congregation.

CHURCH NEWS

Jubilee—We offer the congratulations of the editors and readers of the magazine to Rev. R. J. McIlmoyle of Dervock Congregation on the attainment of his ministerial jubilee. Mr. McIlmoyle, who was brought up in Limavady Congregation, was ordained in Ballyclare on 6th September, 1900. He was inducted in Dervock on 31st August, 1904. He was Moderator of Synod in 1910—11, and has filled many offices in Synod and Presbytery with distinction.

Dervock—The members of Dervock Congregation observed the Sacrament of the Lord's Supper on Sabbath, 22nd October. There was an encouraging attendance, although some were in hospital, some confined to bed through illness, and some absent on account of the infirmity of old age. Rev. R. B. Lyons, B.A., Limavady, assisted. The Congregation were using an Individual Communion Service, the gift of Mr. and Mrs. R. W. McFall, given in memory of their two fathers. Mr. McFall's father was born and brought up in the Congregation, and had been an Elder for many years. The same is true of Mrs. McFall's father, Alexander Carson. These two names—McFall and Carson, were household words in the Congregation, and the members very highly appreciate this loyal and generous act. It is their wish and prayer that these two friends may be blessed through this generous deed and have many years of service for the Master in the Congregation. Mr. R. W. McFall is a member of Dervock Session and following in his late father's footsteps.

Stories the Rev RJ told at socials, as remembered by Mr James L McAfee, 2 Knocklayde Park, Ballymoney, elder in Ballymoney RP Church

(1) Old John and his wife Jane lived in a wee thatched cottage, away high up in a mountain range, miles from anywhere. They kept very much to themselves, grew all their food and were very self-contained; in fact they lived very primitive lives. But one day old John had gone down the mountainside to look for a missing sheep, and came upon a rough mountain track. A foolhardy motorist must have come along this track one day and lost his side mirror. Old John found it. He had never seen a mirror before; he picked it up and on looking into the mirror he exclaimed, "My aul faither, my aul faither". He put it in his pocket and took it home. He didn't show it to his wife Jane, but now and then he would take it out of his pocket and murmur to himself, "My aul faither, my aul faither". Jane got very curious and waited that night until John had gone to bed and was asleep. Then she slipped into his room, took the mirror out of John's pocket, brought it into the kitchen where there was more light, and, on looking into it, exclaimed, "So that's the aul hag he's efter noo".

(2) This farmer called John was invited to a fairly posh dinner where six or seven courses were being served. John wasn't used going to posh dinners, but he was coaxed to go. He enjoyed the company of his friends and at table had a very talkative couple on either side of him. The first course was served and John was half way through it, when he was asked a question by his friend next to him. Before the conversation was finished, the waiter came and whisked away the remainder of his stuffed peaches. The next course, soup, was served and John was half-way through it when his friend started talking again. And before the conversation was finished the waiter's hand reached in and took away the half-full soup plate. The main course was then served and John was really enjoying it when the table companion on his other side engaged him in conversation. Out of the corner of his eye John spied the waiter's hand reaching in and lifting his plate with his unfinished turkey and ham on it. This was too much for John, who lifted his knife and in a voice which all could hear, shouted "Drap it, man, or I'll sned the fingers aff ye".

(3) A farmhand was courting a girl in the neighbour's farm, and, when going to see her at night, always took a hurricane lamp to light his way. One night, coming home, the farmer met and asked him what he was doing with the lamp, and the lad said he had been over seeing his girlfriend at the next farm. The farmer said, "Oil is very expensive, you know. When I was courting I never took a lamp with me". "Ah, it's easy to see you didnae, because luk what ye got!"

On the Art of Public Speaking

I remember one pep-talk, in which the Rev RJ said that if you ever had the occasion to speak in public and were not used doing so, you must never apologise to your audience for not being a good speaker. He said that if you were not a good speaker, your audience would know it soon enough. If you managed fairly well, they might think you were better than you really were. But you must never get your audience down in the dumps before you even get started.

GOLDEN WEDDING, TROCADERO, PORTRUSH: 1951

Back (left): ?, ?, Susan McIlmoyle, Dr Mitchell, ?, ?, Mrs WJ Blair, Mrs J McIlmoyle, Mrs W Lyons, Prof J McIlmoyle, Fergie McIlmoyle, Tom McIlmoyle, Rev RN Lyons; **middle**: Elvina McIlmoyle, Vincent McIlmoyle, Kathleen McIlmoyle, Enid McIlmoyle, Tom Fallows, Pearl Fallows, Mrs Fallows, Mrs F McIlmoyle; **front**: Rev RJ McIlmoyle, Mrs Louise McIlmoyle

1950

Jubilee—At the close of the November meeting, the Northern Presbytery retired to the High Street Cafe, Ballymoney, where at a complimentary lunch, the guests of honour were Rev. R. J. and Mrs. McIlmoyle of Dervock R.P. Church. The Rev. J. R. Wright, B.A., of Ballyclabber, Moderator of Presbytery presided, and after lunch had been served, Mr. Wright explained that it was their intention to do honour to Mr. McIlmoyle, who had completed 50 years in the ministry of the R.P. Church. Rev. William McCullough, B.A., of Drimbolg, a life-long friend of Mr. McIlmoyle, in his own efficient and inimitable way, voiced the congratulations and good wishes of the Presbytery. He outlined the outstanding qualities of Mr. McIlmoyle's character :— his zeal, his sense of humour, his youthful vigour, his love for the Covenanting Church, and the way in which he had used his influence over the whole country for the promotion of the work of God's Kingdom. Mr. McCullough expressed pleasure at the presence of Mrs. McIlmoyle, who had contributed so much in her own way to her husband's success. Mr. McIlmoyle, with his usual flash of humour, suitably acknowledged the compliment he had received from the Presbytery. He spoke o the good health he had always enjoyed, that helped to make his work easier, and thanked the brethren for many happy associations he had had with them. The Moderator of Synod, Rev. W. R. McEwen, of Melbourne, and Rev. Adam Loughridge, Portrush, spoke brief words of tribute, and the meeting was brought to a close by the singing of Psalm 133, and the pronouncing of the benediction by Rev. Prof. Ramsey, LL.B., of Portstewart.

1951

From the *Covenanter*, September:

Anniversaries—We would express the congratulations of all the readers of the Magazine to Rev. R. J. and Mrs. McIlmoyle who celebrated their golden wedding on 24th July; and to Prof. and Mrs. Ramsey who celebrated their diamond wedding on 20th August.

Dervock—The congregation met in a social capacity in the church on 22nd August to do honour to Rev. R. J. and Mrs. McIlmoyle on the occasion of their golden wedding. After tea had been served by the ladies, Rev. W. McCullough, B.A., was called to the chair. Mr. Norman McConaghie read an address from the congregation, expressing their sincere thanks for the long and faithful service of Mr. and Mrs McIlmoyle, and their good wishes that they might be spared and blessed to continue their work for many years. Mrs. R. W. McFall, on behalf of the congregation, presented Mr. and Mrs. McIlmoyle with a well-filled wallet of notes. On behalf of the choir, Mr. R. Bleakley, read an address and Miss Maud Lynas made the presentation of a beautiful clock. Mr. McIlmoyle thanked the congregation and choir for their generous gifts and good wishes, and recalled many pleasant memories of his work in Dervock. Congratulatory speeches were made by Revs. J. R. Wright, B.A., A. Loughridge, B.A., and J. H. Beggs (Toberdoney). A musical programme was contributed by several friends.

Golden Wedding, 1951, Trocadero, Portrush

Enid, Kathleen, Vincent & Elvina with Father & Mother

At the end of 1951 it was reported that:

The Dervock Congregation has suffered heavily under the hand of death within recent months. First of all **Miss McConaghy.** She had been ailing for a few days, but the end was altogether unexpected. She was of a quiet and retiring disposition, and was slow to thrust her opinions on any one else, while at the same time revealing a distinctive personality. An only sister mourns her loss.

Then **Samuel Chestnutt.** While still a boy he contracted the disease usually described as " Sleepy Sickness." From this attack he never rallied. For many, many years he was the constant care of his mother and the other members of the family. He never complained and always appreciated the loving care lavished upon him.

Last of all **Neil Fleming.** After a more or less protracted illness he passed away in full assurance. For many years he had been a member of Session as was his father before him. Well grounded in the faith and with a sound knowledge of the principles of the Church, he was ever a faithful witness to his Master. The Congregation feels this loss acutely as does also his native district. To his widow and boys sincere sympathy is extended.

A selection of stories of the Rev RJ recorded by the BBC, Belfast, in 1953; on an LP 33 1/3 rpm, this was reproduced on tape on 21 May 1991 by Rev Dr Bert Tosh and given to me as a gift - ***RH***

(1) The farmer sent his boy to tell the vet how the cow looked. When the vet heard the story, he gave the farmer a powder and he gave him a tube with a receptacle on the one end of it. "Now" he said, "when you get home, put the powder in the receptacle, put that end of it in the cow's mouth and blow". Early next morning the boy appeared back again and, said the vet, "What about the cow?". Said he, "She is all right, but my father's ill". "What's wrong?", he asked. "The cow blowed first."

(2) Talking about milk, this young man, born and brought up in the city, knew little or nothing about the customs and habits of country life. He went to the country and engaged himself to a farmer. His first job was to go and do the milking. A short time afterwards the farmer went out to see how things were progressing and when he got to the byre the city man had just finished milking the best yielding cow in the byre and she had finished drinking the whole of the milk. The farmer was terribly annoyed and said "Why did you do it?" "Well, sir" said he, "I thought the milk was a bit thin looking and that I would put it through again."

(3) Talking about sheep, a bishop one time went on holiday. He needed a rest. He needed it badly and he chose a little hotel at the foot of a hill, a quiet, quiet place. He didn't go about dressed as a parson or bishop. During his daily rambles he became very friendly with an old shepherd and one day he said to the old shepherd, "What do you do for a living?". "Oh", said he, "I am a shepherd". "Well", said the bishop, "I am a shepherd too." And then the bishop said, "How many sheep have you under your care?" "Ten score." "And how many have you?". "Nine thousand." That was the size of his parish and the old man was thunderstruck, "My, my, nine thousand sheep. You'll have a divil o' a time at the lambing."

(4) This was a sheepdog competition, a champion competition. The team consisted of a shepherd and two dogs and each competing team at this show had won first prize earlier in the season at one show or another. Now here was a team, a shepherd and two dogs, which had never been beaten and people flocked from miles to see the performance. But it didn't come off! The dogs didn't pen a single sheep and they succeeded in driving some of them into a lake. Now the spectators were just flabbergasted and they couldn't understand it. And when that competition was over, a friend went up to the shepherd and asked what happened. "Well, I'll just tell you ... I'll just tell you. There wus that mauney clergymen aboot, I darney use the only language the dogs knew."

(5) A friend of mine was judging sheep at a local show. While he was at his work the Secretary came along and said "I want you to do the goats, for the judge has failed to turn up". So my friend just laughed in his face and said, "I know nothing about goats; not a thing". So he went on with his judging and the Secretary finally came back and said, "There is nobody here that knows anything more". "All right", he said, "I'll not let you down." And when he finished the sheep, he started the goats and did the best he could. And when he had finished he gave himself a pat on the back and said, "Well done". A short time after that a man came up to him and said," "What do you think of Paddy Doherty's goat?" Well, now, he didn't know anything about the men or their names and said he, "Where was she placed?" "First", said he, and then the judge said to him what nobody could contradict, "That is the best goat that ever

The minister calls for one of his flock, but only to powder a sheepish nose

SHOW WINNER HAS FACE-DO FIRST

Farmers take a day out among the gadgets

By EDWARD TROW

THE Rev Robert McIlmoyle opened a brown attache case, took out a towel, a soft handbrush, and a tin of white powder. Then he called for his sheep. He was about to prepare his Border Leicester ram for the judge.

For it was the second day of the Royal Ulster Agricultural Show at Belfast yesterday.

Carefully, the towel was placed round the neck of the sheep. Then the animal's face was whitened with the powder. The brush was used to take off the surplus.

This form of sheep beauty treatment is important for square-backed Border Leicesters, because their wool is dyed a bright yellow. The white powder throws the face into relief.

None in Ulster or Eire is more competent to administer sheep shampoos than the Rev Robert McIlmoyle, breeder of sheep for 39 years, and especially an expert on Border Leicesters. He has 20 at his manse farm at Dervock, Co. Antrim—all of them tip-top show animals.

2,000 prizes

In four years, he has won more than 80 prizes with them. But altogether, since he became interested in sheep, he has won close on 2,000 prizes.

Yesterday his elegant-looking Border Leicester two-sheer ram, dyed in the wool and powdered, took another first ticket to add to the collection.

Presbyterian minister McIlmoyle . . . "I'm nearly seventy" . . . has judged and shown his sheep all over Northern Ireland. He said: "They are my hobby. I can't keep a big flock because I have not enough land. But I am happy to concentrate on rearing a small number into good ones."

Yesterday was Farmers' Day at the show. Hundreds of them from all parts of Ulster arrived at Balmoral by coach, train and car.

Scrap saved

They flocked to the farm implement exhibition in the show yard, and carefully examined everything from a small steel curry comb to the latest thing in heavy tractors.

One of the most important trade exhibits was that of the Scrap Campaign Committee for Northern Ireland. Since this organisation started in 1948, 120,000 tons of scrap iron has been collected from Ulster farms.

The woman who never stopped talking at the show was Miss Lily Wynn, 72-year-old retired domestic science teacher. She is an authority on old Irish farmsteads. And she is an Englishwoman.

All day, in a replica farm kitchen of the period 1850, and standing in front of a peat hearth fire, she told farmers and their wives how Ulster folk managed their homes 100 years ago.

Said Miss Wynn: "I came to Ulster 30 years ago, and liked it so much that I stayed. I have made a study of old farmsteads, but today, I am sorry to say, there are very few left."

Lord Wakehurst, Governor of Northern Ireland, paid an informal visit to the show. He said afterwards: "I have been most impressed."

Rev. R. J. McIlmoyle—Clergyman, farmer and raconteur.

● *Face powder for the Border Leicester ram . . . given by his owner. Then . . . on to win first prize*

I saw". And says he, "What about mine?" "Where was yours?" "She was only fifth." And then the judge said to him what any judge is very apt to say to a disgruntled exhibitor, "You have a real good goat, but she needs time". And many a disgruntled exhibitor has gone forth without the red card, rejoicing that when his animal would mature and get a little older and get more into show form that he would be up and the other fellow would be down. So the judge said to this man, "You have a really good goat, but she needs time". "Hang it all", says he, "mine is the mother of his."

(6) A man on one occasion bought a pig and this was in the days when pigs were cheap and didn't cost much and he bought a pig for £3 and he bought for it £2 worth of meal and sold it later for £5. His friend said to him, "That's foolish, for you couldn't make money that way". "Oh, I know", says he, "but then I had the company!"

(7) Now on to poultry. During the time when eggs were rationed a lady who lived in the city felt that she wasn't getting enough and thought that a farmer friend in the country might help her. She went and told her story. And, said he, "I will be breaking the law and you will too, but I'll risk it". Then he got up separately for her whatever eggs she wanted and took a lot of trouble and pains to do it. And at that time he was getting four shillings a dozen for these eggs and she could have turned round and bought them at the same time, as many as her ration card authorized, the same eggs for two shillings a dozen. And he did a very wise thing and a very fair thing. He charged her four shillings a dozen, what he would be getting at the packing station, but then she went off at the deep end. "Extortion", said she, "extortion with a vengeance. No egg is worth more than a penny." "Well", says he, "I'm only charging you a penny each for these." "But", says she, "I have already paid four pence." "Well", he says, "the other three pence is for the wear and tear of the hen."

(8) Farmers' wives have wonderful experiences. This young man became a minister and he was brought up in the city and was ignorant of a great many country ways and customs. One harvest afternoon he made an awful blunder. He called to make a pastoral visit at a farmhouse. All the men and the women too had been in the fields from early morning. All the women except the mistress of the house and she was left to cope with the whole business that lay to hand. And it was more than she could do. And in the afternoon a knock at the door and when she answered it, it was his Reverence and he had no more loyal member in all his congregation than that lady, but she didn't want to see him then, not then. She took him in and did the best she could and then she began to apologize for her appearance. She was dishevelled and she also apologized for the untidy condition of the house. Said he, "Mrs Brown, don't worry; my mind is on things above". "Dear me", says she, "don't go upstairs; it's far worse up there."

(9) This other man he had a wife, a very nice wife, and young family growing up. He had a business which had prospered and one day he came in, in bad shape. He said, "Mary, the doctor has said that I must take a holiday". "Well", said she, "that is all right. We have been talking about a world tour for ages. Could I take my mother with me?" "No", he says, "certainly not, we are going for a holiday." Now she wheedled until she got him to say yes, and so the three of them went for a world tour, the husband and wife and her mother, his mother-in-law. One day they were in the jungle and then suddenly the mother-in-law was missed. She wasn't there and the wife became frantic. And a search party was sent out and when

R E S U L T S

Royal Ulster Agricultural Show, Balmoral, Belfast Newsletter, 29 May 1953 - Sheep: Border Leicester Ram (two shear and upwards) 1 Rev RJ McIlmoyle, Dervock, Minister's Son; 2 JH Aiken, Dromara, small Holm Field Marshall; **Shearling ram** 1 Messrs Minnis & Bell, Myles Leader; 2 T & J Horner; 3 J H Aiken; **Ewe (over one shear, with lamb at foot)** 1 A Minnis; 2 Messrs Graham & McCrum, Dromara; 3 Rev RJ McIlmoyle; **Shearling Ewe** 1 T & J Horner; 2 A Minnis; 3 Graham & McCrum; **Ewe lamb**: 1 T & J Horner; 2 J H Aiken; 3 A Minnis.

Coleraine Agricultural Show, Belfast Newsletter Monday, 15 June 1953: Sheep: Border Leicester Ram any age: 1 Rev RJ McIlmoyle, Dervock; 2 WL Moore, Risk, Priestland; **Ewe any age:** 1 & 3 Rev RJ McIlmoyle; 2 J McIlroy, Rossdowney House, Derry; **Ram lamb:** 1 WL Moore, 2 J McIlroy, 3 Rev RJ McIlmoyle; **Ewe lamb: 1 & 2** William L Moore; 3 Rev RJ McIlmoyle.

Royal Ulster Agricultural Show, Balmoral, Belfast Newsletter, Friday, 24 May 1957 - Sheep: Border Leicester Ram, two shear and upward: 1 Rev RJ McIlmoyle, Dervock, Humeston Surprise; 2 James Aiken, Carnew, Dromana, Co Down; 3 W A Bell, Fruithill, Hillsborough, Co Down, Millerhill (5 entries); **Shearling ram:** 1 Alexander Minnis, Mossvale, Ballygowan, Co Down, Eglinton Tip Top; 2 Samuel Holden, Ballygowan, Ballynure, Co Antrim, Rockmount Ambition; 3 T & J Horner, Ballyaltikiligan, Comber, Co Down (5 entries) **Ewe over one shear with lamb at foot (ewe only judged):**1 T & J Horner; 2 & 3 W A Bell (8 entries); **Shearling ewe:** 1 Alexander Minnis; 2 T & J Horner; 3 Rev RJ McIlmoyle (11 entries) **Ram lamb:** 1 T & J Horner; 2 W A Bell (14 entries) **Ewe lamb:** 1 J Biggerstaff, Enagh, Dromara, Co Down; 2 Samuel Holden; 3 Wm James Dunlop, Carneal, Raloo, Larne (10 entries).

Ballymoney Agricultural Show, Belfast Newsletter, Wednesday, 12 June 1957 - Sheep, Border Leicester: Ram one year or upwards: 1 Rev RJ McIlmoyle; 2 D McKeeman, Ballymoney; 3 CR Lee, Garvagh; **Ewe:** 1 Rev RJ McIlmoyle; 2 D McKeeman-Gimmer; **1&2** Rev RJ McIlmoyle: 3 CR Lee; **Ram lamb:** 1 WR Gilmore, Garvagh; 2 Rev RJ McIlmoyle; 3 H Dick, Portrush; **Ewe lamb:** 1 Rev RJ McIlmoyle; 2 H Dick; 3 D McKeeman. **Special prize for Best Border Leicester in show:** Rev RJ McIlmoyle

Balmoral Show, Belfast News Letter, Friday 27 May 1960 - Border Leicester Special prize for best animal, Rev RJ McIlmoyle, Dervock; reserve WA Bell, Hillsborough; Black cup for best group, consisting of a breeding ewe, a shearling ewe and a ewe lamb, the Rev RJ McIlmoyle, reserve WA Bell.

Coleraine Agricultural Show, News Letter, Monday, 13 June 1960 - Border Leicester Ram any age: 1 R Smith, Ballymagarry, Portrush, 2 S Black, Portstewart; Ewe are one year old with lamb or lambs at foot, or due to lamb or having produced a lamb or lambs: **1&2** Rev RJ McIlmoyle, Dervock; 2 S Black; **One year old:** 1 Rev RJ McIlmoyle; 2 S Black; 3 R Smith; **Ram lamb: 1&3** S Black; 2 WL Moore, Priestland **Ewe lamb** 1 Rev RJ McIlmoyle; 2 R Smith; 3 S Black

Ballymoney Agricultural Show, News Letter, Wednesday, 15 June 1960 - Border Leicester Shearling ram: 1 R Smith; **Ewe with lamb at foot: 1&2** Rev RJ McIlmoyle; 3 R Smith; Gimmer: 1 Rev RJ McIlmoyle; 2 R Smith; 3 S Black, Portstewart; Ram lamb: 1 W L Moore, Coleraine; **2&3** S Black; **Ewe lamb:** 1 Rev RJ McIlmoyle; 2 R Smith; 3 S Black. Rosette for best Border Leicester and breed society prize - Rev RJ McIlmoyle, Dervock; res R Smith, Portrush.

Royal Ulster Show, Balmoral, 25 May 1961 -Sheep: Border Leicester Black Cup for best group consisting of breeding ewe, shearling ewe and ewe lamb, Rev RJ McIlmoyle; reserve Alexander Minnis, Ballygowan, Belfast. Certificate for best group consisting of ram, one year old and up, ewe one year old and up, and ram or ewe lamb, WA Bell, reserve Rev RJ McIlmoyle.

6 June Ballymoney Show - Pedigree Border Leicester Ram any age: 1 Rev RJ McIlmoyle, Dervock; 2 Robert Smith, Ballymagarry, Portrush; 3 Samuel Black, Portstewart; **Ewe any age with lamb or lambs at foot:** 1 Rev RJ McIlmoyle; **2&3** Robert Smith; Gimmer: 1 Rev McIlmoyle; 2 Robert Smith; 3 Samuel Black; **Ewe lamb:** 1 S Black; 2 Hugh Dick, Portrush; 3 Rev McIlmoyle

Balmoral Show, Belfast Newsletter, Friday 24 May 1963 - Border Leicester Ewe over one shear with lamb at foot (ewe only judged) (seven entries): 1 Alexander Minnis; 2 Samuel Black, Portstewart; 3 Rev RJ McIlmoyle, Dervock.

Ballymena Agricultural Show, Newsletter, Thursday, 13 June 1963 - Border Leicester Ram one year old: 1 Messrs McCrone, Holden and Dunlop, Ballynure; 2 Rev RJ McIlmoyle, Dervock; 3 W White, Dundonald; **lamb dropped in 1963:** 1 S Holden, Ballynure; 2 J M Lees, Coleraine; 3 S Black, **Portstewart Ewe over one year, sucking lamb or lambs:** 1 Rev RJ McIlmoyle; 2 R Smith; 3 S Black; **Ewe over one year old: 1&2** R Smith; 3 Rev RJ McIlmoyle; **Ewe lamb dropped in 1963:** 1 H McCrone, Ballynure; 2 R Smith; 3 Rev RJ McIlmoyle

---

Robert Hanna wrote the centenary history (1974) of Dromara RP Church.

---

they found her, she was standing in a clearing in the jungle, autocratic, upright as ever, masterful. Ten yards in front of her a full-grown lion was crouching in terror and when the wife saw this she says, "John what can we do?". "Oh, nothing at all", he says, "the lion got itself into that scrape and he'll get out of it whatever way he likes."

(10) This lady was burying her third husband. Now a commercial traveller was in the district and this commercial traveller and she had been lovers or thought they were lovers in their early days. But she was now very glad to see him and took him to the graveyard where she showed him the beautiful stone she had erected to the memory of the other two and their names beautifully carved on that stone. And now she says, "Your name might have been there too, if you would have had any spunk at all".

(11) This young couple got married early in life. That is the time to get married. If you didn't get married then, do it now. For a time everything went well and it seemed an ideal union. But then there was a rift, a tiny wee rift. If either of them had been man enough or woman enough to say "Sorry, it was my fault", that would have been the end of it. But neither did; neither would. This rift widened out until it became a yawning chasm. Then there was difficulty in the home. She was very severe on her husband. He took to drink and she was more severe still. Finally the minister was called in, and, when he heard the two sides of the story, he looked at the lady. "Now it's your fault. You have taken the wrong turning. You are travelling the wrong road. Try the other way. Be kind to your husband, gentle, loving, court him." Now she thought it was good advice and she would take it. And the very next night she waited at her own door for his homecoming and then in the distance she heard the slow unsteady footfall. And when he got her length she took him in her arms and gave him a wifely embrace. She took him in and set him down by a good fire, took off his boots, and put on his slippers and gave him a good cup of tea. "Now", says she, "wouldn't you like to go to bed and get a good sleep?" "I suppose so", says he. "When I'm here I might as well, for I'll get a hammering when I go home anyway."

(12) There was a country villa situated in its own grounds and here is another one in an adjoining plot. To the first of these a newly-wed couple came to live and to the other villa another couple came, not so newly wed. Shortly after the honeymoon couple came, the lady in number two noticed that a certain thing happened with clockwork regularity each morning. At a certain hour, the young husband and wife emerged from their home, walked down the garden path, arm in arm, and when they got to the gate he kissed his wife. He kissed her lovingly and then waved her good bye and went to his business in the city. Now number two lady wasn't getting nearly the attention from her husband that she thought that she had a right to and she thought she might manage things to her own advantage. And so purposefully she waited the next morning and, as soon as she saw the newly-wed couple coming out, she said to her husband, "John, come to see this". John came and John and his wife both looked and saw the newly-weds walk down the garden path, arm in arm. He kissed his wife, kissed her lovingly, then waved her good-bye and went away. Then number two lady looked at her husband and said "Now, John,couldn't you do that?" "I might", said he. "I might, but give me time. I don't know her well enough yet."

(13) An Ulster farmer took his wife for a holiday to Paris. One day he took her into a swell restaurant for dinner. There were a great many French dishes which they had never seen nor tasted.

Here was a dish that was to cost one pound (that was the time you could get a good lunch in Belfast in a good hotel for half-a-crown). So when they got the bill it was for four pounds for two lunches. He said to the waiter, "This is extravagant. I'm not paying this, for there is a pound for a dish we never touched." "Well", said the waiter, "that is your fault, for it was there if you wanted it." Again he said, "I'm not paying". Then the waiter bought the manager and he went over the same ground. "A pound for a dish we never touched!" "Well", said the manager, "that is your fault; it was there if you wanted it." "All right", said the farmer, as he got out his wallet and gave him three pounds and ten shillings. The manager said, "This is ten shillings short". "I know that", said the farmer, "but I am keeping that off you for kissing my wife." "Oh", said he, "I never kissed your wife, I didn't kiss your wife." "Oh, I know, I know that, but she was there if you had wanted to."

(14) If there is one thing we need today in this world that is upset (no-one knows where they stand or where they may be tomorrow), if there is one thing we need more than another, it is the spirit of optimism. The pessimist is the one who never sees any good in anything. He never has a word of commendation or praise for anyone. The world is wrong, wrong all the time, and things are upside down. But, thank God for the optimist, thank God for him. You can tell when you meet him in the morning with his cheery smile and firm hand-grasp. He is able to enthuse all with whom he comes in contact. He can take the worst possible situation and make it a little brighter and better than he found it. I heard some time ago of an optimist and, if *he* was not one, where would you go? Where? This man washed his shirt, the only shirt he had, and then put it out to dry. And a whirlwind came and blew it away and, as he saw it go and knew that he would never see it again, he thanked his stars that he wasn't in it.

(15) If there is one person that I dislike more than another and I shouldn't have said that (ministers especially shouldn't dislike anybody, but you can like a person very much and dislike some of the things they do), now if there is conduct that I dislike more than any other, it is that conduct which can be described as negative. There are people like that in the world. They never do anything, they never try to. I would rather see a person spoil a horn than refuse to make a spoon any day. Negative. Two young men were seated in a railway carriage. Right opposite to them was another young man whom they didn't know and in the other corner of the carriage and on the same seat as the young man was a clergyman sitting. As soon as the train pulled out, one of the two young men offered the one across from them a cigarette. "No thanks", he says, "I don't smoke." And the minister was delighted. Now some ministers object very much to smoking, but this one didn't. He didn't, because he drank tea himself and tea and tobacco are both weeds. Then after a while they brought out a pack of cards and asked their friend across the way to join in a game. He said, "No, I never play" and the minister was better pleased still. Then after a while they brought out a flask. Now it wasn't whiskey that was in it, it wasn't whiskey, but the minister didn't know that. They asked the young man across the way to join them in a drink and he says "No, I have never tasted it". By this time the minister was enthusiastic and the minister and the young man got out at the next station. The minister followed him, touched him on the shoulder and said, "Young man, you played a hero's part today. I was proud of you. Come and I'll introduce you to my daughter." "No, thank you. No thank you", said the young man, "I never touch women."

SINISTER SIDE OF THE CUP

Of all the many stories which contributors to this volume have recalled, there is no mention of one which I heard RJ tell at a YFC function in Kilraughts Presbyterian Church Hall, possibly in the early 1950s. The young minister, in making his first visit, came to see an old women whose kitchen was anything but hygienic. However she insisted that this being the first visit of her new minister he must sample her hospitality. For the minister the cups being used presented the biggest problem, as they were less than clean. However he quickly decided that he would not hold the cup in his right hand, but in his left and drink the contents as well as he could. It wasn't long until his hostess exclaimed excitedly "Your Reverence, I see you are left-handed like myself!" RH

1955

Dervock—A very successful Guest Tea, organised by the Ladies' Committee was held in the Town Hall, Ballymoney. Although inclement weather conditions prevailed the hall was filled to capacity. A very enjoyable programme was submitted under the chairmanship of the Rev. R. J. McIlmoyle. Over £500 was realised in aid of the Church Repair Fund.

The congregation has undertaken and all but completed an extensive renovation scheme—new ceiling and windows and installation of electric light and heat for the church building. The Annual Congregational Social was held on 22nd February, with a record attendance—the largest for some time if not ever. When tea was ready, Mr. James Lyons, senior member of Session called upon Mrs. McIlmoyle to turn on the lights. Mrs. McIlmoyle in reply said she wished to thank Mr. Lyons and the committee for the honour done her which she much appreciated. She congratulated the congregation on being the first in the district to instal electric light and heat. She thanked the members for the courtesy and kindness extended to her throughout the years. She recalled the many pleasant visits Mr. McIlmoyle and she had enjoyed in their homes and the kindly welcome always given. She wished all present a pleasant evening and many more of them. After tea, provided by the ladies, Mr. McIlmoyle in reviewing the work of the year said all organizations, Session, Committee, W.M.A., C.Y.P.U. and Sabbath School functioned efficiently and harmoniously during the year. At the last meeting of the committee it was decided to make an appeal to the members for help to meet the financial liability undertaken by the committee, and within a matter of days almost £600 was raised. This liberality was an inspiration to the minister and other office-bearers. The congregation seemed to have taken on a new lease of life, and its future was never brighter than at the moment. A programme of song and verse speaking was introduced and much enjoyed. During an interval Mr. Craig Millar, Superintendent of the Sabbath School distributed prizes to the children and young people.

1956 On 17 May, at the installation of the Rev Thomas Donnelly BA as minister of Ballyclabber congregation, in succession to the Rev James R Wright BA, the Scripture was read and prayer offered by the Rev RJ McIlmoyle. It was interesting to note that the Rev W McCullough BA, Drimbolg, who also took part in the service, and the Rev RJ McIlmoyle had both taken part in the service of installation of the Rev JR Wright BA in Ballyclabber on 25 April 1911.

Men of the Covenant.

Men of the Covenant! We will not
Forget the sacrifice they made,
When for Christ's Crown they nobly fought
By Scotland's mountainside and glade.
The blood-red banner of the Cross
Was placed beside the flag of blue,
And Cameron's men by crag and moss
Did make their vows to God anew.

Men of the Covenant! Fire and Sword
Could not assuage the joyful psalm
That rose from lips by burn and ford
And solemnised the Sabbath calm.
And even at the gallows tree
Fair Scotland's sons did firmly stand,
Their kindred would henceforth be free,
The Covenants* would revive the land.

Men of the Covenant! Through the flood,
They wrestled on, with faith sublime.
In Greyfriar's Churchyard with their blood
They signed the Covenant for all time:
At Bothwell bridge and at Ayrsmoss,
They did not fear the foreman's frown,
What things were gain they counted loss
For Christ and His bejewelled Crown.

Men of the Covenant! We will take
The torch that they to us hand on.
"Christ's Crown and Covenant" we will make
Our motto at life's early dawn.
We'll take the way those brave men trod,
Although the end we cannot see;
A remnant faithful to our God,
God's chosen people e'er to be.

Robert S. Taylor.

* "The Covenants, the Covenants, shall yet be Scotland's reviving."—*Jas. Guthrie.*

1957: Presented with a clock by the Newtownards branch, UFU

1957

Limavady—

—On 13th June the congregation opened a church hall, named the Crawford Hall, in memory of the late John M. Crawford, of Parkersburg, U.S.A., to whose initiative and generosity its erection was mainly due. A short service was held in the church in which Revs. Hugh Wright, Moderator of Presbytery ; J. A. C. Blair, Moderator of Synod and James Blair took part. Then the hall was declared open by Mrs. John McIlmoyle.

On the following Sabbath, 16th June, a special evening service was conducted by Rev. R. J. McIlmoyle, who gave a fine helpful address to a large congregation. On Sabbath evening, 23rd June, another special service was held when Rev. Hugh J. Blair, B.A., Moderator, gave a challenging address.

NOTICE.

ANNUAL MEETING OF SYNOD, 1957

The Annual Meeting of Synod will (D.V.) be held in Ballymoney R.P. Church, commencing MONDAY, 17th JUNE, 1957, at 7.30 p.m. The outgoing Moderator, Rev. J. A. Cresswell Blair, B.A., will conduct public worship and constitute the Court.

The meeting of the Synod at Ballymoney this year will focus attention on an important anniversary in the history of our church. In 1757, William Martin was ordained to the office of the Gospel Ministry at The Vow, Co. Antrim. This spot was undoubtedly chosen for the convenience of Covenanters on both sides of the Bann. The growth and development of the Covenanting cause in the Counties of Antrim and Derry have a close link with that historic occasion, and by the appointment of Synod, the Northern Presbytery is making arrangements for an appropriate commemoration of the event. It is planned to hold a Special Service at The Vow on Sabbath afternoon, the 16th of June, and for Synod to hold another short service there on Wednesday afternoon, the 19th June.

The whole church should be interested in the proceedings of Synod and members of the church are invited to the evening sessions on Tuesday and Wednesday, when the items under review are of special interest.

ADAM LOUGHRIDGE,
Clerk of Synod

29. Synod proceeded to the appointment of a Professor of Church History and Pastoral Theology. Rev. R. J. McIlmoyle and Rev. J. W. Calderwood nominated Rev. Adam Loughridge, B.A., of Portrush, Professor of Church History and Pastoral Theology as successor to Professor McFarlane.

30. The Moderator, in the name of Synod, urged Mr. Loughridge to accept the appointment.

31. Rev. Adam Loughridge thanked the Synod for the honour done to him; and intimated his acceptance of the Chair.

Miss Nan Downs, 33 Portstewart Road, Coleraine, writes: "I belong to Dromore Presbyterian Church (formerly Original Secession). While we were in the Secession body and vacant, the late Rev AR Wright of Ballylaggan RP Church ministered to us and sometimes other RP ministers would deputise for him. I well remember the Rev McIlmoyle doing so once. My mother and I were walking to church and Mr McIlmoyle came along in his car and kindly offered us a lift. My mother got into the seat beside him at the front and I got in at the back, only to find that the back seat had been taken out of the car and the floor space was covered with sheep's wool and droppings. There I was, in a crouched position with nowhere to sit. I had to put my hands under my knees to keep my clothes from the floor. His Reverence never made any comment nor noticed my predicament. I was very cramped and uncomfortable for that half-mile journey to the church and I was very thankful when the car arrived. The Rev RJ had apparently transported sheep in the back of his car and treated me as another of his flock. I also remember him at social evenings in my young days, for he was always the top entertainer."

Stories of the Rev RJ remembered by Mr Boyd McConnell, "Hylands", 24 Greens Road, Saintfield, who is an elder in Ballymacashon RP Church, Killinchy

(1) The young minister was taking a service for a colleague who was well known for the length of his sermons. As his sermon was rather brief, he thought he would have to make some excuse. So he told the congregation that while he was preparing his own sermon the dog came into the study and ran off with two pages. An old chap at the back of the church jumped to his feet and shouted, "Your Reverence, would you keep our minister a pup out o' that dog!".

(2) The minister was taking the Sabbath services for a colleague. He had preached the sermon in the morning and apparently had not been too successful. He arrived back for the evening service and going up the badly-lit stairs he came upon an elderly lady making her way slowly up. He offered his assistance and on arriving at the top she asked him, "Who is the speaker tonight?" "Mr Brown", he said, "the speaker you had this morning", "Oh dear me", she exclaimed, "help me down again!".

(3) The minister happened to be passing a field where one of his parishioners was ploughing. Things were not going too well. The horses were giving trouble, the ploughing was not too good and the man's language left much to be desired. The minister shouted over the hedge, "John, that's terrible, you will have to modify your language." John replied "I might in stubble, your Reverence, but not in lea!"

1958

Dervock—A United C.Y.P.U. meeting was held on 30th May, Mr. George Hunter presiding over a good attendance. Rev. R. J. McIlmoyle led in prayer, and Misses Hazel McConaghie and Sadie Kerr read Scripture. Papers were contributed on the general subject—"Christ our Mediator"—Miss E. Fleming, Ballymoney—"His Birth and Life"; Mr. Wm. Anderson, Cullybackey—"His Death and Resurrection"; and Miss Agnes Hyndman, Kellswater—"His Ascension and Coming Again." A period of voluntary prayer was held. Tea was served to all present by the local members, who were cordially thanked by Mr. John Loughridge.

Bravery—Many members of the church were thrilled to read of a heroic deed performed by Miss Isabel Ramsey in the month of April. Miss Ramsey is matron of Cushendall Hospital, and was sitting in her bungalow when she noticed some excitement among boys on the bank of a nearby river. Hurrying over to them she was told that a boy of seven was at the bottom of a deep pool. Wading into the water up to her neck, she partly raised the boy with her foot until she could grasp him with her hand. She carried him out and applied artificial respiration, in which she was helped by a doctor who came on the scene, and finally their efforts were successful. For this Miss Ramsey has been awarded a testimonial on parchment by the Royal Humane Society. We salute Miss Ramsey as a worthy daughter of Prof. Ramsey, the hero of Niagara.

The Manse family and offspring in the 1950s Back (left): Dr Fred Mitchell, Lewis McIlmoyle, Vincent McIlmoyle; **middle**: Enid Mitchell, Kathleen McIlmoyle, Susan McIlmoyle, Elvina McIlmoyle; **front**: Peter McIlmoyle, Rosemary Mitchell, Rev RJ McIlmoyle, Mrs Louise McIlmoyle, Desmond Mitchell and Haldane Mitchell

Another great entertainer in Ulster was Wilson Guy of Firgrove, Fintona, better known as Mat Mulcaghey (the oul' besom man from the County Tyrone) who died on 5 November 1959 at the age of 84. In his *Ballymulcaghey Calling* he has this chapter:

TOP DRESSING

One of the best story tellers I ever heard is the Rev. R. J. M'Ilmoyle. Some time before the milk subsidy was extended to embrace creamery suppliers of milk, the Farmers' Union had a meeting in a hall in the Clogher Valley. Mr. M'Ilmoyle was one of the speakers. On this occasion he told a story about an oriental gentleman who had taken unto himself a wife. Now it so happens that in this Eastern land the ladies keep their faces covered and have only peep holes to look out of. This is a most unfortunate circumstance for a would-be suitor. He has no idea of what his lady love looks like, and he only sees her face, for the first time, when he has taken her to wife. It was such a lady that the oriental had married.

The next morning the bridegroom was seated outside his house and kept lifting handfuls of clay and piling it on his head. A neighbour, who was passing on his way, looked aside and saw his friend giving expression to some inward sorrow. He paused and asked sympathetically: "Why the clay, brother?"

It was then that the other told his tale of woe. "You see I was married yesterday," he explained.

"Yes, so I understand, brother, but I cannot see reason in that for the application of clay," he argued.

To this his friend replied: "Ah, yes, my friend, but as you know I never saw my wife's face till last night, and I declare that she is the ugliest woman ever created."

The philosophic one reasoned with his disappointed friend, and said that he, too, had married a woman whose face he had never seen till after the wedding. She, too, was one of the ugliest women on earth. She looked positively horrible to him, but after he had lived with her for some time he found that she had so many excellent qualities that he soon forgot her face and grew to love her more than if she had been the greatest beauty on earth. "You, too, brother, will probably have the same experience and you should not give way to grief. All will be well."

The friend was about to pass on his way when the aggrieved one called to him: "I sincerely hope that your prophesy may come true, but I am afraid it is impossible. You will better understand if you just step inside and have a look at her for yourself."

His friend passed inside and after a very short stay came out, and as he passed his friend he said quietly out of the corner of his mouth: "Put on more clay, brother!"

As usual, Mr. M'Ilmoyle's story was well received, but the funniest thing was yet to come.

It so happened that Sir Basil Brooke was then Minister of Agriculture in the Northern Government. He, too, was present on the occasion, and after delivering the first part of his address, paused to remark: "Since coming to your district I have been approached by quite a number of milk suppliers who are sending their milk to creameries in Ulster. They have asked me if I think the subsidy that has already been granted to milk producers in England will be extended to Northern Ireland? I assure you that this matter has already had my closest attention. I have gone very carefully into the question with the various Ministers concerned in the Imperial Government; but it has been pointed out to me that this subsidy is intended only for milk producers who are catering for those who consume whole milk in the cities and towns, whereas you milk suppliers to creameries are using the milk for manufacture into butter. No, I am sorry to say that I can hold out no hope of this subsidy being extended to Northern Ireland."

In the silence caused by this disappointing news, an old farmer, unkempt and unshaven, called from the back of the hall: "Put on more clay, brothers!"

1960

Glenmanus—The Annual Social and business meeting of the congregation was held in the Church Hall on Thursday, 14th January. After tea had been served, Professor Loughridge in the chair made reference to the main events during the past year. It had been one of changes. The congregation had lost valued members like Mrs. Killen and Mr. Nevin through death while others had been compelled to sever their connection with the congregation through migration. The Chairman regretfully announced to the meeting the impending departure, on promotion, to Belfast of their treasurer, Mr. V. H. McIlmoyle. He hoped that these changes would present a challenge to each member to do his best to make good the service and support lost by these changes. The Session report read by Mr. John Gordon expressed sympathy with the Session Clerk, Mr. John Maconaghie in his prolonged illness. Eight members had been admitted to fellowship and three children baptised during the year. The Committee's report, presented by the Secretary, Mr. Joseph Gilmour, commended the congregation for responding so generously to the quarterly collections for the Repair Fund. thereby reducing the deficit from £300 to £20. Mr. V. H. McIlmoyle submitted a very satisfactory financial statement. It showed that in spite of the passing of generous subscribers, the financial position had been well maintained. Mrs. Wm. Wright presented the report and financial statement of the W.M.A. These showed an increase in attendance at the meetings and a record amount contributed to Missions. The reports were adopted on the motion of Mr. Allen Loughridge, seconded by Mr. Marshall McMaster. During the evening Mrs Logan on behalf of the congregation made a presentation to Allen Loughridge in recognition of his services as leader of the praise for 3½ years. She wished him well in his career in the Civil Service. A most enjoyable programme was provided by Mrs. Craig, Misses Patrica Creighton, Sheelagh McKay, Kathleen Black, Eileen Taylor and Dot. Faulkner and greetings and good wishes to pastor and people were brought by Revs. R. J. McIlmoyle, Hugh J. Blair and K. M. Alexander, Portrush.

Dervock—The annual congregational social was held on 22nd January, 1960, when there was a good attendance of members and friends. Tea was served by the ladies of the congregation. Rev. R. J. McIlmoyle presided and introduced an enjoyable programme of songs, music and recitations. A pleasant feature of the evening came when Mrs. Lynas on behalf of the congregation presented Miss Boyd with a wallet of notes as a token of appreciation of her services as choir-leader for a number of years. Sabbath school prizes for answering and attendance were distributed by Messrs C. Millar and A. McConaghie. Prof. Loughridge congratulated the prize winners and commended the congregation for team-work and the smooth running of congregational affairs. At the close Mr. McIlmoyle thanked all who had contributed to the success of the meeting.

RJ McILMOYLE & THE ULSTER FARMERS' UNION

When the Ulster Farmers' Union was formed in 1918, the Rev RJ McIlmoyle, representing County Antrim on its Council and Executive, was involved in much of the work dealing with the multiplicity of matters concerning farmers at that time. Before Partition, Mr McIlmoyle took part in negotiations with the Irish Farmers' Union and the Irish Agricultural Organisations Society in Dublin to clarify the relation between the UFU and the IFU and to establish the UAOS to service the co-operative societies in the North. The completion of the schemes to buy out landlords, which had been postponed for the duration of the 1914-18 war, came to the fore again when the Northern Ireland government was established. Mr McIlmoyle was one of the principal speakers at mass meetings of farm tenants and in 1925 he was on a deputation to urge the Prime Minister to take action to complete the transfer of the remaining farms to the tenants. He urged a meeting of the Unbought Tenants to accept the terms offered in the 1925 Land Purchase Act. In promoting the new Union throughout the Province, Mr McIlmoyle took an active part as a member of the Organisation Committee which requested him in 1920 to become a part-time Organiser for the Northern part of the province. The early Union oversaw the publication of the *Farmer's Journal* as a means of communication with its members and as a magazine of general interest for farmers and their families. Mr McIlmoyle was one of the first shareholders in the *Journal* and sat on its Board of Directors from 1919 until it was reorganised in 1950, having maintained a valuable record of the agricultural world in those years. In the 1920s and 30s, when the depression in agriculture resulted in the early enthusiasm of farmers for their organisation giving way to despondency and the lapsing of many branches of the Union, Mr McIlmoyle travelled widely, encouraging farmers to unite to meet the difficulties of the times. In one of his reports to the Executive he stated that he had addressed twelve meetings in the preceding month.

As prices for farm produce fell, the income of the Union dropped and in 1929 the bank told the Union that it must reduce the overdraft of which Mr McIlmoyle was one of the guarantors. When the Executive of the Union was reviewing its expenditures, it stated that the work done by Mr McIlmoyle was worth more than all that he had been paid for his part-time work. Mr McIlmoyle was active in schemes to increase the Union's income to meet its needs. He supported a plan to persuade 200 members to contribute £5 a year and he proposed a scheme to raise 20,000 shillings for the Union. He also took part in negotiations with the Government to obtain a subsidy of £1,000 a year for the education work of the Union. An Education Committee was formed to administer this grant, from which part of the salaries of the staff was paid. Under this arrangement Mr McIlmoyle's position was entitled Lecturer instead of Organiser. The Union sought in many ways to help farmers to carry on during the years of depression. In 1925 Mr McIlmoyle accompanied a delegation to meet County Councils on the increasing of rates to improve roads for motor cars which most farmers at that time could not afford. In spite of the current financial difficulties of the industry the Union considered the long-term welfare of agriculture when a committee, of which Mr McIlmoyle was a member, agreed with the Ministry of Agriculture to use part of the grant for the relief of rates to establish the Agricultural Research Institute at Hillsborough. Mr McIlmoyle also took part in the negotiations with the National Farmers' Union Mutual Insurance Society to extend its operations to Northern Ireland and to use the branch secretaries of the Union as agents. This brought valuable financial support to the Union both locally and at its headquarters. In 1923, when the Farmers' Union set up the Farmers' Produce Company, to enable farmers to obtain their supplies economically and to market their produce efficiently, Mr McIlmoyle canvassed members to support this co-operative venture. He also took a leading part in meetings to protest against the importation of subsidized farm products which undermined the prices for home-produced food.

As well as all Mr McIlmoyle's work for farmers in general, his own personal interest in agriculture was in the breeding of pedigree sheep. He took a leading part in the work of the Ulster Ram Breeders' Association, being Secretary for many years. In the Farmers' Union he was a member of the Livestock Committee, campaigning on arrangements for the importation of pedigree livestock from Scotland and the shipment of lambs to England. He was also a member of the Ministry of Agriculture's Advisory Committee for Sheep. In the Union's efforts to deal with the ever-continuing menace of sheep-worrying by dogs, Mr McIlmoyle persuaded the Northern Ireland Parliament in 1927 to pass a Dogs Act, one clause of which protected farmers from a claim for damages if they shot a dog when it was attacking livestock. In 1930 he was on a deputation to the Ministry to discuss a Livestock Breeding Bill. Mr McIlmoyle's work was not confined to sheep, as he also sat on the Union's Committee for Eggs and Butter and was appointed a member of the Ministry of Agriculture's Advisory Committee on Eggs. He supported the General Secretary of the Union, Mr Humphrey Jamison, and Mr W S Armour, Editor of the *Northern Whig*, in the formation of the Young Farmers' Clubs of Ulster and in the administration of the grants obtained to support them through the Education Committee of the Union, until the Young Farmers' Clubs took on the whole administration of their affairs in 1937.

Mr McIlmoyle was a member of many deputations on a variety of matters to England and Scotland. He urged the use of the radio to promote the work of the Union, which led to a talk on the BBC by Sir Basil Brooke, President of the Union in 1930, on "The UFU: What It Is and What It Does", and another such talk by Sir Arthur Algeo in 1946. When hostilities again broke out in 1939, Mr McIlmoyle was on the Executive which offered to the Government the services of the Union in organising agriculture in the War Effort. He was on the Union's War Emergency Committee and in 1940 urged farmers to grow more flax in response to the Government's appeal for 100,000 acres of flax to supply the needs of the armed forces.

Mr McIlmoyle always maintained the importance of the social side of the Union's activities, which brought together the members and their families. In 1924 he organised a party of members to visit the Wembley Exhibition in London. He arranged visits to the Spring Show in Dublin and the Highland Show in Inverness. After the War he was one of the most popular speakers at Branch Socials and County Dinners throughout the Province, where his seemingly endless fund of humorous and witty stories led on to his call on all farmers to unite in the support of their Union. In a more serious vein, the repetition of his story of the sale of "The Old Violin" was frequently requested by leading members of the Union. When he was over eighty the Union insisted on supplying a driver for his nocturnal journeys. As late as 1962, after the Fermanagh County Social in Enniskillen, when the President intended to stay the night, Mr McIlmoyle arranged to take him home to Limavady on his way to Dervock in the small hours of the morning. When the Garvagh branch of the Union was making a presentation to Mrs O'Kane who had been chairman of the branch for some years and also a founder of the Women's Institutes, she recalled with pride that the presentation had been made to her, a Roman Catholic, by the Master of the local Orange Lodge and that the citation had been held for them by a Covenanting minister (Mr McIlmoyle). This was an instance of the good relations between all the members in the Farmers' Union which Mr McIlmoyle did much to foster. This is by no means a complete record, as RJ McIlmoyle seems to have been involved in nearly every aspect of the Union's work from its earliest days. Any account seems inadequate without a selection of the humorous stories with which he delighted meetings throughout the country, but such stories cannot be the same without his personality to tell them. **Alastair McLurg**

Presentation by Ballymoney Branch of UFU **Back left**: TV McClenaghan, Sir Arthur G Algeo CBE, JP, Rev RJ McIlmoyle, president of the branch, Wm Pinkerton OBE, Mrs Sam Boyd, Sam Boyd JP, David Moore, Mrs Mary Stevenson, Wm Stevenson; **front**: Myra Stevenson, Ann Stevenson

1959/60

PRINCE OF "STORYTELLERS"

Ballymoney Tribute to Rev. R. J. M'Ilmoyle

A PRESENTATION was made to the Rev. R. J. M'Ilmoyle, Dervock, at a social meeting of Ballymoney Branch of the Ulster Farmers' Union in Dalriada School on June 5th. Mr. M'Ilmoyle was described as the prince of story tellers and as the father of the social movement of the Union. Mr. D. Moore presided.

Mr. Moore explained that he was deputising for Mr. Alan Taggart, the branch chairman, who was ill. Welcoming those present, the Chairman said they were met to pay tribute to Mr. M'Ilmoyle. Calling on Mr. W. A. Pinkerton, O.B.E., B.Sc., he mentioned that Mr. Pinkerton had been made an Honorary Life Member of the U.F.U. Council for his long service. This was the first time such a thing had been done.

FIRST SECRETARY

Mr. Pinkerton described the honouring of Mr. M'Ilmoyle by the branch as an historic occasion. Mr. M'Ilmoyle had given long service to the Union. He (Mr. Pinkerton) had been connected with Ballymoney Branch for probably a quarter of a century, and he thought Mr. M'Ilmoyle had been connected with the Farmers' Union before that. When the Ballymoney Branch had been started at the end of the first war Mr. M'Ilmoyle had been the first secretary; after a time the surrounding branches of Kilraughts, Dervock and Finvoy had branched off, and Ballymoney ceased to be a branch of the Farmers' Union. It was later reorganised and he (Mr. Pinkerton) had been appointed chairman. He would like to pay tribute to the loyalty with which he had been served. It was owing to the loyalty of the members that Ballymoney Branch had such a respected name at the headquarters of the Union. He was very glad to see present that night, Mr. William Warnock, one of the oldest members of the Farmers' Union. Mr. Warnock had been in the branch before him (Mr. Pinkerton) and had been at the inaugural meeting, and had been a very loyal attender. It was only right that they should pay a tribute to a man of Mr. Warnock's standing in the Farmers' Union.

MUCH TRAVELLING

Referring to the tribute they were paying to Mr. M'Ilmoyle, Mr. Pinkerton thought it was fitting that they should honour a man during his lifetime; it was all very well to have obituary notices and a lot of things on the man's tombstone, but it was more fitting to be honoured while alive. It was right that they should pay some tribute to Mr. M'Ilmoyle for what he had done for the Union. Most of Mr. M'Ilmoyle's activities for the Union had been carried out during the winter time, and these involved much travelling at night to the different branches. Mr. Pinkerton wondered how he had stuck so much travelling, often in the small hours of the morning. He was sure Mr. M'Ilmoyle had been to every branch and had served them well. If ever there was a social occasion Mr. M'Ilmoyle was called on to be on the platform. The Ballymoney Branch had had many socials, and he thought Mr. M'Ilmoyle had attended most of them.

Mr. M'Ilmoyle had a happy knack of illustrating his point by a story, and Mr. Pinkerton had not heard his equal; there was no man, to Mr. Pinkerton's knowledge, who could tell a story so well as Mr. M'Ilmoyle. A dry speech was nothing. but Mr. M'Ilmoyle could bring in humour and that was the reason for his popularity as a speaker in the Farmers' Union and other circles. A great deal of the popularity of the social meetings in the Farmers' Union was due to Mr. M'Ilmoyle. Concluding his tribute, Mr. Pinkerton hoped the Rev. M'Ilmoyle would live long and enjoy life.

Mr. A. G. ALGEO

Mr. A. G. Algeo, C.B.E., J.P., a Past-President of the U.F.U., recalled that when he was President how helpful Mr. M'Ilmoyle had been in collecting money for the Union's new headquarters. They had meetings night after night; sometimes Mr. M'Ilmoyle was on his own, sometimes both of them were together. Mr. Algeo spoke of one occasion when they had returned from Lisnaskea in the small hours of the morning, but Mr. M'Ilmoyle said he would go home and make himself a cup of tea and start off his day's work. How he was able to do that, Mr. Algeo didn't know; but Mr. M'Ilmoyle was still carrying on at the same work. He was an exceptional man in every respect.

Not only was he the prince of story tellers but he had also been the father of the social movement of the Ulster Farmers' Union, and Mr. Algeo thought that if it had not been for the social movement which Mr. M'Ilmoyle had inaugurated they would have had a very small Union at the present time.

Quoting some lines of verse concluding with the point that a man "cannot read his tombstone when he's dead," Mr. Algeo supported what Mr. Pinkerton had said. He thought that the Ballymoney Branch in paying the tribute to Mr. M'Ilmoyle was only paying something that was due. Mr. M'Ilmoyle had always been at their call no matter when they had wanted him to attend a social meeting, and there were very few social meetings of the branch that [illegible] was absent from. He congratu[illegible]ed Mr. M'Ilmoyle on having been able to stand up to all the work during the last number of years, when his journeys got more frequent and times got more difficult in the work he was doing for the Union. He hoped that Mr. M'Ilmoyle would be long spared along with his good wife, to carry on the good work.

THE PRESIDENT

Mr. S. Boyd, J.P., President of the U.F.U., said he was present to bring Mr. M'Ilmoyle best wishes not only from the Ballymoney Branch but from farmers all over Northern Ireland. He was very proud to be present and to be President of the Farmers' Union at the time when honour was being paid to Mr. M'Ilmoyle. He thought Mr. M'Ilmoyle had given more pleasure to more people than any other man he knew. He wished Mr. M'Ilmoyle and his wife long life and great happiness to enjoy the tribute that was being paid that night.

A cheque was handed over to Mr. M'Ilmoyle by Mrs. Boyd who said she had great pleasure in presenting him with the token of the esteem in which the branch held him. It carried the good-wishes of every individual in the branch.

RESPONSE

Mr. M'Ilmoyle, in returning thanks, congratulated Mr. Boyd in carrying for the coming year the highest honour the Farmers' Union could give to any of its members. He pointed out that the Union had come more than once to the Ballymoney district for its President. Mr. Algeo had been President more than once, and now that they had another President from the district they ought to congratulate themselves.

Referring to the honour which had been done him, Mr. M'Ilmoyle said this was one of the times when he felt he had nothing to say; the subject was altogether beyond him. He could not find one reason why they should have honoured

"Prince of Storytellers"

him, but he appreciated it ; it was very nice of them to give it, and very nice of the speakers to speak as they had done. If someone would deputise for him, and say to them the things that ought to be said, he would promise much to that person. It was a time when one felt almost dumb, but he hoped they would take the wish for the act, and accept his sincere thanks. He didn't think he had done so much for the Union until he had heard the speakers. The wish had been expressed that night that he might be able to carry on for some years still, and he hoped he would.

EARLY U.F.U. STAFF

He went on to say that the Farmers' Union had been born during the first World War. Agriculture had taken a turn for the better, prices were going up, wages weren't at the level they were at now, and everything was going well. The Farmers' Union was organised, and money kept flowing in. In those days they had a very small staff. The late Mr. M'Dowell was secretary for a long time. Mr. M'Dowell was a very able man and a great orator. Mr. M'Dowell and his typist were the only people in the office, and as their expenses were not high they heaped up a balance until it reached a fairly good height.

As the first World War dragged on the appeal was made to the farmers as the only men who could save the country. They were patted on the back and told that the country would never forget them. **But every single promise to them was broken. The Corn Production Act, that promised a little amelioration, was scrapped still-born, and the farmer was left high and dry. But for the farmers we would have lost the war because there wouldn't have been enough food to feed the armies in the field or the people at home. Old grasslands had been ploughed up, and they hadn't come back to their original state of fertility when the second World War broke out. He felt that the Farmers' Union had been too late in being born.**

FAITH IN FUTURE

Recalling that he had been brought in to help in the work of the Union, he said he had been asked to go round the country, and he agreed he was the father of the Union's social movement, which he claimed was one of the strongest planks of the Union's platform. He was proud of the fine, lusty boy into which the social movement had grown. The Union had socials going during the years of prosperity, and they succeeded in keeping some of them alive during the years of adversity, when they got the people out and to laugh, although there had been very little to laugh about. When the slump came branches lost members, and the Union lost branches. Then the tide had turned, and he suggested that this had come about because people had had faith in the future and had held on.

ARISTOCRACY

He spoke of it as being fortunate that he had got settled in a country congregation : he would break his heart in a city and maybe even in a town. The soil was in his blood, and anything he could do for agriculture and the farmer was only a pleasure. He declared that the farming community were the aristocracy of the countryside. He asked his audience to imagine what it would be like if the farmers went on strike. The townspeople couldn't do without the farmer, and he would like to see the chasm between the town and the country blotted out.

He concluded his expression of thanks with the assurance that any time they wanted him, his services were at their disposal.

A gift was presented to Mrs. Boyd by Miss Ann Stevenson.

The proceedings began with an enjoyable tea, served by Mrs. Moore and other helpers. Later there was a musical programme, with Mr. William Stevenson as compere. Songs were rendered by Miss Betty Stirling, Miss Myra Stevenson, Messrs. William Lyons, John Ramsay, William M'Corriston and William Kane, and there were also recitations by Miss Stevenson. The accompaniment for the musical items was played by Mr. Kane.

A vote of thanks to the artists was passed on the motion of Mr. Algeo, seconded by Mr. Pinkerton, and supported by Mr. Matthew Cameron.

UTA chief who was farmers' champion

NOV 1967

The death has occurred at the Royal Victoria Hospital, Belfast, of Sir Arthur Algeo, chairman of the Ulster Transport Authority. He was 66.

Sir Arthur, who lived at Coleraine Road, Ballymoney, was one of the farming community's most active leaders and served a record number of four one-year-terms as president of the Ulster Farmers' Union.

He became a member of the Ulster Transport Authority in 1953, being appointed vice-chairman in 1962.

On becoming chairman in 1963, Sir Arthur devoted his energy to giving Northern Ireland a modern and efficient public transport system, heading the authority through the most critical period of its history.

He was a director of the Northern Ireland Farmers' Bacon Company Ltd., Cookstown; the Northern Ireland Bacon Agency Ltd., and was managing director of Robert Holmes Ltd., Ballymoney.

Sir Arthur was born in Sligo, where his father, who later became Mayor of Enniskillen, was inspector of the line with the Sligo, Leitrim and Northern Counties Railways.

Sir Arthur was also a member of the Electricity Board of Northern Ireland, from which he retired earlier this year after 18 years' service.

He was awarded the C.B.E. in 1949 in recognition of his services to agriculture and in the Queen's birthday honours list in June, 1966, he was knighted.

As president of the U.F.U. in 1946-47 and in 1954-55, he guided the agricultural community through two vital stages in its history.

His first term saw the passing of the 1947 Agricultural Act while the second

coincided with the discontinuing of the purchase of the major items of U.K. farm produce by the Ministry of Food.

He was also concerned with the negotiations which led up to the remote area grant arrangements applying in Northern Ireland.

Sir Arthur was formerly a member of Antrim County Council and served on five committees, on three of which he was chairman. He was chairman of North Antrim Unionist Association for the 1966-67 term.

Keenly interested in education, he was also chairman of the North Antrim Regional Technical Committee, but on his appointment as chairman of the U.T.A., he gave up all council activities.

Sir Arthur is survived by his wife and four children.

PRIZE-WINNING SHEEP IN TAXI AT YORK ROAD STATION!

I knew the Rev RJ McIlmoyle only in the latter years of his life, but I recall him as a dignified and gracious old gentleman. He seemed to represent an age fast disappearing and to bring something of its style and manners into our more mundane world. He was always dressed in a long black or grey coat, black hat and clerical collar, which gave him an added air of distinction and even a touch of severity. I never saw him without his clerical collar and even when he was going to feed his sheep, with a bucket of food on his bicycle, he was still dressed as a minister and was wearing the collar. When he attended Farmers' Union meetings and concerts, he was similarly dressed and when he appeared on the platform and started telling his stories, people could not believe that this rather severe-looking figure before them could be so humorous. That was part of his impact. He shocked them and they started to laugh, perhaps a little scared to do so too much when he began, but then the laughter grew, as story followed story, until he virtually "brought the house down". His dead-pan expression (he never laughed at any of his jokes), his fine resonant voice, his perfect timing and his ability to hit the punch-line "dead on" every time combined to make him quite the most skilful performer of his day. But it was not just a performance which he gave. He used his stories really as an introduction to what he wanted to say. I remember him telling me that when you got a group of farmers laughing, and that was quite a feat in itself, then they were in a much better mood to receive the information you wanted to put across to them.

Similarly at church functions he always ended with a word of uplift from the Bible, a sentence or two to make people think, a message which they could take home and remember. He built up a great reputation throughout Ulster and when it was known that 'McIlmoyle' (he had the honour only given to a few to be popularly known by his surname alone) was on the programme, it would be a big night. Farmers' Union branches organising concerts and meetings knew that they must procure his services. One man said to me that if you could not get McIlmoyle you just need not bother having the concert or public meeting, for nobody would come. If he was on the programme, it was a different matter; they were there by the hundred. His material was gathered from everyday affairs of rural life, matters which interested farmers and country folk. People told him of incidents and he adapted what he heard to his own requirements. He often told stories about new developments in agriculture, country characters, sheep and agricultural shows.

When RJ was quite old he found driving by car to Belfast too much for him; so he often went by train from Ballymoney Station. I recall him on the train with one of his special prize-winning sheep, on the way to Balmoral. He sat with the sheep in the guard's van and, when we got to Belfast, he hired a taxi to get to Balmoral. I recall standing at the bus-stop at York Road Station and seeing him driving out in the back of the taxi with the sheep sitting on the seat beside him. It was a memorable picture and just could not happen today. **S Alex Blair, Dungorbery, Kilraughts**

LAUGHING AT THE RITZ ... I can still remember the Rev RJ McIlmoyle appearing at an Ulster Farmers' Union County Concert in the Ritz Cinema in Enniskillen when there was a full house. It was about 30 years ago and the Farmers' Union County Quiz took place during the concert. The Rev RJ gave a talk which was very much appreciated. I remember his rich Co Antrim brogue which gave a special quality to the yarns he told. I wish I could remember some of them, but they were certainly very enjoyable and were received with enthusiasm by the audience. As they were related to farming and country life, they went over very well. I think it was probably RJ who told the anecdote which highlights the Co Antrim rural dialect: "Two United States airmen were ferrying a new Flying Fortress bomber over to Britain during World War II. When they were over Northern Ireland they either ran out of fuel or had a major engine failure and had to make a forced landing. They managed to get the Flying Fortress down on the Antrim plateau without too much damage. However, they had no idea where they were. As they had lost direction, they started walking across the mist-covered bogland and eventually saw a man sitting fishing on the bank of a burn. They did not want to reveal that they were lost or what country they were from; so the captain decided to make general conversation at first. He asked the fisherman: "Have you caught anything yet?" Turning round, the elderly angler replied: "Yin young yin!" said the captain to his co-pilot, "We must have landed in China!"

Although the Rev RJ would have been a fair age, I remember that he had a good clear voice and that he could spice his talk with both jokes and good, sound advice. At that time the Fermanagh farmers respected the Co Antrim men for their sagacity and knowledge, and the thriftiness resulting from their Scottish ancestry. Although the UFU concert did not finish until quite late, the Fermanagh people liked getting value for their money. The Rev RJ would probably have set off to drive home to Dervock, irrespective of the weather and at that time when the roads were not so good and cars not as comfortable or reliable as today. This is really all I can recall of the Rev RJ. He probably came to other UFU gatherings in Fermanagh. George Cathcart of 'The Sheelin', Bellanaleck, was a prominent figure in the UFU and in farming generally at that time. He has a most retentive memory and must recall some of the Rev RJ's visits.

Mervyn Dane, *The Impartial Reporter & Farmers Journal*

Mr. A. Maclurg, president, Ulster Farmers' Union (right), presenting an illuminated address to the Rev. R. J. M'Ilmoyle, Dervock — to mark his recent election as an honorary life member — at yesterday's Council meeting of the Union. Mr. M'Ilmoyle is a foundation member of 42 years' standing. In centre is Mr. George Cathcart, deputy president, UFU.

I have taken an active part in the Ulster Farmers' Union since 1942, when we founded the Bellanaleck Branch of the UFU here in County Fermanagh. I had the honour of being the Union's President in 1961. Mr McIlmoyle was then a part-time lecturer with the Union and I formed a lasting friendship with him. I have been a member of the Fermanagh County Committee of the Union since 1942. In those days the County Committee organized the UFU annual social in Enniskillen Town Hall. We engaged professional artists from Belfast, but Mr McIlmoyle soon became the star. He always requested to come on stage half-way through the programme. I can picture him yet, a smallish slim man, with a face that never seemed to smile, even when the audience exploded with laughter. He had a pleasing Antrim accent and an uncanny knack of throwing his voice so that everyone could hear every word. There was always a microphone on stage, but he waved it aside. Occupancy of the stage was so easy and natural to him. He only glanced occasionally at a postcard with the story headings, as he led one story into the next, sometimes standing still, at other times strolling with measured steps, but always facing the audience. The annual social became so popular, mainly because of him, that we were forced to abandon the Town Hall for the local cinema, which could accommodate some 1500 people. RJ's stories always covered the natural wit of the inhabitants of our beloved Province. He always wore his clerical collar and never failed to bring tears to the audience and unlimited applause when he finished with the immortal poem "The Old Violin". In its final lines it gave the message of the Gospel which was the Rev McIlmoyle's mission in his long life. Incidentally he was always very careful not to reveal the date of his birth and when on one occasion he had a slight car accident (he was insured with the NFU Mutual Insurance Company), the General Secretary of the UFU, Mr JT O'Brien, said to me "We will get to know his date of birth now, as he will have to put it on the claim form"; but, true to form, RJ simply completed that part of the form by stating that he was over 21. I am now in my 80th year and I am hoping to have my memories in book form before the end of the year. I shall let you have a copy and will be very interested to receive a copy of your book on the Rev RJ.

George A Cathcart, "The Sheelin", Bellanaleck, Enniskillen

MINUTES

OF THE

Proceedings of the Reformed Presbyterian Synod of Ireland

ANNUAL MEETING, 1960

in the Reformed Presbyterian Church

Grosvenor Road, Belfast

SESSION I

Monday Evening, 20th June, 1960, at 7.30 o'clock.

1. The Synod of the Reformed Presbyterian Church of Ireland met. Rev. W. Norman McCune, B.A., outgoing Moderator, conducted public worship, preached from Mark 16: 19, 20—"So then after the Lord had spoken unto them, he was received up into heaven, and sat on the right hand of God. And they went forth, and preached every where, the Lord working with them, and confirming the word with signs following. Amen"; and constituted Synod while leading in prayer.

---

8. The outgoing Moderator addressed Synod on his year of office, thanked members for their courtesy and helpfulness, demitted his office, and called upon the Court to appoint his successor.

9. Rev. Isaac Cole and Prof. A. Loughridge nominated Rev. Robert John McIlmoyle, Dervock, for the office of Moderator for the ensuing year.

10. Rev. R. J. McIlmoyle, elected to the office, was warmly received by Synod, and addressed the Court on the theme: "Introspection in the Christian Life."

---

107. Committees, etc., of Synod were appointed.

108. It was agreed that the Moderator, Rev. R. J. McIlmoyle, be appointed to convey the greetings of Synod to the General Assembly of the Presbyterian Church in Ireland next year.

109. It was agreed that Synod meet next year in Cullybackey on Monday, 19th June, at 7.30 p.m.

1960 (continued)

119. Psalm 72, verses 7 to 11, was sung in praise to God.

120. The Moderator welcomed Rt. Rev. A. A. Fulton, M.A., PH.D., D.D., Moderator of the General Assembly of the Presbyterian Church in Ireland, and invited Rev. W. N. McCune to introduce him to the Court.

121. Dr. Fulton addressed the Synod and conveyed the greetings of the Presbyterian Church in Ireland.

122. The Moderator thanked Dr. Fulton for his presence and for his stimulating address.

123. The Moderator welcomed to the platform Rev. S. R. Archer, Convener of the Committee on Irish Evangelisation, Mr. T. J. McKee, colporteur, and Mrs. McKee, from Cork.

124. Rev. S. R. Archer moved the adoption of the report and statement of accounts of the Committee on Irish Evangelisation; seconded by Rev. David J. Magee, and passed. (Report p. 32.)

125. Mr. T. J. McKee addressed the Synod on his work in Cork on behalf of the Irish Mission.

126. Mrs. McKee who addressed Synod on her work among women and children in Cork and was thanked by the Moderator.

132. The Moderator conducted devotional exercises, dissolved the Court, and brought the meeting of Synod to an end.

R. J. McILMOYLE, *Moderator.*
ADAM LOUGHRIDGE, *Clerk.*

Attested by me,
ADAM LOUGHRIDGE

Rev RB Lyons BA, Limavady, as an editor of *The Covenanter*, reported as follows:

SYNOD, 1960

The Annual Meeting of the supreme court of the Reformed Presbyterian Church opened in Belfast on Monday evening, 20th June, under most favourable conditions. There was a good attendance of office-bearers and members of the church, when the outgoing Moderator, Rev. W. N. McCune, conducted public worship. His sermon on " The Church in Action" was on his usual high level of clear thinking, happy expression and devotional fervour.

Thanking the members of the court for their support during the year, Mr. McCune asked for a successor in office. The Northern Presbytery furnished this by a man who has made records in many fields, Rev. R. J. McIlmoyle, minister of Dervock congregation, who comes to the chair a second time, fifty years after his first appointment. The years have not dimmed his quickness to see a point in argument and to set in motion the necessary procedure. A glance round the Synod shows new faces year by year as sons and grandsons take the place of the fathers and many were regular in their attendance throughout the meeting. Two changes of field and one ordination were reported. Two ministers were unable to be present at any of the meetings.

1560-1960

In 1960 the Reformed Presbyterian Church of Ireland was associated with the Church of Scotland at the commemoration, in Edinburgh, of the fourth centenary of the Scottish Reformation. The Synod of the RP Church of Ireland was represented by its Clerk, the Rev Prof Adam Loughridge, who deputised for the Moderator, the Rev RJ McIlmoyle. Rev Prof Loughridge concluded thus a report of that memorable and historic occasion:

There were many highlights and stirring memories for those who were privileged to attend. Not least of these were the excellent arrangements for hospitality. The fellowship with a Church of Scotland minister and his wife in the home ; the reception given by the Moderator and the gift of his latest work, " A Church History of Scotland," as a memento of the occasion ; the many tokens of friendship from members of the Committee on Arrangements ; the thoughtful attention given each day to the wives of delegates, these will not soon be forgotten. But one would be less than human to refrain from recording that the special memory will always be the visit to the Palace of Holyrood house as guests of Her Majesty the Queen, and the privilege of having been selected—two Covenanters from Ireland, for presentation to her. The outstanding impression of this opportunity for speaking with the Queen is not her undoubted grace and charm, but her warm appreciation of the work of the Reformation and her wide knowledge of the details of Scotland's commemoration.

It was right and profitable for Scotland to remember the Reformation of 1560. It was a privilege to have been associated with the Church of Scotland on a historic occasion in which history was made. It is a pleasure to record the impression that, while there is a wide range of views within the Church of Scotland, she is sound at heart and has a great contribution to make to the maintenance and propagation of the Reformed Faith in the modern world.

A.L.

'Capital of Covenanting': Kellswater Reformed Presbyterian Church
(Jacqui McNeill)

1960

Dervock— The Northern Presbytery met in Dervock on Wednesday, 3rd August, for the visitation of the congregation. Rev. Isaac Cole, Moderator of Presbytery, presided, and put the prescribed questions to the minister, Rev. R. J. McIlmoyle, and representatives of the congregation. Messrs. David Miller and James Simpson represented the Session ; Messrs. James Miller and Daniel McKeeman, the Committee ; and Messrs. John Fleming and Joseph Kerr the congregation. A most satisfactory finding was prepared by the Committee of Presbytery, consisting of Revs. Hugh J. Blair, S. M. Calderwood and Mr. W. M. Aicken. The Presbytery congratulated Mr. McIlmoyle on his completion of sixty years in the ministry, fifty-six of which have been spent in Dervock. Tribute was paid to the great services rendered to the congregation by Mrs. McIlmoyle, notwithstanding her physical handicap within recent years. The congregation was commended for their spirit of loyalty and harmony in the work of the church. The church property was found to be in excellent repair. Tribute was paid to Mrs. McIlmoyle and the ladies of the congregation for the generous support of Mission work ; and to the young people for their active interest in the work of the church.

The Presbytery made certain recommendations which, it was felt, would result in still greater effectiveness in the congregation's witness. After the meeting the Presbytery and friends were hospitably entertained by the congregation to luncheon in Moore's Restaurant, Ballymoney. A cordial vote of thanks was proposed by Rev. Hugh J. Blair, and seconded Mr. James McNeill.

Dervock—Mrs. Jas. Kerr, Vice-President of the Woman's Missionary Association, presided at their Annual Meeting held in the church on Thursday, 4th August. There was a very good attendance of members and their friends, and all were very glad to have Mrs. McIlmoyle, the President, with us after her illness—she is an inspiration to us all. Rev. H. J. Blair, Convenor of our Foreign Mission was guest speaker, he gave a challenging Missionary address, and we feel, through his message, stimulated to greater things regarding our Foreign Mission. A vote of thanks to Rev. Blair was proposed by Mrs. D. Millar. The Treasurer's report was read by Miss M. Millar in the absence of our Treasurer, and the adoption of this report was proposed by Mrs. N. McConaghy. A synopsis of the W.M.U. Meeting held in Belfast during Synod week was given by one of the delegates appointed to the Union Meeting. All present were entertained to supper by the members of the Association.

The happy relationship was furthered by an outing of the Dervock W.M.A. on Saturday, 13th August. The company travelled by cars to Cushendall, where tea was partaken of, then to Cushendun and Ballycastle. All enjoyed the social fellowship and hopes were expressed that the outing would become an annual event.

Dervock—Friends from the congregations of the Northern Presbytery and neighbouring churches packed the church to capacity on Wednesday, 26th October. Rev. R. J. McIlmoyle who presided welcomed the visitors and introduced the speaker, Mr. Herbert J. Mateer of the European Missionary Fellowship. Mr. Mateer showed his film, " Journey through Ireland," which depicts various aspects of religious life in Ireland, and gave a commentary, after which he spoke of the need of the South of Ireland and of the need of a personal experience of Salvation. The offering which was in aid of the European Missionary Fellowship, amounted to over £40. The ladies and young people of the congregation served tea to the visitors. On behalf of all present Mr. George Hunter proposed a vote of thanks to Mr. Mateer, which was seconded by Mrs. Hugh Blair, Ballymoney, who also expressed the thanks of the visitors to the Dervock congregation.

THE MINISTER'S PROBLEM*

Mr Robert Dunlop, 88 Garryduff Road, Ballymoney, who often heard RJ tell the story of the donkey which died, was inspired (6.8.1979) to put it into verse form:

A very decent minister, who owned a farm of land,
Quite often was tormented, by a crowd which he had banned
The gypsies always camped nearby, to settle for the night
And put their horses in his field to graze till morning light.
He chained the gates, put padlocks on, for he had common sense,
And did not want his sheep to stray, through a bad or broken fence.
But all his efforts were in vain, the gypsies did prevail
And in some field, he'd find their stock, of horses, hoof and tail.
For weeks this practice lasted, annoying all agree,
But when patience got exhausted, he rang the RUC.
To the Sergeant told the story, who said 'twould not be long,
Till he would send a convoy out, to move the gypsies on.
True to the promise of that day, an officer made a call,
Gave orders for the group to move, their horses one and all,
Quite willingly they said they would and, long before 'twas dark
They moved a few miles up the road and their caravans did park.
The minister thought he'd take a stroll, to see his flock of sheep,
To find if they had pasture which the horses did not eat;
And in a quiet corner, beside a grassy mound,
There lay the gypsies' donkey, stiff dead upon the ground.
He felt sorry for the animal, its ribs were bare, poor thing;
It had seen a lot of summers, and many a hungry spring.
He thought of how the Saviour rode upon an ass one day,
So at least he would report its death and have it taken away.
So home he went directly, and picking up the phone,
Rang the local barracks, and, in an earnest tone,
Related to the sergeant, just how that he was led
To make the sad discovery, the poor wee donkey dead.
The sergeant was most helpful, but, after all, he said
Your Reverence, it's your duty that you should bury the dead.
Thank you, said the Minister, the job I will begin,
But I also felt it was my place, to inform the next-of-kin.

* This familiar story, as floated by James G Kenny in the Roamer's column in the *Belfast News Letter* of 2 December 1989, re-surfaced in no less a tome than Elizabeth D Svendsen's *Bumper Book of Donkeys* (Sidmouth, 1991). In the same snippet from the Ballygarvey stable there is the lament that "it was a real tragedy that the clergyman's repertoire was never recorded". Better late ...

---

(1) Keep a few sheep and keep them good.
(2) Benweeds in a field are the sign of a good farm, but a very bad farmer. Keep sheep and there will be no benweeds.
(3) If you want anything done, go to the busy man. The other fellow has no time.
(4) A sheep's worst enemy is another sheep.
(5) One man is as good as another, until he makes himself worse.
(6) The hill always seems steeper when you are late.
(7) Don't put all your eggs into one basket.

Do you know any other McIlmoylisms?

SOME OF THE THINGS I HEARD HIM SAY; THE OTHERS I HEARD ATTRIBUTED TO HIM...

A sheep's worst enemy is another sheep... Keep them [sheep] few and keep them good.

(1) When confronted about his smoking cigarettes, the Rev RJ replied, "You eat dulse (seaweed), which is as bad as my smoking cigarettes (a land weed)". (2) A police officer answered the door at the police station to find the Rev RJ McIlmoyle standing waiting to report the carcase of a donkey, which had been left behind by some gypsies who had recently been camping in the neighbourhood. The officer suggested to the Rev RJ that he understood it was part of his routine duty to bury the 'dead'; to which Rev RJ McIlmoyle replied, "Yes, but not until the next-of-kin have been informed". (3) It is said that in 1933 when the Pigs Marketing Board was being set up, at a time when the Rev RJ McIlmoyle was Lecturer for the Ulster Farmers' Union, there were several public meetings of farmers held to discuss the pros and cons of such a Board. At one such meeting, one of the audience addressed the Rev RJ and said, "Sure you are a sheep man; you know nothing about pigs. Do you even know how many ribs there are in a pig?" His Reverence replied, "I do not; but if you come up, I can soon count them". (4) He often told of the young man who went to work in Glasgow. On returning from his first day's work, he was asked by his landlady if he found his lunch OK. The young man replied, 'Yes', but went on to remark that she need not butter the bread on both sides; to which she replied that she had not buttered the bread on both sides. "Did you not?", asked the young man, "I didn't notice any difference". (5) Again he often told the story of the young man who also emigrated to Scotland, to his first job, and also found his lunch less than satisfying. He let this be known to his landlady, who kept supplying an additional sandwich nearly every day, but never seemed to be able to satisfy this young man's appetite. Eventually, one day, in frustration, she sliced a loaf of bread in two, put some butter and a few slices of ham in the centre and pressed the two halves together again. When the young man returned from work that evening, the landlady enquired how his lunch had satisfied him. He replied that it was quite good, but he had noticed that she was back to just one sandwich.

(6) The story which I like best of all was the one the Rev McIlmoyle often used when called upon to say Thanks for a meal. He told of the young man who started off in business, selling herrings from a box on the footpath. He then expanded to a bicycle, with parcel-carrier in front, and then to a hand-cart. He eventually succeeded to a pony and flat van. One spring day he was in the country with his pony (which had seen better days) and his flat van, selling herrings. The pony heard the cry of a bugle-horn, for there was a hunt nearby. The pony, reminded of those better days, increased its pace from a walk to a trot, then from a trot to a gallop, by which time the herrings were jumping or bouncing through the box, some of them on to the van and even some on to the road. A surfaceman tried to hail the fishman, to tell him that he was losing his herrings; to which he replied, "Och, what about a herring or two when you are riding with gentry". (I should have stated at the outset that the Rev RJ McIlmoyle resented the tag of storyteller. He preferred to be described as one who used illustrations. This was of course an accurate description in that all these stories were used to illustrate or emphasise a point.)

Dervock,
Ballymoney
Sept. 6/60.

Dear Mr. Orr,

Now that the excitement of the Show & Sale has died down I feel I ought to write you.

It was a great success. From the start of the judging till the close of the sale not a hitch.

This was due to your ability as an organiser.

Then a record attendance. This was due partly from the fact that Ballymena is nearer to the bulk of our customers than Belfast, but principally to your advertising.

Then the best sale ever — this to your outstanding ability as an auctioneer.

On behalf of the Association I thank you.

Your office staff were a model of all such a staff should be. Courteous and willing to oblige.

Your outdoor staff gave full satisfaction and went far out of their way to make the event a success.

Then Mrs. Orr. Please thank her for me for the efficient and dignified way in which she did her part.

The dinner capped it all. All present enjoyed themselves to the full.

The 1960 sale will not soon be forgotten.

Thank you for all you did to make my work as Sec. not only easy but pleasurable.

Yours sincerely,
R. J. McIlmoyle

Having been a minister for so many years, Mr McIlmoyle had many stories relevant to his work. (7) He often spoke of the minister who had married a couple when times were hard in the Thirties. The bridegroom was unable to offer the minister a fee, but explained that, very shortly, he would pay his debt by making the minister's young son a toy barrow. Unfortunately, things were not going too well between the recently-weds; so badly, in fact, that the bridegroom went to see the minister and promised to make him a cart if he would loose the knot he had tied and for which he had not so far been paid. (8) Two men who had been to school together, had gone their respective ways and had done well, met again, quite unexpectedly, one by now a bishop and the other a stationmaster. The bishop had grown into an enormous corpulent gentleman and, recognising his old school-friend, immediately approached the stationmaster and sought directions about a train to his destination. The stationmaster clearly and efficiently supplied the required information, but then taking another careful look at the bishop's profile, added the warning that he thought the bishop, in his apparent condition, ought not to travel. Here Mr McIlmoyle said, "One should always leave the table feeling one could eat more". He further said that "So many in these days dig their graves with their teeth". He claimed that we only need one-third of what we eat; the other two-thirds keeps the doctors busy.

I have many happy memories of times spent in the Rev R J's company and recollect so clearly his days as secretary to the Ulster Ram Breeders Association when I was a young auctioneer in Allam's, Belfast, and then here in Ballymena. My latest memories of the McIlmoyles are distressing in that in the last weeks of his Reverence's life, when I went to visit him at Dervock, I found him confined to bed and was admitted by Mrs McIlmoyle who was in a wheelchair. How sad!

Robert L Orr MBE

(We are grateful to Mr Orr for a gift towards the cost of publication)

Left: AC Gibson, Rathsherry; William Linsday, Glenuig, Kirriemuir; Rev RJ McIlmoyle MBE, Secretary URBA; Robert L Orr & AA Whyte, Spott, Kirriemuir

1960 During their few years in Belfast and before being transferred to Limavady Mr & Mrs Vincent H McIlmoyle were in membership of the Cregagh Road Reformed Presbyterian Church and Vincent was chairman of the Congregational Committee. His sisters Elvina and Kathleen were also in membership in the Cregagh Road congregation at that time. The compiler of this biography of their father, after supplying the Cregagh Road pulpit on at least one occasion, was hospitably entertained by Elvina and Kathleen in their home at 16 Commons Brae, Saintfield Road, Belfast.

FAMILY OF REV RJ McILMOYLE data supplied, November 1990, by Mr Vincent McIlmoyle. Five children:

(1) Lewis: born in Ballyclare; started with LMS railway in Belfast and became chief civil engineer there before going to Euston, London. He became assistant chief civil engineer (Mew works) & was made an MBE. He had many letters to his name: C Eng, FICE, MAREA (& others). 88 years of age.

(2) Enid: qualified as a nurse, and after a time in the Royal went as theatre sister to Tyrone County Hospital. Married Dr Mitchell. Now a widow aged 86. Her son Haldane is now a doctor in Omagh.

(3) Elvina: a graduate of Trinity College, Dublin, in 1928. Teacher for a time in England, who finished her days teaching in Mersey Street School, Belfast. Died 1973.

(4) Vincent: retired 1971 as manager of Belfast Bank, Limavady. Aged 82.

(5) Kathleen: supervisor of school meals. Aged 81.

The Rev RJ and Mrs McIlmoyle with (from left) Enid, Lewis, Kathleen, Vincent and Elvina

SOME SENIOR MINISTERIAL MEMORIES

Rev Robert B Cupples, Newry Road, Banbridge, Co Down, a retired Reformed Presbyterian minister, remembers well being invited to Dervock Manse, prior to his conducting a pre-communion service. There was ample time for him to inspect the pedigree flock of Border Leicesters. Then Mr Cupples was further invited to stay until the Lord's Day to assist in the Dervock Communion. He acceded to this request of the Rev RJ, although it meant making a journey back home for another sermon!

Rev David J Magee, 54 Sleepy Valley, Rathfriland, Co Down, recently-retired Reformed Presbyterian minister, has written: "Regarding the late Mr McIlmoyle, I'm sorry that I didn't know him even better than I did, since he was a unique person. He didn't approve of some of the changes which he saw taking place in farming methods in his day. He believed that there were great dangers ahead in the switch to highly intensive farming. On one occasion I heard him remark: 'No farmer should put all his eggs in one basket'. I wonder what he would have to say about the situation today? Intensive farming is causing serious environmental pollution. One farmer who told me about his visits to this area many years ago was impressed, not only by his lively wit, but also by the way he was able to turn the thoughts of his audience to a higher plain as he recited 'The Touch of the Master's Hand'. He was able to hold the attention of his audience in a remarkable way.

From *Farming Life*, Wednesday, 26 June 1991: "the **Rev W J Watson, Roseyards Manse, Kirk Road, Ballymoney,** was official judge for the hackney driving, and driving for Shetland ponies, Highland ponies and the private driving at last week's Royal Highland Show. The Rev Watson, who is a household name in the driving world throughout the British Isles, judged at Royal Windsor last year, the Royal Show at Stoneleigh in 1987 and the Royal International at Birmingham in 1988. A keen hackney competitor himself, the Rev Watson is also a talented artist and craftsman, with an impressive array of oil paintings of equines and horses which he carves from wood".

Mr Watson now recalls: "My earliest recollection of the late Rev RJ McIlmoyle was when my father pointed him out to my brothers and myself at an agricultural show, either during the World War II or shortly afterwards. Dressed in clerical garb, over which he wore a dust-coat, the Rev RJ was tending a pen of Border Leicester sheep. It was not until I came to Roseyards that I had the pleasure of meeting and getting to know that remarkable man. I remember him well at Ballymoney and other local shows, where his famous Border Leicester sheep were always among the prizewinners. He knew his sheep and how to produce them in the show ring. His fellow exhibitors had the greatest admiration and respect for him and enjoyed his friendship and conversation. As a neighbour and a colleague I shared services at the local British Legion War Memorial on Remembrance Day and at funerals. I will never forget the first time I heard him offer prayer at a graveside. It was just as if he was having a friendly chat with his Lord whom he knew so intimately and trusted so implicitly. A statement made by the late Very Rev Dr J Ernest Davey, Principal of Assembly's College, Belfast, in one of his lectures, so aptly epitomizes the Rev RJ McIlmoyle, "When a man is humble, he looks up to God".

Elizabeth R

Elizabeth the Second, by the Grace of God of the United Kingdom of Great Britain and Northern Ireland and of Her other Realms and Territories Queen, Head of the Commonwealth, Defender of the Faith and Sovereign of the Most Excellent Order of the British Empire to Our trusty and well beloved The Reverend Robert John M'Ilmoyle

Greeting

Whereas We have thought fit to nominate and appoint you to be an Ordinary Member of the Civil Division of Our said Most Excellent Order of the British Empire.

We do by these presents grant unto you the Dignity of an Ordinary Member of Our said Order and hereby authorise you to have hold and enjoy the said Dignity and Rank of an Ordinary Member of Our aforesaid Order together with all and singular the privileges thereunto belonging or appertaining.

Given at Our Court at Saint James's under Our Sign Manual and the Seal of Our said Order this Thirty first day of December 1960 in the Ninth year of Our Reign.

By the Sovereign's Command.

Philip

Grand Master.

Grant of the Dignity of an Ordinary Member of the Civil Division of the Order of the British Empire to The Reverend Robert John M'Ilmoyle.

Dervock co-op

Rev. Robert John McIlmoyle, of Dervock, Ballymoney, outside Buckingham Palace after he had been invested with the insignia of the M.B.E. by the Queen Mother.

With him are his two daughters, Kathleen and Elvina, and his son, Vincent.

The Covenanter

(Established 1830.)

"For Christ's Crown and Covenant"

JANUARY, 1961

A NEW YEAR MESSAGE

From Our Moderator.

The successful business man takes stock regularly and often. Why does he do so? It is not out of idle curiosity, and not that he may boast to his friend as to the success of his business undertakings. He looks upon this step as an absolute necessity, the life-blood of his business career. He knows that without this safeguard he may go floundering on in the dark, not knowing where to turn. In short, he takes stock in order to get necessary information about the progress of his business.

Some may hesitate about taking this step. They are afraid that all is not well with their undertakings. They are afraid of the shock which the auditor's report may bring them. So they delay the day of reckoning, and arrange a postponement in the hope that at the next turn in the road things may have sufficiently improved to allay anxiety. The wise man looks on and says—" You are wrong. Your inaction may leave you in ignorance of something you ought to know. Through want of knowledge you may lose ground that otherwise you could occupy to advantage."

This is as true in the spiritual world as in the material. As the believer stands on the threshold of another year it is right and proper that he should look himself in the face and say to himself—" How is it with me? Am I gaining or losing? Am I going forward or slipping back?" So spiritual stocktaking is an absolute necessity. But here again man delays, and shrinks from the task. He is afraid in this case too things are not as they should be with him. Then his Teacher replies—" The sooner they are put right, the better."

How little man knows about himself. The tragedy is that in many cases he doesn't want to know. A distinguished philosopher on one occasion wandered into the Royal Gardens in Berlin. He had not gone far until he was met by an officer of the guard, who put to him the question—" Who are you?" The philosopher replied—" I don't know. I shall be pleased if you can tell me!"

Man needs introspection so as to gain information about himself. The business man would not be satisfied to audit his own accounts. He employs a chartered accountant, a person competent to handle figures, and capable of pointing out the lesson the figures teach. So in spiritual things man is altogether incompetent of himself to make a true report. But God is standing by, and says—" Come along, I will show you."

The person who gets into trouble and has to employ a lawyer to defend him in court realises that his first step is to tell the lawyer everything. If he fails here, he will fail all along the line. God knows all about us, about everyone; and yet He wants to be told all, and that by ourselves.

If we have carried out this stocktaking as we should, there will, we hope, be good grounds for thanksgiving, and ground, maybe also, for weeping and tears. What thanks we should render unto God for all His mercies, mercies which seem to many just commonplace happenings, but which nevertheless are mercies from the hand of God. Ours is still a land of religious light and freedom. We have the privilege of worshipping God when and where we please. We can meet in the Sanctuary and there worship in the way we consider right without any Gestapo official being present to see and hear and report, with subsequent arrest and maybe death. While we have these privileges, we need to remember that there are thousands and tens of thousands of men, woman and children who are afraid of the rising of to-morrow's sun because of what that rising may bring them. What shall I render to the Lord for so great a privilege? And for so many others also?

What about the weeping and tears? Well may we weep when we think of the present unsettled state of the world in spite of all the influences for good. Social morality is perhaps at a lower ebb than ever before in the history of our nation. Juvenile delinquency, due to want of parental

control in the home, makes headlines in almost every paper we lift. Never have we had national backsliding on such a scale as we have to-day. The nations of the world are drifting on the great sea of time without captain or compass or chart.

Truly there is cause for tears. But we are not to be too despondent. Whenever a child of God sits down to mourn over the desolations of the earth, God says to him—" What doest thou here?" The earth is the Lord's and the fulness thereof. He is King among the nations. The heathen may rage, but He that sits in heaven shall laugh. The cup of the enemies' iniquity may not yet be full. God may let Satan have power still to carry on his nefarious work.

Even then there is no need for pessimism. Even then there shall be a remnant whom the Lord shall call. The important thing for us is to be among the faithful few. Some of the most notable military victories recorded in history were won, not by a big army dashing over the countryside, leaving death and destruction in its trail, but by the few brave men and true who held the pass until reinforcements arrived.

Quit yourselves like men. Have implicit confidence in your Guide, and wait God's time. One of the Old Testament saints wanted very much to see the promised Messiah. He prayed earnestly about it. But God said—" No, my child. He will come. Men shall see Him, but it would be too long for you to wait up."

R.J.McI.

Amongst those who received the M.B.E. is Rev. R. J. McIlmoyle, of Dervock, Moderator of the Synod of the Reformed Presbyterian Church of Ireland, and one of the Province's best known figures in agriculture. His name is always associated with the breeding of Border-Leicester sheep for which he has won over 1,500 rosettes and many cups.

The senior minister of Brigh & Albany, the **Rev Robert Fisher, "Ardeevin", 22 Seafield Park, Portstewart**, tells us that "RJ was in full flight when I was going to school in Kells and Connor and one of the stories I heard him tell was of the minister who preached very loud and shouted and then at times lowered his voice almost to a whisper. At a service he noticed a women in church weeping and the minister felt that he was at last getting through with his message. After the service he mentioned to her about her weeping in repentance and distress of soul. 'It was nothing like that', she said, 'but your roaring reminded me of a young bullock we had years ago and it became unwell and was in severe pain and it roared all the time until it died'."

TWO NEPHEWS' MEMORIES

It is nice to know that a book is being written about my uncle, and I feel all of us in the family are indebted to you for undertaking such. My uncle was very widely known and travelled extensively to all parts of Northern Ireland. I recall him speaking at my installation reception in Druminnis in 1955, and, though coming on rather late in the programme, he held the audience spellbound. He was a special attraction at many a Farmers' Union Social or concert. I have no doubt that you will receive much material. I don't think that I can add a great deal, but I do appreciate your asking. Speaking to my sister the other evening on the phone, I learned that she has sent on some cuttings and photographs. Here's wishing you all success with your venture, and I do look forward with interest to the publication of the book.

Jack Lyons, Richhill

COSTA DEL DERVOCK

Mr Lex McIlmoyle, 6 Strandview Gardens, Ballycastle, recalls these anecdotes in the life of his late uncle RJ: (1) When he retired from the active duties of the congregation of Dervock, where he had spent practically all his ministry, he decided to continue to reside in the village. Someone remarked to him that they thought he might have moved to the seaside, where so many retired folk have gone, but he is reported to have replied, "When you've lived in the city most of your life, it's hard to leave it". (2) He seemed to be unwilling to disclose his exact age and in his later years, when someone asked him, he stated "Well, they say I'm 90". Mr McIlmoyle also remarks, "It is good of you to undertake this book. I was very glad to hear a recording of his voice in the Radio Ulster programme before the service from Dervock some months ago."

SOBER SENTIMENTS

Mr Wm C Anderson, Grange Avenue, Ballymena, remembers the Rev RJ saying "Life is an incline; we either go up or down", and Willie also recalls RJ's words in prayer "We thank thee, O God, that while others have been called away, we are still left as the spared monuments of Thy mercy."

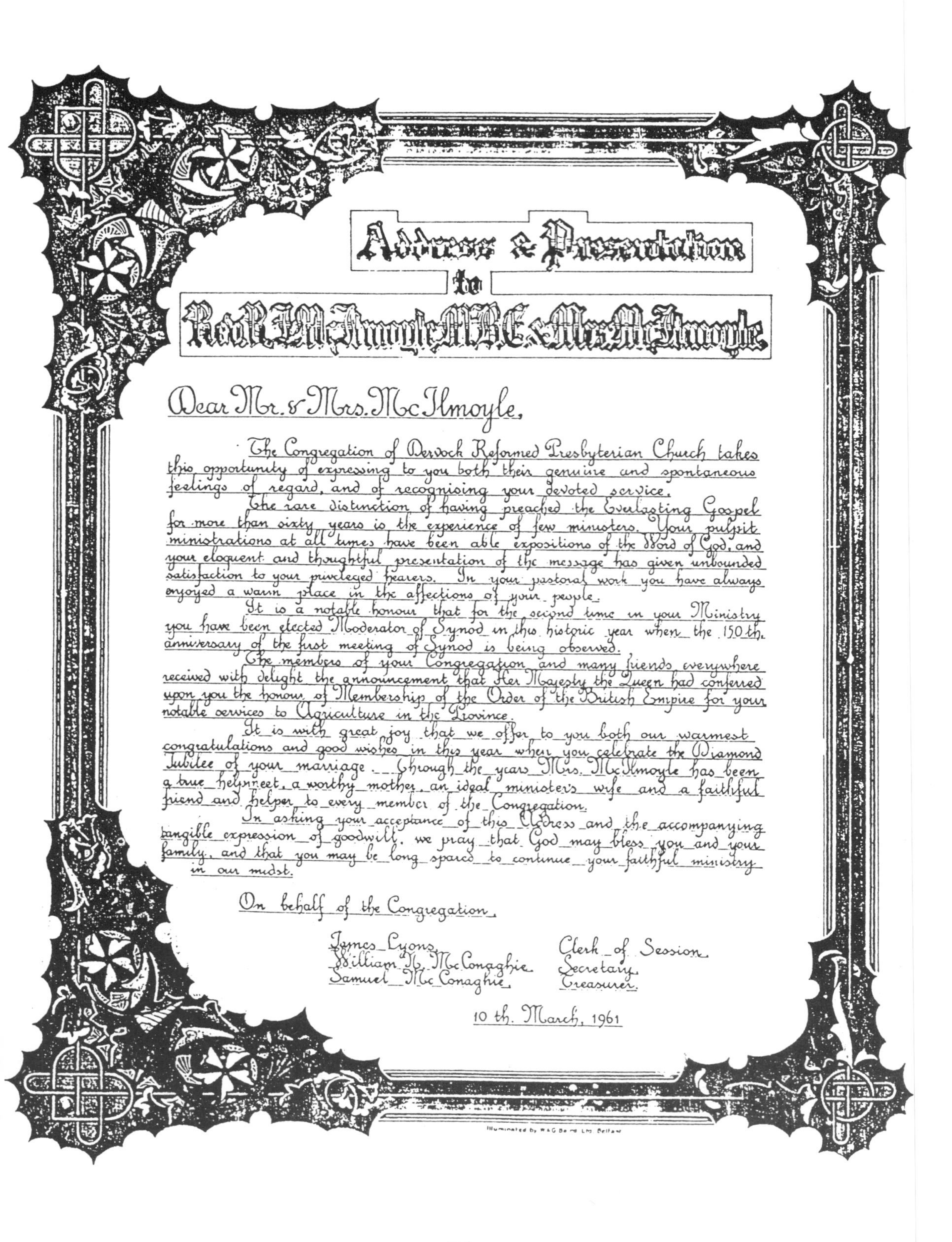

Address & Presentation to Rev. R. J. McIlmoyle M.B.E. & Mrs McIlmoyle

Dear Mr. & Mrs. McIlmoyle,

The Congregation of Dervock Reformed Presbyterian Church takes this opportunity of expressing to you both their genuine and spontaneous feelings of regard, and of recognising your devoted service.

The rare distinction of having preached the Everlasting Gospel for more than sixty years is the experience of few ministers. Your pulpit ministrations at all times have been able expositions of the Word of God, and your eloquent and thoughtful presentation of the message has given unbounded satisfaction to your privileged hearers. In your pastoral work you have always enjoyed a warm place in the affections of your people.

It is a notable honour that for the second time in your Ministry you have been elected Moderator of Synod in this historic year when the 150th. anniversary of the first meeting of Synod is being observed.

The members of your Congregation and many friends everywhere received with delight the announcement that Her Majesty the Queen had conferred upon you the honour of Membership of the Order of the British Empire for your notable services to Agriculture in the Province.

It is with great joy that we offer to you both our warmest congratulations and good wishes in this year when you celebrate the Diamond Jubilee of your marriage. Through the years Mrs. McIlmoyle has been a true helpmeet, a worthy mother, an ideal minister's wife and a faithful friend and helper to every member of the Congregation.

In asking your acceptance of this Address and the accompanying tangible expression of goodwill, we pray that God may bless you and your family, and that you may be long spared to continue your faithful ministry in our midst.

On behalf of the Congregation,

James Lyons, Clerk of Session
William H. McConaghie, Secretary
Samuel McConaghie, Treasurer

10 th. March, 1961

Illuminated by R & G Baird Ltd. Belfast

10 March 1961

DERVOCK R.P. CHURCH

Minister and wife receive gifts

The congregation of Dervock Reformed Presbyterian Church held their annual social evening on Friday. Before tea, served by the ladies, the minister, the Rev. R. J. M'Ilmoyle, pronounced the blessing. Afterwards, Mr. R. W. M'Fall asked Professor A. Loughridge to take the chair.

Mr Loughridge welcomed members and friends present, and said the main item of the evening was to honour and congratulate their minister (Mr. M'Ilmoyle) on receiving the M.B.E. from the Queen.

Mr. and Mrs. M'Ilmoyle were then made the recipients of an illuminated address, a well-filled wallet of notes, a diamond brooch and an electric blanket. Both Mr. and Mrs. M'Ilmoyle expressed their appreciation of the gifts.

The Sabbath School prizes for answering and attendance were handed over to the children. A varied programme was contributed by the following: Misses L. Halliday, S. Stirling, L. Watton, R. Scott, E. Cochrane and H. M'Conaghie; Rev. J. H. Beggs and Messrs. J. Scott and W. M'Corriston.

Congratulations and good wishes were expressed by the Rev. J. Blair, Rev. J. H. Beggs, Rev. J. G. Leitch, Rev. A. M'A. Owens and Rev. H. J. Blair, and by Mr. A. G. Algeo, C.B.E.

REV. R. J. M'ILMOYLE DERVOCK

Honoured by Northern Presbytery of R.P. Churches

The Northern Presbytery of the Reformed Presbyterian Church met in Ballymoney and passed a vote of sympathy with the Rev. J. R. Wright, B.A., in the death of his wife.

The Moderator of Presbytery, the Rev. Isaac Cole, B.A., Drimbolg, referred to the fact that the Rev. R. J. M'Ilmoyle, Dervock, had received the award of the M.B.E. in the New Year's Honours List.

A minute of congratulations was moved by the Rev. James Blair, Kilraughts, seconded by the Rev. T. Donnelly, Ballyclabber, and cordially passed.

At the close of the meeting members of the Presbytery entertained Mr. M'Ilmoyle to luncheon in Moore's Cafe, in recognition not only of the honour conferred on him by the Queen, but also to mark his completion of 60 years in the ministry. Rev Professor A. Loughridge, clerk of Presbytery, presided.

Congratulations and good wishes were expressed on behalf of the members by the Rev. S. M. Calderwood, Kellswater, and Mr. T. A. Warnock, Coleraine.

Mr. M'Ilmoyle acknowledged the compliment in his own inimitable way.

Ballyclare—A special service was held on Sabbath evening, 4th June. The preacher was Rev. R. J. McIlmoyle, M.B.E., a former minister, who was ordained in Ballyclare in 1900. Extra seating had to be provided for the large congregation. The offering was in aid of the Repair Fund. Thanks are tendered to the collectors and to the members of other denominations in Ballyclare and district who co-operated in the service.

Rev McIlmoyle still continued to have extra duties during his year as Moderator of Synod

Broadcast Service—The B.B.C. has arranged to broadcast the evening service on the Northern Ireland Home Service, on June 18, at 7.45, from Ballymoney R. P. Church. The service will be conducted by Rev. R. J. McIlmoyle, M.B.E., and Rev. Hugh J. Blair. The prayers of the whole Church are requested for this broadcast service.

TENTACULAR TALE

Mr Alex Chestnutt, sitting in the office of his mill in Stranocum, related two of the Rev RJ McIlmoyle's favourite yarns. These were used particularly when he was addressing an audience of young folk. (1) A young fellow went to see a young girl and sat looking at her for quite a while, but he was shy and backward. Eventually he said to her, "I wish I was an octopus". "What on earth is that sort of animal? And what would you do?", she asked, "if you were an animal like that?" "Oh", said he, "I would put all eight arms around you." "Well", said she, "if you would make use of what you have got!" (2) Alex Chestnutt also recalls how Rev RJ often referred to the warm welcome he received at the meetings and socials in Moycraig. RJ once told of the young minister who was beginning to visit the homes. He made his way, for the first time, to an old house with the path to the front door overgrown with weeds; and the hall door was seldom opened and was swollen with damp. There were small windows at the side of the door, which gave the occupants a good view of any stranger who sought admission and who didn't know to use the back door. A hatchet was kept in the hall to give leverage. The young minister made his way to the door and knocked several times. From inside he heard an old man shouting excitedly, "Run for the hatchet, for it's our new minister!"

LOST LEICESTER

Mr Gordon Chestnutt, Dervock, whose garage appears in the photograph on our front cover, can remember the Rev RJ coming very early one May morning to his house to ask him to drive him to Belfast, as one of his Border Leicesters had been left behind at Balmoral Show. Gordon, who was still in his pyjamas, asked, "When do you want me to go?" "Now", came RJ's reply and, as Gordon readily agreed, RJ made his usual appreciative comment, "That's very good ... very good ...". Gordon Chestnutt recalls taking the Rev RJ to many different meetings and socials, particularly in Co Down, from 1953 to 1961, and his father often drove him before that.

ORCADIAN OBSERVATIONS

Although absent from his native North Antrim for many years, the **Rev Joe Creelman**, the Ballymagarry man who is now minister of Westray United Free Church, Orkney, can vividly recall that the Rev RJ McIlmoyle said that he looked after sheep six days a week and goats on the Sabbath. Here are two stories of the Rev RJ remembered by Joe. (1) The minister was visiting a man and his wife at whose wedding he had officiated many years earlier. As the minister approached the door, he heard the wife's voice calling her husband "Come oot, come oot". As the minister stood at the open door looking in, he saw the man of the house hiding under the table and his reply was "Ah'll no' come oot - Ah'm boss in my ain hoose". (2) The second story illustrates that benweeds are the sign of good land. A son and his blind father went by horse and cart to buy a farm. When they arrived at their destination, there were few trees nearby and the son asked his father "Where will I tie the horse?" The father answered "To a big benweed". "Oh, Father", the son declared, "there are no benweeds at all here." "Then", said the father, "Put the horse again back into the shafts of the cart, for I'm for home."

FLOCK 435

Rev. Robert J. M'Ilmoyle, M.B.E., Dervock, Ballymoney, Co. Antrim

Tel. No. Dervock 212.

RAMS.

Rams used in 1960.	Sire.	Dam.		
(18447), Skerrington Delight	(17110), Balig Perfect Colours	(B L 255),	E	4
(19071), Fruithill Fifty Fifty	(18799), Norman Sir Michael	(B L 85G),	F	4
(19119), Kininmonth Aristocrat	(18839), Skerrington Jackpot	(B L 8K),	F	13
(19301), Albanagh Satisfaction, K 1	(19071), Fruithill Fifty Fifty	(B L 34P).	I	1
J 2	(18447), Skerrington Delight		G	2
J 4	Do.	(B L 557),	D	6
(B L 59J). J 32	(18845), Skerrington Policy	(B L 6G),	H	7

1961

WINNERS OF AWARDS OFFERED BY THE SOCIETY IN 1960

ROYAL HIGHLAND AND AGRICULTURAL SOCIETY OF SCOTLAND, EDINBURGH, 21st-24th June, 1960.

£10 for Best Male; Awarded to Robert M. Forsyth, Chapelheron, Whithorn, Wigtownshire, with Shearling Ram (19149) Lindiferon Ambassador.

£10 for Best Female; Awarded to Hugh L. Stewart of Struthers, Ltd., Cupar, Fife, with Gimmer 471-J3, by (17799) Balig Smasher.

Best Groups of 4 with not more than one from any class: Awarded to—
£5 Hugh L. Stewart of Struthers, Ltd., Cupar, Fife.
£3 Alan H. B. Grant, Thorn, Alyth, Perthshire.
£2 James W. Findlay, Bogardo, Forfar, Angus.

ROYAL AGRICULTURAL SOCIETY OF ENGLAND, CAMBRIDGE, 5th-8th July, 1960.

60 Guinea Challenge Cup and £10 for Breed Champion: Awarded to Hugh L. Stewart of Struthers, Ltd., Cupar, Fife with Ewe 471-H2, by (17799) Balig Smasher.

ROYAL ULSTER AGRICULTURAL SOCIETY, BELFAST, 25th-28th May, 1960.

£5 for Breed Champion: Awarded to Rev. R. J. M'Ilmoyle, M.B.E., Dervock, Co. Antrim, with Ewe 94B-H2, by (17965) Kinross Special.

ROYAL DUBLIN SOCIETY, DUBLIN, 3rd-7th May, 1960.

£5 for Breed Champion: Awarded to James Mulligan & Sons, Brague, Corbet, Banbridge, Co. Down, with Ram (18819) Priestland Brigadoon.

(19433) CULTS BONDHOLDER. B L 46P. Lambed 1960
Breeder—James McLaren, Cults.
Owner—William Brown, Millmoor.
Sire—(17635), Milton Good News ; *breeder*—James Butters.
Dam—B L 17H, I 3.
S.D.—(17734), Struthers Bond ; *breeders*—Trs. late John Stewart
S.G.D.—(17280), Muirside Overdraft ; *breeders*—A. B. Howie & Son
S.G.G.D.—(16520), Honey Bee ; *breeder*—John Duncan.

(19434) DALHOUSIE SIX-FORTY A.M. B L 14K. Lambed 1960
Breeder—Robert Barr, Upper Dalhousie.
Owner—Francis Watson, Meikle Ernambrie.
Sire—(18526), Angus Superlative ; *breeders*—J. & C. D. Findlay
Dam—B L 67B, I 1.
S.D.—(18451), Skerrington Perfect Blend ; *breeder*—William Young.
S.G.D.—(16482), Fortytude ; *breeders*—J. & C. D. Findlay.
S.G.G.D.—(14456), Lee's Verdict ; *breeder*—John W. Lee.

(19435) DERVOCK JOY. B L 89B. Lambed 1959
Breeder—Rev. R. J. M'Ilmoyle, Dervock.
Owner—James A. Gamble, Bridgehill.
Sire—(18447), Skerrington Delight ; *breeder*—William Young.
Dam—B L 557, D 6.
S.D.—(16615), Prince John ; *breeder*—John J. Minnis.
S.G.D.—(15921), Prince Alexander ; *breeder*—Walter Alexander.
S.G.G.D.—(13947), Blackburn ; *breeder*—Thomas Black.

(19436) DITTON GAY GORDON. B L 2H. Lambed 1960
Breeder—Matthew Steel, Ditton Farm.
Owner—John L. Coltherd, Hoebridge.
Sire—(18959), Bogardo Gay Gordon ; *breeders*—J. W. & A. B Findlay.
Dam—B L 23C, I 6.
S.D.—(18502), Whinbush Expectation ; *breeders*—Thomas S Frame & Son.
S.G.D.—(16251), Park Admiral ; *breeders*—William Gray & Sons.
S.G.G.D.—(14158), Quality Street ; *breeders*—R. & D. Wardrop.

(19437) DRENNAN'S SHOW WINNER. B L 72P. Lambed 1960.
Breeder—John Drennan, Hillhouse Farm.
Owners—William Paterson & Son, Denbie Mains.
Sire—(18933), Balig Ambition ; *breeders*—John McIlwraith & Son.
Dam—B L 96M, F 3.
S.D.—(17375), Skerrington Welcome ; *breeder*—William Young.
S.G.D.—(16486), Future Outlook ; *breeder*—David Russell.
S.G.G.D.—(14875), Prince Consort ; *breeder*—William Young.

NEWRY AGRICULTURAL SOCIETY—James H. Aiken, Carnew, Dromara, Co. Down, with Ewe 466-G 11, by (17745) Tullyvallin Champion.

NEWTOWN ST. BOSWELLS & DISTRICT FARMERS' CLUB—William Mitchell, Bank House, St. Boswells, Roxburghshire, with Shearling Ram (19068) Fordafourie Victor.

NITHSDALE AGRICULTURAL SOCIETY—James Howie & Son, Muirside, Dumfries, with Ewe Lamb 282-K 14, by (19093) Hillend Substantial.

NORTH ANTRIM AGRICULTURAL ASSOCIATION—Rev. R. J. M'Ilmoyle, M.B.E., Dervock, Co. Antrim, with Ewe 94B-H 2, by (17965) Kinross Special.

NORTH WEST OF IRELAND AGRICULTURAL SOCIETY—Rev. R. J. M'Ilmoyle, M.B.E., Dervock, Co. Antrim, with Ewe Lamb 435-K 2, by (18723) Kinpurney Cashier.

NORTHERN COUNTIES AGRICULTURAL SOCIETY—W. R. Cumming, Allanfearn, Inverness, with Ewe 40-H 40, by (17791) Balbinny Sunrise.

NORTHUMBERLAND AGRICULTURAL SOCIETY—Rock Farms Ltd., Rock, Alnwick, Northumberland, with Ewe 21-H 7, by (17856) Charter Monarch.

ORKNEY AGRICULTURAL SOCIETY—James W. Taylor, Northfield, Burray, Kirkwall, Orkney, with Ewe 83N-I 1, by (18369) Lindifferon Pride.

ORKNEY WEST MAINLAND AGRICULTURAL SOCIETY—William G. Kirkpatrick, Newhall, Stromness, Orkney, with Ewe Lamb 57H-K 1, by (19274) Thorn Perfect Flash.

OSWESTRY & DISTRICT AGRICULTURAL SOCIETY—H. L. Wrench, Southfields, Penyffordd, Chester, with Gimmer 788-J 17, by (18538) Avon Bright Times.

PERTHSHIRE AGRICULTURAL SOCIETY—Alan H. B. Grant, Thorn, Alyth, Perthshire, with Gimmer 36E-J 52, by (18469) Struthers Standby.

ROYAL MANX AGRICULTURAL SOCIETY—The Isle of Man Board of Agriculture, Knockaloe Experimental Farm, Peel, Isle of Man, with Ewe 89J-I 17, by (18095) Sypland Swell.

SAINTFIELD Y. F. CLUB & DISTRICT AGRICULTURAL SOCIETY—T. & J. Horner, Ballyaltikilligan, Comber, Co. Down, with Ewe Lamb 557-K 2, by (19200) Noble Classic.

RJ's stories recalled by Mr Wilson Ross, Union Street, Ballymoney

(1) This man was hired by a farmer at the hiring fair. The first day he was there dinner consisted of potatoes and turnips; second day the same; third day turnips and potatoes. When the end of the week came, the man said to the farmer that he wasn't for staying. "Why?", said the farmer. "Well", said the man, "I have been here all week and haven't seen a piece of meat since I came." "Well", said the farmer, "you stay and I'll see that you get meat." So he said to his wife, Mary Ann, "When you do the shopping tonight, get a good roast of meat, cook it, slice it, put it on a plate and at dinner time this man can take as much as he wants; for, unless he gets meat, he won't stay". So Mary Ann did as she was told. At dinner it was potatoes as usual and turnips plus the meat. The servant man was told to take as much as he wanted and when he had almost finished the farmer says, "John, if you eat much more of that meat, that cow will be roaring inside you". "Well, if she does", says the servant, "it will not be for the want of turnips."

(2) This young man took his girl friend out for a drive in his car. On the way back the car began to boil and he called at a little house further down the road to get some water. He returned with a bucket of water, filled the radiator and threw the remainder of the water over a hedge on the other side of the road. Suddenly, up jumps a man whose language was not too choice. The motorist said to him, "Hush, keep quiet, I have a bird in the car". The man replied, "What do you think I have here, a flaming water hen?"

(3) This couple had been married a short time. Things were not going well, or not as well as married life should, and one day John saw the minister who married them. He says to the minister, "Thon's a terrible woman you married me to". "Oh", says his Reverence, "it can't be as bad as all that. Go home, be nice to her and things will be all right." A week later John saw the minister again and, when he asked how they were getting on, John just told him that they were going from bad to worse. "And I want you to come with me and see if you can talk to her." So, after some persuasion, the minister said, "I'll go with you now", and when they came near the house John says to the minister, "Now you wait here till I go in and get her started".

(4) A young man came to visit his girl friend. They were seated comfortably in front of a nice fire. After a short time the girl went down to the kitchen and shortly afterwards her young brother came up to the parlour. The young man started talking to the little boy and said, "I will give you sixpence if you turn down the parlour lamp when your sister comes back". "Ah! away you and your sixpence. She has given me a shilling to put it out altogether."

(5) There were three daughters in this family. They each married well. The first felt she had married best, because she married a bank manager and he made her rich for nothing. The second felt she had married best because she married a doctor and he made her well for nothing. The third said she had married best, because she married a minister and he had made her good for nothing.

(6) This man was bringing home a load of turf with a donkey and cart. At the foot of a steep hill the donkey was struggling with the heavy load. The minister on his bicycle overtook them and, seeing that the donkey was in difficulty, he left down his bicycle, put his shoulder to the cart and pushed it to the top of the hill. When they got to the top, the man thanked the minister very much

and said, "You know I believe the one donkey never could have done it".

(7) This minister was a bit long winded and during the sermon one of the members began to snore. The minister, still speaking, could listen to this no longer and asked the gentleman sitting beside him to waken him and he replied, "Just waken him yoursel. It was you that put him to sleep."

EARLY ENCOURAGEMENT I read today (5 February 1991) with delight in the *Belfast News Letter* of your intention to compile a book about the late Rev RJ McIlmoyle. I remember him with great affection and respect. My lifelong pastime has been music and entertainment, and, until very recently, I regularly enjoyed playing at functions for churches, charities, etc. From the early 1950s to the early 1960s I was based in Co Londonderry, in Maghera, Coleraine and Garvagh, and during that period I often appeared on the same programme as the Rev RJ McIlmoyle, usually at Young Farmers' Clubs, Farmers' Union and church functions. In those days the Rev RJ was the king of country entertainers. However, he had the wonderful knack of making the inexperienced and extremely nervous amateurs, such as myself, feel quite professional and completely relaxed before going on stage. At that time I was fond of relating old monologues, which were invariably of a solemn and quite sad nature, and, on an occasion when I asked the advice of the Rev RJ about performing these, he passed the following comment which has remained in my mind all those years: "Our sweetest songs are those that tell of saddest thoughts". I recall the Rev RJ reciting on several occasions the lovely old monologue, "The Old Violin", but never at the same venue twice. He was meticulous in his recording of venues, to ensure that he never repeated his repertoire before the same audience. He also, on one occasion, portrayed a beautiful verbal picture of life, likening it to the journey of a steam train: starting off slowly and, with some puffing and slipping in early life, speeding up and steaming swiftly and steadily through the middle years, until, nearing the end, it first began to get slower, and slower, until, with a few final deep breaths, it ground to a weary halt, having travelled through the journey of life to the Final Destination. I look forward to seeing your forthcoming publication on the shelves of our bookstores and would take this opportunity of wishing you well in your search for material about a wonderful character and a great man. **Drew Coid**

TARDREE TALES I have happy memories of the Rev McIlmoyle when, as a speaker for the Ulster Farmers' Union, he was greatly in demand at socials of the different branches throughout the country. One such branch was formed in Tardree School in County Antrim, where I enjoyed his wit and humorous stories. Sadly, very few of the members of that first branch are now living, but I think the first secretary of that branch was Mr John Bell of Springmount, Tardree. Although of advanced years, like myself, he may be able to recall some of Mr McIlmoyle's jokes. I remember one he told. When there was a recession on the railway, there was only one man on the train. When he alighted at his home-town station, he shouted to the driver, "Ye neednae bring her oot the morra, for ah'm no goin'". Another one I recall was about the Sunday School teacher explaining to his pupils about the Devil. He told them he was chained, but the chain was so long he could reach any length. One young lad pointed out, "Sure, he micht as weel be lowse". As I am in my eighty-third year, and Mr Bell may be five years older, memories are not so sharp. However I wish you all success in the publication of the book and, if God spares me, I may have a chance to read it. With sincere wishes. **James Brown, Forthill, Kells**

SAM'S 'SPEEDY' RECOGNITION OF PRIZE EWE

Rev. R. J. McIlmoyle, of Dervock, Co. Antrim, with his Border-Leicester ewe, prize-winner in the sheep section of Limavady Agricultural Show last year.

This photograph, from the *Londonderry Sentinel* of 14 June 1961, was inserted in the *Coleraine Chronicle* by Mr W 'Speedy' Moore in February 1991 when he appealed to readers for help with material. Mr Samuel Black, 'Albanagh', Portstewart, was the one who responded immediately with ready information. "That ewe was bred by John Howie, Hillhouse, Kilmarnock, off a ram called Kinross Special. That ewe won the championship at Balmoral and there was a lot of talk that it shouldn't have won, but the next year it won again and Mr McIlmoyle said 'That will keep them quiet'." Sam Black further adds that Mr McIlmoyle always liked to win and never liked to be beaten. When Sam first won at Ballymoney Show with a ewe lamb, the Rev RJ became interested in this new winner and from that time a great friendship began, with many hours spent together in journeys and in visiting each other or other breeders and exhibitors throughout the country. Together they travelled to Scotland to the Lanark Sheep Sale and that meant taking the Belfast to Glasgow boat and travelling overnight. Although Rev McIlmoyle had a berth, he would confess "I hardly slept a wink". The remainder of the journey was done by train.

From Northern Ireland, on the same errand to Lanark, there would have been other sheep breeders and exhibitors, but none was as well known and respected as the man from Dervock. He was on the most friendly terms with the Youngs, Skerrington Mains, Hurlford, Ayrshire, and attended at least one wedding within that family. One of the family was William Young who came over one year to Dervock and helped the Rev RJ to dress and prepare the Border Leicesters for Balmoral Show. Alas, one of the sheep broke away

Behind the sheep's ear, Jimmy Moody, RJ's shepherd, who lived in Dervock, is wearing the cap and zipped jumper.

and fell into the midden. Both men then had to devote all their time in getting it washed again and dried in front of the fire in the room. All the extra work was not in vain, for the next day at Balmoral it was the winner. Sam Black tells the story that at a local show someone asked the Rev McIlmoyle why he had to spend so much time preparing the sheep. "Why don't you show the sheep in their natural condition?" The quick reply was "You would be a nice fellow in your natural condition, with a beard down to your belly".

The morning that I was interviewing Sam Black, my wife and I were hospitably entertained by his wife, Mrs Toye Black, who is the Mayor of Coleraine. She could recall the Rev RJ many years ago at the Ballylaggan RP Church Socials. Sam Black was impressed by several commendable features in the Rev RJ. One was his punctuality, for, although he was always so busy, he was never late. He preferred being some minutes early and waiting until the set time with Sam in the car, before going to the door of the house which they were visiting. In later years RJ appreciated the help of Sam in driving the car. Robert Smith often accompanied them and he would drop the hint, "Sam will drive us". That was felt to be safer, as RJ's driving had become erratic! Sam Black also recalls RJ's generosity, not only to the shepherd, Jimmy Moody, but to anyone who helped him with the sheep. When his sheep were over at Sam Black's, the same generosity was shown to anyone there. RJ was kind to anyone who was kind to his sheep. As Sam Black says, "Mr McIlmoyle fed his sheep well and was always caring for them, for he couldn't understand how anyone could neglect sheep". He practised well his own precept, "Keep a few sheep and keep them good".

MAYORAL MEMORIES The former Mayor of Ballymoney, **Mrs Mollie J Holmes OBE, JP, 'Lismoyne', Charlotte Street, Ballymoney,** appreciated the visits from time to time of the Rev RJ & Mrs McIlmoyle. Her late husband Harold looked forward greatly to those occasions for a good chat and Christian fellowship. Mrs McIlmoyle, in times of increasing infirmity, sometimes stayed with the Holmes family, when her husband had to go in the evenings to keep an engagement at some function across the Province. Mrs Holmes recalls that the Rev RJ usually referred to his wife as "Mammy". Does this not remind us of the prevalent usage of this title by the husband and father in the presence of the children and when the mother's Christian name would not have been used?

MID-ULSTER MEMORIES

Mr Verdun Wright, 66 Molesworth Road, Cookstown, has been very helpful in supplying material for this biography. He tells of the Rev RJ being invited one Lord's Day afternoon to conduct a special service in Coagh Presbyterian Church, County Tyrone, when there was a full attendance to hear him preach. It seems that the church had clear glass windows and in the fields around, that spring day, there were many sheep to be seen. From the beginning of the service the Rev RJ kept looking out at the sheep and then began to focus more particularly on one particular window. This was having an adverse effect on the large congregation, being very distracting and not easily understood. Suddenly he gave his congregation undivided attention as he declared "I had my eyes on a ewe out there and she has lambed all right; so now we'll get on with the preaching!" Mr Verdun Wright speaks of the delight he experienced in the Rev McIlmoyle's company: "it was like a breath of fresh air on a spring morning". When the Rev RJ was at farmers' meetings in and around Cookstown during the Second World War, the windows of a shed at Tullylaggan had to be blacked out. Rev RJ was always given a standing ovation and after his night's entertainment he enjoyed a cup of tea and a cigarette. Mr Wright also recalls that Mr George Shannon, principal of Loughry Agricultural College, was invited to speak at the same farmers' meeting as the Rev RJ, somewhere in the County Down. The former was to speak on poultry and the latter on sheep. Mr Shannon insisted that he be asked to speak first, for if he was on the programme after the Rev RJ no-one would listen to him! In February 1942 the *Mid-Ulster Mail* reported on the visit of the Rev RJ McIlmoyle to Moneymore, when he outlined the activities of the Ulster Farmers' Union and its democratic constitution. He used anecdotes to illustrate his address and concluded by stating that the UFU was as necessary as the soil in which they worked. Mr Wright also remembers that Cookstown Court House was packed to capacity, when the YFC was formed in 1944. The welcome given to Rev McIlmoyle had to be seen to be believed. A quotation often used by the Rev RJ was: 'there is your work and my work and work for all to do, but, if you shirk your work, someone else must do not only his own work, but your work too'.

Mr John Dunlop, Moneymore, former Member of Parliament for Mid Ulster, recalls that he knew Rev McIlmoyle during and after the War. The Epworth Hall in Moneymore was the venue for meetings of the UFU and YFC and the Rev McIlmoyle was always the special speaker with "his inexhaustible supply of stories and anecdotes".

Mrs RR McCorry Upper Malone, Belfast, writes: "My father (James Woods of Glentimon, Sion Mills, Co Tyrone) was also a great exhibitor, not only of sheep, but of anything from Clydesdales to Bantams! A friendly rivalry existed between the Rev McIlmoyle and my late father, in exhibiting outstanding Border Leicesters. I wasn't very old at the time, but I could read my Dad's expression, if he had been 'on top' at a particular show. The dipping, clipping and preparation of these animals before the show was time-consuming work. It is well that hired hands, for the rest of the work on a large mixed farm, were easily obtained and paid in those far-off days. They were as interested in success as "the master" himself. In the summer months the exhibitors attended all the more important shows and to busy farmers these days "off" made up their summer holidays. I remember looking with awe at the great man (Rev McIlmoyle) after he had won many crimson rosettes. Then the rosette would have meant more to me than if he had presented me with one of his valuable animals!

This was one of the rare occasions when Mr. McIlmoyle was seen at a show—without sheep! He was judging the goat section at the North-West Show this year. 1961

GREAT CHARACTER I am simply delighted to learn that something is being done to perpetuate the memory of the Rev RJ McIlmoyle, who was one of the great characters of Ulster agriculture, and was simply unique. He always claimed to be the father of the social movement of the Ulster Farmers' Union. Of course, he had a retainer from this body because of his great gift of story-telling and because, in many cases, he was the main attraction in any meeting to be addressed by the President or some senior members of the Union. His presence greatly enhanced the attendance at such meetings. It was always amusing to British Ministers of Agriculture, when they visited us, to discover that Ulster agriculture made such use of Presbyterian clergymen. In the Minister of Agriculture's office at Dundonald House, amongst the many photographs of former NI Ministers of Agriculture, was one of the Rev Robert Moore. When the visitors were told that, in addition, the Farmers' Union had on its staff the Rev RJ McIlmoyle, it caused great hilarity. During my year as President of the Ulster Farmers' Union the whole Province was peppered with branches, 106 in all, whereas now these branches are condensed into groups. My predecessor in the UFU was Sir Arthur Algeo of Ballymoney and in his year he visited each one of the 106 branches throughout the Province and, of course, as his successor, I was expected to do likewise. At a great many of these meetings the Rev RJ would appear, to the great applause of all present, even if the meeting were in South Armagh, South Fermanagh or some other equally remote part of the Province. And, despite the many pressing invitations to stay the night, particularly in inclement weather, the Rev RJ always insisted on returning to Dervock the same night. Although I heard his stories at almost every meeting I attended, I could nevertheless enjoy them, because of his special way of telling them. The passing of the Rev RJ marked the end of an era, the like of which will not be seen in Ulster again for a very long time, if ever. **Harry West, Rossahilly, Enniskillen** (*who has been generous in his support for this publication*).

Mr Tom Johnston, 1 Windsor Gardens, Ballymoney, a Ministry of Agriculture employee who knew the Rev RJ for very many years, has referred to him as one of nature's gentlemen, who just loved to hear people laughing. "One afternoon we were busy inspecting the Rev RJ's flock of Border Leicester sheep with the purpose of selecting a ram lamb to be shown at Balmoral Show. When the best lamb was selected, a neighbour asked, 'Your Reverence, what name are you giving this special ram lamb?' Without hesitation the Rev RJ replied, 'The Minister's son'."

Mr Wm ES Fullerton, an ex-President of the UFU, who is at present Vice-President of the RUAS, Balmoral, and Vice-Chairman of the Milk Marketing Board, is a well-known farmer from Hillsborough, Co Down. From the mid-1950s he can recall hearing the Rev RJ speak at a National Pig Breeders Association meeting in Belfast, when he was impressed by the ease with which the speaker could use stories to illustrate his address. Mr Fullerton also heard the Rev RJ conduct a service in Bailiesmills Reformed Presbyterian Church, near Lisburn, during the ministry of the Rev John Watters, and has remembered vividly the Rev RJ's gift of speech in prayer as he thanked the Almighty "for our forefathers who in the difficult times in the hills and moorlands of Scotland were faithful".

William Fullerton deputy president of the Royal Ulster Agricultural Society

THE ANNUAL MEETING OF SYNOD, 1961

The Annual Meeting of Synod for 1961 will D.V. be held at Cullybackey.

Rev. R. J. McIlmoyle, M.B.E., will conduct public worship and constitute the Synod on Monday evening the 19th June, at 7.30 p.m.

A cordial invitation is extended to members of the Church to attend the evening Sessions when special note will be taken of the 150th Anniversary of the constitution of Synod in 1811.

It is hoped to keep the evening Sessions reasonably free of routine business and to provide an agenda that will make a wide public appeal.

Special speakers expected at the evening Sessions of this historic Synod include Rev. A. S. Horne Moderator of the R. P. Synod of Scotland ; Rev. Robert B. Tweed, of Geneva College, representing our sister Church in the United States ; Rev. Ray A. King, Professor-elect of Church History in the Associate Reformed Presbyterian Church of America ; Rt. Rev. W. A. A. Park, Moderator of the General Assembly of the Presbyterian Church in Ireland ; and Rev. William Lytle, senior Missionary of the Church in Lebanon.

ADAM LOUGHRIDGE,
Clerk of Synod

The Coleraine Chronicle on Saturday June 24 1961 reported as follows on:

150th Anniversary of Reformed Presbyterian Synod

Rev. R. J. McIlmoyle's Unique Distinction

SERVICES to celebrate the 150th anniversary of the constitution of the first Reformed Presbyterian Synod are being held this week in Cullybackey. It was in that village that the first Synod was formed in May, 1811.

The Synod opened on Monday evening with a service conducted by Rev. R. J. M'Ilmoyle, M.B.E., Dervock, the outgoing Moderator, who has completed 60 years' ministry. He was the outgoing Moderator in 1911 and conducted public worship in Cullybackey when Synod celebrated its 100th anniversary.

Rev. Hugh Wright, minister of Trinity Street congregation, Belfast, was appointed as new Moderator. Born at Ballybay, County Monaghan, he is a son of Rev. James R. Wright, formerly minister of Ballyclabber Reformed Presbyterian congregation.

Mr. Wright was educated at Coleraine Model School and Coleraine Academical Institution. He continued his studies at Magee University College and graduated B.A. in Mental and Moral Science from Trinity College, Dublin, in 1930.

He studied at the Reformed Presbyterian Theological Hall, Belfast, and the Reformed Presbyterian Theological Seminary, Pittsburgh, U.S.A. He graduated in 1933 and spent the summer months of that year doing mission work in Canada. Mr. Wright began his ministry in Winnipeg, and in 1938 returned to Northern Ireland and was installed in Londonderry in that year. He has been minister of Trinity Street, Belfast, since 1959.

Mr. Wright has taken an active part in the work of the St. John Ambulance Brigade, his services being recognised by his appointment as a serving brother (assistant chaplain) of the Most Venerable Order of the Hospital of St. John of Jerusalem.

The new Moderator, in his address, said on taking up the high and responsible office to which they had been pleased to call him his first words must be of appreciation.

Only Time in History

In a reference to Rev. R. J. M'Ilmoyle he said it was the only time in the history of their Church when a member of the Court was in the Moderator's chair, fifty years after he had first been Moderator. "Well did he discharge his duties, as indeed we all expected he would, and we thank him for the service he has rendered both to the Church and to its Lord and Head, in this way," said Mr. Wright.

The new Moderator said he was pleased to be called to the chair, in Cullybackey, on account of the associations with the name of Wright in that place. Grandfather, father, uncle, brother and cousins had all sought to play their part, and some were still seeking to do so, in the work of the Synod and the Church. "I count it an honour that a humble representative of the Wright-Reid connection should be so privileged on this occasion. I count not the honour just as an honour to myself but to all the others who have served or are still seeking to serve," he said.

REV. HUGH WRIGHT

Rev Prof John McIlmoyle MA (a cousin) minister of Dublin Road RP Church, Belfast and an editor of *The Covenanter*, reported as follows on:

SYNOD, 1961

Many thoughts must have surged through the minds of members of Synod as they gathered in Cullybackey R.P. Church for the opening sederunt on Monday, 19th June. One hundred and fifty years had elapsed since the first meeting of the Irish Synod of the R.P. Church had taken place there and fifty of these had gone since the last meeting was held in the same place. The changes that time brings were reflected in the roll of Synod. The fingers of one hand would suffice to count the ministerial members of the 1911 Synod who are alive to-day and all the elders of that Synod, the average age of whom would be higher than that of the ministers, have gone to their reward.

But those present at the Synod of 1961 were also reminded of the fact that God binds us by a living link with the witness of the past. Fifty years ago Rev. R. J. McIlmoyle, Dervock, with ten years ministerial experience behind him ascended the Cullybackey pulpit to preach the outgoing Moderator's sermon and constitute the Synod. It was with extreme joy that members of the present Synod and the extremely large audience watched him ascend once more, now with sixty years of outstanding service to his Church behind him and having completed a year of office with distinction during which his wider service had been recognised by his country and his Queen through the bestowal of the M.B.E. On few have the ravages of the years left less of their mark, and in his usual arresting style he preached the outgoing sermon on Psalm 121 : 1, and constituted the Synod.

The other four who had been present in 1911 and all of whom were present on this occasion were Prof. T. B. McFarlane, Revs. J. R. Wright, James Blair and A Gilmour.

Ministers and elders at the 150th Synod at Cullybackey in 1961

Back: WS McCune, Rev AS Horne, Rev HJ Blair, HA Steele, R Miller, RJ Pinkerton, JRG McIlmoyle, CD McCluggage, JC MacQuigg, H Tadley, G Crawford, SK Cromie, Rev SR Archer, Dr J McKelvey, Rev R Hanna, WC McDowell, Rev JAC Blair, Rev FS Leahy, J Armstrong, Rev DJ Magee, HW Stewart; **middle**: Rev J Watters, AB McCarroll, Rev JR Patterson, Rev WJ Gilmour, Rev WN McCune, Rev JH McGladdery, WN McConaghie, WJ Stevenson, Rev RB Lyons, HC Lyons, Rev AR Wright, Rev W Young, WM Aicken, T Carson, RA Stevenson, G Archer, A Wilson, J Fryer, Rev R Tweed, Rev Dr D Calderwood; **front**: Rev Prof J McIlmoyle, Rev W Dodds, Rev W Lytle, HW Reid, Rev JR Wright, Rev RJ McIlmoyle, Rev Prof TB McFarlane, Rev J Blair, Rev J Campbell, Rev Prof A Loughridge (Clerk), Rev Hugh Wright (Moderator), Rev T Donnelly, Rev RA Watson, Rev JR Wright, Rev I Cole, Rev SM Calderwood, WJ Lyons, Rev JW Calderwood

MINUTES

OF THE

Proceedings of the Synod of the Reformed Presbyterian Church of Ireland

ANNUAL MEETING, 1961

in the Reformed Presbyterian Church

Cullybackey

SESSION I

Monday Evening, 19th June, 1961, at 7.30 o'clock.

1. The Synod of the Reformed Presbyterian Church of Ireland met. Rev. R. J. McIlmoyle, M.B.E., outgoing Moderator, conducted public worship, preached from Psalm 121, verse 1, "I will lift up mine eyes unto the hills from whence cometh my help," and constituted Synod while leading in prayer.

NORTHERN PRESBYTERY

MINISTERS	ELDERS	CONGREGATIONS
Thomas Donnelly, B.A. ...	James McCollum,* *alt.* Thomas Carson	Ballyclabber
Alex. R. Wright, B.A. ...	Hugh Creelman, *alt.* James McNeill*	Ballylaggan
Hugh J. Blair, B.A.	Wm. John Lyons, *alt.* John Brewster	Ballymoney
Wm. J. Gilmour, B.A. ...	Dr. John McKelvey	Cullybackey
R. J. McIlmoyle, M.B.E., G.A., M.C.	Wm. Norman McConaghie	Dervock
Isaac Cole, B.A.	Wm. M. Aicken	Drimbolg
....	....	Garvagh
S. M. Calderwood, M.A. ...	James Warwick, *alt.* Alexander Wilson	Kellswater
James Blair, G.A., M.C. ...	Robert J. Pinkerton, *alt.* David Robinson*	Kilraughts
Prof. Adam Loughridge, B.A.	Robert Miller, *alt.* Wm. Wright	Portrush
Wm. Lytle, B.A.	Missionary to Lebanon	
James R. Wright, B.A. ...	Retired Minister	

SOUTHERN PRESBYTERY

MINISTERS	ELDERS	CONGREGATIONS
Wm. Dodds, B.A.	....	Ballenon
	....	Ballylane
....	William Hamilton,* *alt.* James Brown*	Clare
J. Robin Patterson, B.A. ...	Graham Crawford, *alt.* Adam Moffett*	Creevagh
David J. Magee, B.A.	Joseph Armstrong	Fairview
	John T. Shanks*	Tullyvallen
Robert B. Cupples, B.A. ...	Thomas Cromie, M.P.S., *alt.* John Gilmore*	Loughbrickland
Prof. T. B. McFarlane, B.A.	Henry C. Lyons, *alt.* Hugh Wm. Stewart	Newry
Samuel R. Archer, B.A. ...	R. J. Cromie, *alt.* S. K. Cromie	Rathfriland

EASTERN PRESBYTERY

MINISTERS	ELDERS	CONGREGATIONS
John Watters, B.A.	Wm. J. Martin, *alt.* H. B. Hanna, M.A.*	Bailiesmills
	John T. McClure, *alt.* George Archer	Knockbracken
J. F. McGladdery, B.A. ...	James McKeown,* *alt.* Thomas W. Kennedy*	Ballyclare
Frederick S. Leahy	W. J. Stevenson, *alt.* R. M. Watson*	Cregagh Rd., Belfast
Prof. J. McIlmoyle, M.A.	J. McCarroll, *alt.* J. R. G. McIlmoyle	Dublin Rd., Belfast
Wm. Young, B.A.	W. C. McDowell, *alt.* T. J. Barr	Grosvenor Rd., Belfast
Hugh Wright, B.A.	Hugh McFerran, *alt.* W. S. McCune	Trinity Street, Belfast
J. Renwick Wright, B.A. ...	Bailie Bell, *alt.* Joseph Fryer	Dromara
....	Martin Mateer, *alt.* W. J. Finlay*	Killinchy
James Campbell, B.A.	Gardiner McCluggage,* *alt.* Charles D. McCluggage	Larne
J. ... Cresswell Blair, B.A.	John Henry McEwen,* *alt.* John Lyons	Newtownards
Alexander Gilmour, M.A.	Retired Minister	
J. Claude Macquigg, M.A.	Minister without Charge	
Charles Presho, M.A., B.D.*	Minister without Charge	

WESTERN PRESBYTERY

MINISTERS	ELDERS	CONGREGATIONS
J. W. Calderwood, G.A., M.C.	R. A. Stevenson, *alt.* John Buchanan*	Bready
W. N. McCune, B.A.	H. Adair Steele, *alt.* Harry Tadley	Faughan
Robert B. Lyons, B.A.	Marcus S. F. McCollum	Limavady
....	Alexander B. McCarroll	Londonderry
Robert Hanna, B.A.	James McNutt,* *alt.* William Hay*	Milford
....	....	Mulvin
Robert W. Lytle, B.A. ...	John McClean	Stranorlar
	James A. Stuart	Convoy
Robert A. Watson, M.A., H.DIP.ED.	Minister without Charge	

AUSTRALIAN PRESBYTERY

MINISTERS	CONGREGATIONS
Alexander Barkley, M.A.*	Geelong
Wm. R. McEwen, B.A.*	McKinnon, Melbourne

*Absent from all Sessions of Synod

7. Apologies for absence from the opening sederunt of Synod were accepted from Rev. J. Claude Macquigg, Rev. S. R. Archer, and Rev. Wm. Dodds, and from the meeting of Synod from Rev. Charles Presho.

8. The outgoing Moderator addressed the Court, demitted the office, and called upon the Court to appoint his successor.

9. Rev. Wm. Young and Rev. John Watters nominated Rev. Hugh Wright, minister of Trinity Street Congregation, Belfast, for the office of Moderator for the ensuing year.

10. Rev. Hugh Wright, elected to office unanimously and cordially, addressed the Synod on The Church's Task.

11. Psalm 102, second version, verses 13 to 18, was sung in praise to God.

12. Professor A. Loughridge moved the adoption of the Report of the Historical Committee; seconded by Rev. A. R. Wright, and passed. (Report p. 60.)

13. The Moderator introduced a period of Commemoration and Thanksgiving in connection with the one hundred and fiftieth anniversary of the organisation of the first Synod at Cullybackey in 1811.

14. Professor A. Loughridge addressed Synod on the Story and Challenge of One Hundred and Fifty Years.

15. The Moderator led Synod in a prayer of thanksgiving to God for all His mercies through the years.

16. Psalm 48, verses 10 to 14, was sung in praise to God.

17. The Report of "The Covenanter" Business Committee was submitted by the Convener, Mr. T. S. McCune. Its adoption was moved by Mr. Hugh McFerran; seconded by Rev. Hugh J. Blair, and passed. (Report p. 61.)

18. Rev. Robert Hanna was appointed to conduct devotional exercises at the opening of the sederunt on Tuesday morning.

The Moderator brought this sederunt to a close by pronouncing the Benediction.

SESSION II

Tuesday Morning, 20th June, 1961, 10 till 12.45 o'clock.

Synod resumed, Rev. Robert Hanna conducting devotional exercises.

The minutes of the previous sederunt were read and passed.

19. Leave of absence from the morning sederunt was granted to Rev. A. R. Wright to officiate at a wedding, and from the afternoon sederunt to Revs. Thomas Donnelly and R. B. Lyons and Messrs. Thomas Carson and Marcus McCollum to attend a funeral.

20. Rev. A. Sinclair Horne, Moderator of the Synod of the R.P. Church of Scotland, and the official deputy to this Synod, was invited to his seat in Court.

21. The Moderator welcomed Rev. Wm. and Mrs. Lytle from Lebanon. He further welcomed Rev. Robert B. Tweed from our sister Church in America and a number of visiting elders from our home congregations and invited them to deliberate with the Synod.

22. Rev. Wm. Young moved the adoption of the Report of the Committee on Church Extension; seconded by Rev. J. Renwick Wright, and passed. (Report p. 59.)

23. Dr. John McKelvey moved that Synod authorise the Committee on Church Extension, in consultation with the Northern Presbytery, to undertake church extension work forthwith at Castleroe, Coleraine; seconded by Rev. James Campbell, and passed.

24. Synod authorised the Committee on Church Extension to launch at their discretion a special fund to meet the needs of church extension in any sphere.

25. It was moved by Rev. R. J. McIlmoyle, seconded by Rev. James Campbell, and agreed—That any money obtained from the sale of any property where the work had ceased to exist should be devoted to the Church Extension Fund.

The shepherd of Dervock

Profile

Rev. R. J. McIlmoyle

"NOBODY knows my age," notes R. J. McIlmoyle. "Not even myself. I couldn't tell you my own age unless I counted . . . I couldn't count unless I had the time . . . and, if I had the time, I wouldn't take it."

Whatever his age, however, the years have been kind to this sprightly clergyman. He was ordained in the Reformed Presbyterian Church as long ago as 1900, and has been at Dervock for more than 50 years. His flock of Border Leicester ewes—probably the smallest in the British Isles—is still winning prizes. He continues a heavy programme of lecturing for the Ulster Farmers' Union — which to-day paid tribute to him as its only surviving honorary life member.

McIlmoyle was born in Limavady, and—as he puts it—"the soil's in my blood." When he came to Dervock, therefore, he chose to work the 14-acre manse farm—to which he added another 22 acres several years ago. By now his sheep have won him close to 2,000 cups and medals.

"They keep me healthy," he adds, with a story of a sheep-owning neighbour to illustrate the pride that can be felt in a good flock. One day, the neighbour's wife asked her son to feed the sheep for his father. "I might feed them for him," replied the son, "but I couldn't look at them for him." Many an hour McIlmoyle has spent simply looking at his ewes.

He is similarly attached to his small congregation at Dervock, and has refused 11 calls to other churches since he came to the Co. Antrim village. He even turned down a chance to go on a goodwill mission to America a few years ago, for it would have kept him away too long, and has never been farther afield than England and Scotland.

Within his church he enjoys an unusual distinction, for a gap of fully 50 years separated his election as Moderator in 1910 and 1960. As a farmer, he was a founder member of the Union, and is secretary of the Ram Breeders' Association. He even finds time to be secretary of the co-operative store in Dervock.

"I'm a better preacher, because I have these outside interests," McIlmoyle adds. Certainly he is a more entertaining one for, in his travels throughout the Province, he reaps a rich harvest of stories. Indeed, he takes the same sort of connoisseur's pleasure in these stories—retold in his dry countryman's voice—as he does in his pedigree sheep. "It's not the story, it's the way it's told . . . it's the personality behind it," he comments. "I've heard a good story murdered, and you could shed tears over it."

Martin Wallace

Portrait by Staff Photographer Edward Sterling

BELFAST TELEGRAPH SEPT 1st 1961

Committees and Boards of the Synod of the Reformed Presbyterian Church of Ireland on which Rev RJ McIlmoyle was serving in 1961:

Trustees of Synod's Funds:

Mr. H. C. Lyons.
Mr. Jas. Dick Russell.
Mr. W. M. Graham.
Mr. R. A. McEwen.
Mr. H. B. Holmes.
Mr. J. R. Graham.
Rev. Isaac Cole.
Rev. R. J. McIlmoyle.
Rev. Prof. A. Loughridge.
Mr. A. C. McIlmoyle, Secty.,
14 Broughton Park, Belfast, 6.

Honorary General Treasurer:

Mr. JAMES DICK RUSSELL, Silhill, 1 Sheridan Drive, Helen's Bay,
Co. Down; and
c/o J. H. R. Adams & Co., 7 Howard Street, Belfast.

Committee on Australian Mission:

The Moderator.
Mr. Harold B. Holmes.
Rev. F. S. Leahy.
Rev. W. J. Gilmour.
Rev. R. J. McIlmoyle.
Mr. H. Graham Crawford.
Rev. Robert W. Lytle.
Rev. David J. Magee.
Mr. T. A. Warnock.
Rev. Hugh Wright (Convener).

Ministers' Sick Benefit Fund Committee:

Rev. R. J. McIlmoyle.
Rev. J. Campbell.
Rev. J. A. Cresswell Blair.
Rev. J. R. Patterson.
Rev. W. N. McCune (Convener).

Board of Administrators of the Congregational Aid Fund:

The Moderator.
Rev. R. J. McIlmoyle.
Rev. A. R. Wright.
Rev. J. W. Calderwood.
Rev. Alexander Gilmour.
Rev. Prof. T. B. McFarlane.
Rev. Prof. J. McIlmoyle.
Mr. W. C. McDowell.
Mr. John H. McEwen.
Mr. John Henry.
Mr. John W. McCloy.
Mr. Thomas Cromie.
Mr. David H. McCollum.
Mr. J. D. Russell (Secretary).

Committee on Code Revision:

Clerks of Presbyteries.
Rev. R. J. McIlmoyle.
Rev. Hugh Wright.
Rev. Wm. Young.

Clerk of Synod (Convener).

Board of Management of the Australian Mission of the Irish and Scottish R.P. Churches:

Irish Members

The Moderator.
Rev. David J. Magee.
Mr. T. A. Warnock.
Mr. Harold B. Holmes.
Rev. F. S. Leahy.
Rev. J. H. McGladdery.
Rev. W. J. Gilmour.
Rev. R. J. McIlmoyle.
Mr. H. Graham Crawford.
Rev. Robert W. Lytle.
Mrs. A. C. McIlmoyle.
Miss J. Kennedy.
Mrs. S. R. Archer.
Rev. Hugh Wright (Secretary).

Committee on Friendly Relations with Other Churches:

The Moderator.
Rev. Prof. T. B. McFarlane.
Rev. Prof. J. McIlmoyle.
Rev. A. Gilmour.
Mr. John Willdridge.
Rev. R. J. McIlmoyle.
Rev. W. Dodds.
Rev. R. Hanna.
Rev. J. W. Calderwood.
Clerk of Synod (Convener).

A unique double

FARMING LIFE 25.5.1968

Mr. Sam Black, of Portstewart, with his 10-week-old Border Leicester ram, the youngest ever to win the breed championship at the Royal Ulster May Show, and its mother, which was placed reserve—a unique double.

310 gns for champion ram

FARMING LIFE 11.9.1976

Mr Sam Black, of Portstewart, with his champion Border Leicester ram lamb which made the top price of 310 gns at the breed show and sale at Ballyclare.

Top price of 310 gns was paid for the supreme champion ram lamb at the Border Leicester sheep show and sale at McClelland's Mart, Ballyclare.

The champion came from the flock of Mr Sam Black, Portstewart, who had a field day, winning several awards. In addition to the top proce he received 240 gns for a ram in his second - prize group.

Mr Black won the Supreme Championship, the Allam Cup, the Association's Challenge Cup, the McIlmoyle Memorial Perpetual Trophy, the BOCM Tankard and the championship prize sponsored by the Northern Bank, plus several other awards.

The runners - up to Mr Black in these trophies were Messrs. Graham & McCrum of Dromara, Dromore, Co. Down, who were awarded the reserve championship and won the Jacob Horner Memorial Cup, the Thompson Memorial Cup for the best group of three ram lambs and the prize sponsored by the Northern Bank.

The Shearling cup was awarded to Alexander Minnis, Comber, and the Anderson Cup for the best ewe went to Harold Dickey of Ballymena.

The overall average for the 159 ram lambs rocketed to an average of £77.75, compared with last year's entry of 161 which averaged 37 guineas.

Scottish judge, Mr Hugh Guthrie was very impressed by the high quality of the top rams.

Prizewinners and prices in gns.:

Ram (shearling upwards) — 1, J. H. McConnell, Rathfriland, 55 gns; 2, James H. Aiken, Dromara, 48; 3, F. Hutchinson, Carntall, withdrawn.

Shearling ram — 1, Alex Minnis, Comber, 75; 2, S. Holden, Ballyclare, 90; 3, Alex. Minnis, Comber, 68; 4, Sam Agnew, Ballyclare; Non - prizewinners — Eric Wright, Castlewellan, 80 gns; Jas. Mawhinney & Son, Newtownards, 75.

Ram Lambs (excluding animals entered for the Group class) — 1, Robert Mulligan, Banbridge, 200 gns; 2, John Agnew,

R. J. McIlmoyle, Dervock, Co. Antrim, pinning up the rosette for his fourth first prize in the Border Leicester classes for sheep.

COLERAINE
3 15PM
21 AUG
1962
CO. LONDONDERRY

S. Black, Esq.,
89 Strand Road,
Portstewart.
Co. Derry

Samuel Black tells us that Rev McIlmoyle kept carefully all the rosettes he won and that Mrs McIlmoyle always made sure that children visiting the Manse would not get near the box.

Mr Samuel Black has judged at Aberdeen Show & Sale, Antrim Agricultural Society, Athlone and Midland Agricultural Show Society, Ayr Agricultural Association, Banbridge Agricultural Society, Ballymena (County Antrim) Agricultural Show, Ballymoney (North Antrim) Agricultural Association, Bonagee & North-West Show Society Ltd, Caithness County Show, Castlewellan Show, Coleraine Young Farmers' Show, Clonmany Sheep Dog Association, Dalrymple Show, Denbighshire & Flintshire Agricultural Society, Fermanagh Farming Society, Fife Show, Innishowen Agricultural Society, Letterkenny Agricultural Show, Londonderry & Limavady Show, Lanark Show & Sale, Newry Agricultural Society, North-West of Ireland Agricultural Society, Oldcastle Agricultural Show Society, Omagh & Tyrone Farming Society, Portadown Show, Royal Highland Agricultural Society of Scotland, Royal Ulster Agricultural Society, Saintfield and District Agricultural Society, Shropshire and West Midland, Turriff & District Agricultural Association and the Welsh Ram Sales (Builth Wells)

Dervock,
Ballymoney.
Aug. 21/62.

Dear Mr. Black,

I enclose cheque for £115.

I am more than pleased with my purchase.

The pleasure of looking at the Champion is worth a lot.

Yours sincerely,
R. J. McIlmoyle.

All three local ministers were involved in the presentation arrangements and ceremony in 1962 when

Dervock Doctor was Honoured by Patients and Friends

Presentation tributes to "great gifts of heart, hand and head"

When it became generally known that Dr Thomas McKee would retire from his medical practice in Dervock and district in September last, the desire was widely expressed that the occasion should be marked by a tangible expression of the affection and gratitude felt for him by his patients and friends. With this object in mind, a small committee was formed to put the wishes of the people concerned into practical form. All the members realised that Dr McKee, ever ready to have the worth of others recognised, would be very reticent about his own services receiving any special mention. It was decided, therefore, that all gifts to a presentation fund would be given, or sent, rather than collected. As expected, the response was immediate and wholehearted. The only regret was that, through lack of full knowledge in the matter, some people, who would have wished to have been associated with the tribute, were not informed. The committee realised also that Dr McKee would not wish a public ceremony for the presentation of any tokens of esteem to him. Instead, a very happy function took place at The Stroan, Dervock, the home of Dr and Mrs McKee on Monday last, when a deputation of clergy, the Rev RG McBride, the Rev RJ McIlmoyle and the Rev DF Moore, made the presentation of a solid silver salver, refrigerator, and an Eddystone wireless set.

The inscription The inscription on the salver reads: "Presented by his patients and friends to Dr Thomas McKee, MB, BCh, BAO on retiring from his medical practice, 30th September 1961, as a tribute to his great gifts of heart, hand and head, humbly and unsparingly used in the interests of their health and happiness from 1st October 1929 to 30th September 1961. 'To live revered in hearts you cheered along life's way is rich retirement'." Introducing the subject of the presentation, Mr McBride said he felt highly honoured and pleased to be present, with his two nearest ministerial neighbours, to convey with them to Dr and Mrs McKee their sincere and very best wishes in well-earned retirement. The people of the locality where Dr McKee spent over 30 of the best years of his life, when they heard of his retirement, wanted to do him honour in some tangible way. They knew, however, that, true to the man he is, humble and modest, Dr McKee would not want to be thus honoured. Mr McBride said that if ever a man deserved a heartfelt Thank You as he unbuckled his armour and handed it over to his successor, it was Thomas McKee, their beloved, trusted and talented doctor. The small committee formed to arrange the presentation fund, decided that not a penny would be collected, so if ever there was a spontaneous tribute it was indeed this one. "Congratulations, Dr and Mrs McKee", said Mr McBride. "You should feel pleased and proud tonight, as I feel sure you do, that after 32 years you should command such respect and trust, and be so esteemed and beloved by those who know you so well. I feel greatly privileged in being allowed to say this on behalf of your legion of grateful and generous friends. Quite a number of the subscriptions came to me. Some were handed to me and some came by post. With many there were notes of appreciation of your worth and good wishes for a long and pleasant retirement. Dr McKee, you have had, as you still have, treasured gifts of heart, hand and head, and we have reaped the benefits and blessings of these. You have been to us in this area a God-sent blessing and we thank you for all that, by God's grace, you have been and for all you have been enabled to do for us. Above all, you have been an asset and a shining example in your great profession."

Mr Moore said he agreed wholeheartedly with everything Mr McBride had said. Their friend, whom they desired to honour and thank, was one who had made an indelible mark for good in this district. For some 32 years he had, in an unassuming and highly efficient way, rendered wonderful service to the needs of all creeds and classes. Throughout the entire district he was trusted, respected and beloved. This was a spontaneous tribute to a highly skilled doctor who has done a grand day's work.

Gratitude "We have come", said Mr Moore, "to voice the feelings of gratitude and appreciation of the host of friends and admirers that you have, Dr McKee, in this community, where you have lived and laboured in such an uplifting, efficient and helpful way for so long. We cannot adequately voice these sentiments. However, the spontaneity and extent of the response to this tribute must leave you and Mrs McKee in no doubt regarding the place you hold in our thoughts and affections. We wish you both a long and a very happy retirement. Our great consolation and joy is that, although you have retired from your medical duties, you and Mrs McKee will continue to live amongst us." Mr McIlmoyle, in handing over to Dr McKee a solid silver salver of beautiful design and exquisitely engraved said: "Dr and Mrs McKee, in presenting this salver and the other gifts that form this presentation, I convey to you the gratitude and sincere good wishes of a people who have been comforted, helped, cheered and blessed by your skill and devoted attention for many years. They are most appreciative and deeply grateful to you. We are here to present to you and Mrs McKee their gifts and to express to you their high regard for you and their heartfelt gratitude. All through the years you have been an asset to your noble profession and we in this locality have reaped the benefit of your skill and devoted services. We thank you with sincere hearts and we wish you many happy years of retirement amongst your friends and neighbours."

Thanks Dr McKee replying said: "I cannot adequately express my gratitude to you who have come this evening to say such flattering things about me and my work and to all the good people who have contributed to his wonderful presentation. As I listened to your complimentary remarks I began to wonder if indeed you had made a mistake and were talking about the Ideal Doctor. I have not always succeeded as I should have wished. Indeed, I am very conscious of my own shortcomings, but I always tried to do my very best for my patients and for their comfort and well-being. Whilst I am humbly grateful for my successes I must also have had my failures. However, in your goodness of heart you have overlooked these and have pointed to my achievements only. I am deeply grateful to all those who have subscribed so generously to this tribute. I know I am not worthy of it. What you have said, the gifts and the good wishes of appreciative friends, makes me very humble. At the same time they make me very glad. Please convey to all who have done me this honour and paid me such a wonderful tribute my heartfelt thanks. My wife and I are deeply touched and we would like our friends to know that we sincerely appreciate what they have done and the good wishes they have expressed." Afterwards Dr and Mrs McKee entertained their visitors to supper.

Tribute To A Man Of The Church . . . And Of The Land

BY AN EX-COLLEAGUE

ON Friday next, one of the best-loved figures in Ulster farming circles will be honoured by his fellows in a ceremony in Belfast and it is fitting that the venue should be the head office of the Ulster Farmers' Union.

This is the organisation that Rev. R. J. McIlmoyle has served faithfully for 43 years, and through his selfless devotion to duty he has become known to almost every farmer in Northern Ireland.

"R. J." was a founder member of the Ulster Farmers' Union in 1918 and was the first honorary secretary of the Union's Ballymoney branch. He has been on the staff of the Union for many years as a lecturer and in the course of his duties has travelled tens of thousands of miles over a period of 40 years, speaking to members at branch meeting and social gatherings.

Distance means nothing for Mr. McIlmoyle. He will quite casually set out at four o'clock in the afternoon from his home at Dervock to motor to Enniskillen, speak at a meeting of farmers and leave the Western county at midnight to motor home again. Then he will rise again at 5 o'clock in the morning to attend to his farming duties, and could well repeat the process the next day.

One of my most vivid memories of Mr. McIlmoyle was the occasion of the County Fermanagh U.F.U. re-union in December 1959. He had spoken to 1,200 farmers and their wives in the cinema in Enniskillen and some of us had returned around 1 a.m. to the Imperial Hotel, where we intended having a chat before retiring. Mr. McIlmoyle sat with us enjoying a bowl of hot soup, and how he must have smiled at we "young bloods" as we held up our hands in horror at the thought of him motoring all the way home to Dervock at that hour.

STORY-TELLER

Perhaps the best story-teller in Ulster, it is strange that this gentle figure should have become famous in a profession other than the one he chose as a career. As a concert entertainer, with a moral at the end of every performance, he will be forever rememberd by thousands of rural dwellers in Ulster.

As a breeder of Border Leicester sheep he is known all over the United Kingdom and is perhaps the most successful exhibitor of that breed in the British Isles. He long ago passed the 2,000th milestone in first prize rosettes at the various shows and sales over the past 40 years.

Lord Glentoran said of him in 1959: "He has served his fellowmen with ability, distinction and zeal. In spite of his other activities, he has not spared himself in giving time to the affairs of the Ulster Ram Breeders' Association, of which he was elected President on August 9, 1917."

Mr. McIlmoyle was chairman of the U.F.U. Sheep Committee for many years and it was the pioneering work done by him, and endless speeches and representations made by him that led to a change in the law over the worrying of sheep by dogs.

He has been honorary secretary of the Ulster Ram Breeders' Association for over 40 years.

As a chairman he has not gone unrecognised, either.

A native of Limavady, he was ordained in Ballyclare Reformed Presbyterian Church in September, 1900. After a brief ministry at Ballyclare he was called to Dervock and installed there in August, 1904.

UNIQUE RECORD

Mr. McIlmoyle was Moderator of the 100th Annual Synod of the R.P. Church in 1910 and in June 1960 he was appointed Moderator again for the 150th Synod—a unique record. A fluent and acceptable preacher he has had calls to other churches but chose to remain in Dervock.

He has broadcast frequently and has appeared on television programmes. The peak of his career was achieved when Her Majesty the Queen awarded him the M.B.E. in the New Year Honours in January this year.

During the last ten years he has been the recipient of dozens of gifts and presentations from grateful farmers all over the Province, but he will receive the most important of all on Friday when the president of the Union he has loved for so many years declares him a life member of the organisation—the second man in the Union's history ever to receive the honour.

Although he keeps his age a strict secret, he must be approaching 90.

He presents to the world a picture of eternal youth and he is forever increasing in stature and popularity.

Readers will join with us in wishing this grand old man of farming many more years of good health and many more appearances in the show rings of his native Ulster.

Rev. R. J. McIlmoyle

Ballymena Weekly Telegraph, Thursday, September 13, 1962.

Mr. A. C. Gibson, Broughshane, receiving the Championship Cup, won at the Ulster Ram Breeders' Association Show in Ballymena, from Mrs. R. L. Orr at the annual dinner.

EWE, B L 94B—H 2.

Sire (17965) Kinross Special ; dam, B L 94B—A 3, by (15316) Arbrack Supreme. Breed Champion at the Royal Ulster Agricultural Society Show, Belfast 1960. Bred by Messrs. John Howie & Son, Hillhouse, Kilmarnock, Ayrshire. Exhibited by Rev. R. J. M'Ilmoyle, M.B.E., Dervock, Co. Antrim.

Photograph by The Farming News.

Country of the kirk and co-operative

The first of a new series on people and places which give Ulster its character takes in the lie of the land at the hub of the Route

DERVOCK lies in the centre of Presbyterian Route. It has more churches than public houses, claims to possess the most progressive co-operative society outside Belfast, and has produced an Olympic marathon winner and equally successful greyhounds.

It also has Rev. R. J. McIlmoyle, who shepherds Border Leicesters and Reformed Presbyterians, and has won cups for the former.

Around Dervock there is some of the best agricultural land in the North; the country that stretches away from Ballymoney down to Bushmills produces fine crops of barley and potatoes. Over the years it has also produced a fine crop of churches.

The churches are mostly Presbyterian, reformed and unreformed. It is open country, scoured clean in winter by strong winds and hard frosts. From the slightest rise it is unusual if at least three solid kirk buildings are not discernible. There are no mission halls, for this is well north of the Mid-Antrim mission-hall belt.

Rev. R. J. McIlmoyle has been in Dervock for more than half-a-century.

He is secretary of the local co-operative, and a regular lecturer at Farmers' Union meetings, as well as minister of the Reformed Presbyterian Church.

A neighbour put his age at 86; he himself says he does not know it, and does not want to—"If I did, I would probably collapse on the spot."

He boasts the smallest registered flock of Border Leicesters in the country—six ewes — and one of the best show-ring records.

"There is a great change in the countryside," he said. "Not nearly so much life as there used to be, though there are plenty of dances—they call them parties hereabouts; that looks better to Presbyterian eyes."

Life there is, however. Young Farmers' Clubs, like Kilraughts with more than 100 members, can keep the enthusiast busy three or four nights a week. Drama alternates with films on fertilisers.

"Boyd's Shop" can draw a full house of perhaps 300 in Dervock on a freezing cold night, with icy roads, even though it has already been produced in several neighbouring districts.

And the area is still sufficiently Presbyterian for the producer's chief worry to be the clerical reaction to St. John Ervine's occasional profanities.

Physically, Dervock is dominated by the Co-operative. On the left of the main street, at the bridge, is the cupola-topped original building, which now houses the grocery shop. Behind it is an egg-packing centre, with the very latest in egg-grading machines. Here, too, five mobile shops load up each day for their rural rounds.

Across the road stands the large grain-drying unit. The Co-operative mixes its own feeding stuffs. The manager is a Ballymoney man, Mr. Hugh McDowell.

"We began as an egg-packing centre in 1901. Now we have an annual turnover of half-a-million pounds, and like to think we are the most progressive co-op outside Belfast."

Surveying this scene of obvious well-being from an adjacent wall is an equestrian King William, flanked by orange lilies. His future is less secure than the Co-op's; the local artist who refurbished him annually has joined his subject.

In Derrykeighan, a few miles to the north, the artists, less talented but more prolific, are still going strong. At the cross-roads in this tiny, pub-less village the keen-eyed motorist can, at the time of going to press, read :

Ulster we will maintain. No surrender, 1961. Remember 1690, Derry, Aughrim and the Boyne. God save the Queen. Up Ulster. In Derrykeighan we are sons of Ulster. 1690 King William III. No surrender Derry 1688. Aughrim and the Boyne. Up Ulster. We stand firm, no surrender, Derry's Walls, 1688. No I.R.A. Up Ulster. 1688-1690

There is also the rather superfluous exhortation to "Remember us when we are not here."

Ironically, all these sentiments are displayed on a wall that surrounds Drilly Knowe—the field where the United Irishmen drilled in the days of '98.

For this was United Irish country. It is the district which produced President McKinley for the United States and Kennedy K. McArthur for the Gold Medal in the 1912 Olympic Marathon. It produced, it claims, the father of Master Magrath for the Waterloo Cup and J. B. Armour for Liberalism.

To-day it is solidly Unionist and Orange. Or almost so.

The country has a prosperous look. Farms are large by Ulster standards; the man with 30 acres being a small man. There are signs that a less conservative attitude is spreading among the hard-headed country men.

Sugar

One example is a group-buying scheme, with small and big farmers co-operating to get materials, for example, barley seed, at cost. The Ballymoney sugar project is pressing ahead with plans and agitation for the promotion of a sugar beet industry in the area.

There are several "big houses" in the district which seem to ooze prosperity from every pore of their tar-macadamed driveway and yards.

But many of the old families have been forced out by death duties and rising costs. Those that remain are hard-working farmers rather than idle gentry.

Contrast

The towns and villages provide a contrast to the country. There is no work. There are new housing estates, but derelict cottages give an air of depression. Liscolman looks like a deserted village with its decaying jute mill and rows of cottages.

There are, as they say in Dervock, a lot of people "working to the Queen."

COMMISSION
OF THE EUROPEAN
COMMUNITIES

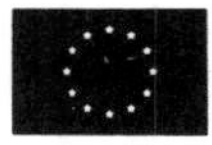

OFFICE IN NORTHERN IRELAND

Windsor House
9/15 Bedford Street
Belfast BT2 7EG

Tel: (0232) 240708
Fax: (0232) 248241
Telex: 74117 CECBEL G

Head of Office
Dennis Kennedy

4-4-91

Dear Rev Hanna,

Thank you for your letter of March 25th, and yes I had noticed the piece in the Telegraph on your book on R J McIlmoyle. In fact I had recognised the photo as one taken at the time I interviewed him in 1963.

I fear there is not too much I can add to what appeared in the interview. I had gone to the Ballymoney-Dervock area to try to find some remnants of North Antrim liberalism, and I must say the Rev McIlmoyle was one of the few such remnants around. I found him most courteous, with a dry sense of humour.

What I do vividly remember was that he had two very large Border Leicester ewes in the small front room of the manse. These, he explained,had been cleaned, brushed and prepared for a show the following day, and had been brought into the yard for safe-keeping. However it had turned wet overnight, the yard was getting muddy..... and it was vital to have the ewes in prime order for the show. He told me all this in a matter of fact way, clearly assuming that,as a sensible man, I would see nothing too unusual about two lumping great, and rather boisterous, sheep, scattering the furniture in the front room.

Best of luck with the book,

Regards,

Dennis K.

Dr Dennis Kennedy

MINNIE'S MINISTERIAL MAGGOTS

Miss Minnie Savage recalls the Rev RJ preaching in Ballenon in the Rev William Dodds' time and she remembers him coming to Portadown and speaking at an area meeting of the UFU. I think on that occasion he told of two clergymen meeting on the train. They were both doing a bit of farming and their talk covered their work in general. One leaned over and asked, "And what about your flock?" The other answered, "Not bad, not bad, but still a few inclined to have maggots!" (*see below*)

James S Throne, Bready: After reading the Roamer's paragraph in the *News Letter* concerning the Rev McIlmoyle, I think it would be of great interest to the public at large throughout Ulster to have a history of RJ, especially in the country districts where he was known best. And the fact that he was also a minister adds to the interest as well. I can remember him being in Bready district hall one night. At first, when he appeared on the platform, he may have seemed to present a sombre appearance to an audience that was waiting to be entertained. But he was not long started until everyone was in stitches... The schoolmaster was teaching mathematics to the class and he says to one of the boys, "If there were 100 sheep in the field and if 99 went over the ditch, how many would be left?" The boy answered, "There would be none left". The teacher said, "I doubt you know nothing about figures". "You know nothing about sheep", the boy replied ... if wellwishers met RJ and asked him, "How were his flock?" (meaning his congregation), RJ replied "Well, I had them examined and found that one of them had scabs, so I just dipped the lot".

Jean D Clarkson, 121 Inveraray Avenue, Pitteuchar, Glenrothes, Fife (*nee* Fullerton of Blaris, Lisburn): I read with much pleasure the 'Ulster Diary' article about the Rev RJ McIlmoyle. He used to speak at our Farmers' Union meeting and, never using a note, he delivered a speech well peppered with humour to a packed house. Though I am now in my seventies, I've never forgotten him. The story I liked best was the one about the little boy who pleaded with his mother to get him a bantam. So he had a bantam's egg for breakfast most mornings, although he complained it was very small. He decided to put a goose egg near the place where the bantam laid its egg and a note which read 'Keep your eye on this and do your best'. I would love to buy a copy of the book on the Rev RJ. I'm sure it will be a worthy tribute to a great man.

Miss Margaret F Willdridge, 8 Delhi Parade, Belfast: Rev RJ's two daughters attended Grosvenor Road RP Church for many years and were very active in the congregation. He was invited to speak at a social evening in Grosvenor Road, possibly the annual congregational meeting, and I remember laughing until the tears ran down my cheeks and I was not the only one. He had a remarkable memory and certainly dispelled the idea that Christians were kill-joys.

One man is as good as another, until he makes himself worse

Dervock Reformed Presbyterian Church

Minister:
Rev R. J. McIlmoyle, M.B.E.
Tel.: Dervock 212

Dervock,
Ballymoney.

Rathleane Hospital.
Coleraine.

Nov. 24. 80.

Dear Mr. Orr,

I have been through a very serious ill-ness but have now turned the corner and am on the road to complete recovery.

I am very sorry about the delay re your statement & cheque.

Meantime my son in Belfast has been down almost every other night. He took my correspondence with him & replied to it on my behalf.

I imagine your letter some was sent at home and so escaped him.

However I have it here now — Statement & Cheque for £95.4.10.

Again apologising. R. J. McIlmoyle.

Ulster Farmers' Union

Head Offices
18 DONEGALL SQUARE EAST, BELFAST, 1
Telephones:
BELFAST 32571/3
Telegrams:
"FARMERS, BELFAST"

MEMBERS OF COUNCIL 1964/65

President:
MR. J. MARTIN, J.P., Crossways, Donaghadee (Groomsport 258).

Deputy President:
MR. W. M. BUCHANAN, The Bawn, Aughnacloy (Aughnacloy 235).

Junior Deputy President:
MR. R. B. MARTIN, Springfield House, Clontonacally, Carryduff, Bel (

Vice-Presidents:
MR. G. N. ROBSON, The Cottage, Kilbride. Doagh.
MR. P. BYRNE, Armagh Road, Newry.
MR. T. J. BOYD, Orchard Hill, Dundonald.
MR. IVAN LOANE, Ruskin House, Bellanaleck, Enniskillen.
MR. A. F. DANTON, Raspberry Hill House, Londonderry.
MR. R. J. HAMILTON, Galliagh House, Londonderry.

U.F.U. Headquarters Staff

General Secretary: J. T. O'BRIEN, B.SC. (ECON.).
Assistant Secretary: S. WHITE.
Administrative Officers: J. B. ANDERSON, B.AGR.; F. A. ESPLEY, B.A. (AG
J. MURRAY, B.SC.(ECON.).
Public Relations and Publicity: J. E. LAMB, B.A., B.COMM.
Lecturer: REV. R. J. MCILMOYLE, M.B.E.

Bankers
NORTHERN BANK LTD., Royal Avenue, Belfast, 1.

Auditors
JAMES BAIRD & CO., Murray Street, Belfast, 1.

Legal Adviser
J. MORRIS MCKEE, M.B.E., 109 Victoria Street, Belfast, 1.

Property Trustees
G. ERVINE, Tullychin House, Killyleagh, Co. Down.
MAJOR P. TERRIS, Knappagh House, Killylea, Co. Armagh.
H. W. WEST, M.P., Mullaghmeen, Enniskillen, Co. Fermanagh.
R. A. BROWN, J.P., Moneyhaw, Moneymore, Co. Derry.
H. DUFF, J.P., Ultimo House, Coagh, Co. Tyrone.

The Farmers' Journal

(Official Organ of the Ulster Farmers' Union)

Editorial and Publishing Offices: 18 DONEGALL SQUARE EAST, BELFAST, 1.
Telephone: BELFAST 23633/4. *Telegrams:* 'FARMERS, BELFAST'.
London Agents: HANNAFORD & GOODMAN, 69 Fleet Street, London, E.C.4. (Telephone Fleet St. 5453).
Printers: EDWARD FOX & SON, LTD., Greenhill Street, Stratford-on-Avon.
Directors: Robert Gibson, J.P. (Chairman); A. E. Swain, C.B.E. (Vice-Chairman); Major P. Terris; T. L. Orr; Samuel Boyd, J.P.; John Martin, J.P.; Samuel Ritchie; George Ervine; A. G. Algeo, C.B.E., J.P.; H. J. Perkes; W. Fullerton; R. J. Hanna, J.P.

Editor and Secretary
JAMES E. LAMB, B.A., B.COMM.
Advertising Assistant
MISS E. MAGILL
List Secretary: MRS. A. MCMAHON

ULSTER RAM BREEDERS' ASSOCIATION

President: Mr. Duncan McLeod.
Vice-President: Mr. Robert Mulligan.
Secretary: Rev. R. J. McIlmoyle, Church Street, Dervock, Co. Antrim.

U.F.U. Presidents

1918—23 MR. D. JOHNSTON, J.P., Lurgan.
1923—24 MAJOR R. J. MCCORMACK, Holywood.
1924—25 MR. A. J. PILKINGTON, J.P., Glens of Antrim.
1925—26 MR. W. R. MORROW, J.P., Dundonald.
1926—27 MR. WILLIAM JACKSON, J.P., Coleraine.
1927—28 MR. T. H. HARDY, J.P., Richhill.
1928—29 MR. J. M. MARK, M.P., Roe Valley.
1929—30 MR. C. B. SMITH, J.P., Islandmagee.
1930—31 SIR BASIL BROOKE, BART., M.P., Colebrooke (Viscount Brookeborough).
1931—32 MR. W. W. B. KEERS, Finvoy.
1932—33 MR. W. JACKSON, J.P., Coleraine.
1933—34 MR. JOHN RITCHIE, Comber.
1934—35 MR. GEORGE THOMPSON, J.P., Dundrod.
1935—36 MR. W. F. MCMORDIE, J.P., Moneyrea.
1936—37 MR. CHARLES MAGEE, Jerrettspass.
1937—38 REV. R. MOORE, M.P., Coleraine.
1938—39 MR. R. J. HALE, J.P., Banbridge.
1939—40 REV. R. MOORE, M.P., Coleraine.
1940—41 MR. D. EWART, J.P., Mid-Ards.
1941—42 REV. R. MOORE, M.P., Coleraine.
1942—43 MR. D. EWART, J.P., Mid-Ards.
1943—44 MR. GEORGE ERVINE, Killyleagh, Co. Down.
1944—45 MR. A. E. SWAIN, C.B.E., Moira.
1945—46 MR. GEORGE ERVINE, Killyleagh, Co. Down.
1946—47 MR. A. G. ALGEO, J.P., Ballymoney.
1947—48 MAJOR P. TERRIS, Killylea, Co. Armagh.
1948—49 MR. J. M. WADSWORTH, Lisburn.
1949—50 MR. A. E. SWAIN, C.B.E., Moira.
1950—51 MR. GEORGE M. FULTON, Eglinton, Co. Derry.,
1951—52 MR. A. G. ALGEO, C.B.E., J.P., Ballymoney.
1952—53 MR. JOHN MARTIN, J.P., Donaghadee.
1953—54 MR. GEORGE ERVINE, Killyleagh, Co. Down.
1954—55 MR. A. G. ALGEO, C.B.E., J.P., Ballymoney, Co. Antrim.
1955—56 MR. H. W. WEST, M.P., Mullaghmeen, Enniskillen Co. Fermanagh.
1956—57 MR. S. SHAW, Craigy Dairy Farm, Saintfield.
1957—58 MAJOR P. TERRIS, Killylea, Co. Armagh.
1958—59 MR. R. A. BROWN, O.B.E., J.P., Moneyhaw, Moneymore, Co. Derry.
1959—60 MR. S. BOYD, J.P., Ballywindland, Ballymoney, Co. Antrim.
1960—61 MR. H. J. CROMIE, J.P., Springmount, Ballygowan, Co. Down.
1961—62 MR. A. MACLURG, B.A., Templemoyle, Limavady, Co. Derry.
1962—63 MR. G. CATHCART, Bellanaleck, Enniskillen.
1963—64 MR. A. G. ALGEO, C.B.E., J.P., Ballymoney, Co. Antrim.
1964—65 MR. J. MARTIN, J.P., Crossways, Donaghadee.

Sheep Committee

(Four Meetings)

Chairman: Mr. J. Hamilton (4)
Vice-Chairman: Mr. G. Hamilton (3)

Mr. J. Anderson	(3)
Mr. J. Armstrong	(–)
Mr. J. Anderson (Cross)	(3)
Mr. A. Barr	(2)
Mr. H. Gordon	(–)
Mr. O. A. Gorman	(3)
Mr. J. F. Henry	(4)
Mr. R. Irvine	(2)
Mr. J. T. Lamberton	(2)
Mr. J. Little	(3)
Mr. W. B. Loane	(–)
Mr. J. Marshall	(1)
Rev. R. J. McIlmoyle	(–)
Mr. W. Rankin	(3)
Mr. S. Shaw	(3)
Mr. H. E. Taylor	(4)
Mr. B. Wilson	(2)
Major W. Wilson	(1)

ULSTER WOOL GROWERS LTD.

Regd. Office: Muckamore, Co. Antrim.
Telephone: Antrim 2131.
Committee of Management:—
ANTRIM—R. A. C. Allen, J.P.; W. J. Crawford, M.B.E. DOWN—M.B.E., J.P.; Rev. R. J. McIlmoyle, W. A. Bell; I. F. Orr. ARMAGH—P. McCaffery; Major P. Terris. FERMANAGH—G. Rogers, J.P.; Major W. Wilson, M.B.E. (Chairman); S. F. W. T. Barton-Loane. TYRONE—J. A. Gamble; H. McMenamin; A. Wauchob LONDONDERRY—Allison Barr, J.P., R. A. Brown, J.P., O.B.E.
Manager and Secretary: W. L. Pullan.

May 1964

REV. R. J. McILMOYLE TO RETIRE

REV R. J. M'ILMOYLE, of Dervock, who has been a minister of the Reformed Presbyterian Church for over 60 years, is to request permission from the Northern Presbytery, meeting in Ballymoney next week, to retire.

Mr. M'Ilmoyle, who has spent most of his time as a minister in Dervock and will continue to reside there, is a native of the Limavady area.

On two occasions he has been Moderator.

For many years he was an Ulster Farmers' Union lecturer, and in that capacity visited most of the halls throughout the Province. Combining business with pleasure, Mr. M'Ilmoyle was probably the greatest comedian Ulster has ever produced, even though he usually confined his "acting" to occasions when he was addressing gatherings of farmers.

Farmers everywhere have been able to rely on the advice offered by Mr. M'Ilmoyle, realising that he had an immense amount of practical knowledge at his finger-tips.

As a sheep - breeder, his Border-Leicester flock has won more than 2,000 cups, medals and prizes. Those are remarkable figures, if only because the flock is the smallest in the British Isles comprising six ewes. Nevertheless, all the ewes are exceptionally well bred, as has been the case with their predecessors.

The Dervock flock has been exhibited at the principal shows in Northern Ireland and has won championships everywhere, including Balmoral.

Everyone will join me in wishing Mr. M'Ilmoyle every happiness in his well deserved rest from his duties as a Presbyterian minister, but I doubt if the Ulster Ram Breeders' Association would ever accept his resignation as secretary after his being so long in office.

Mr. and Mrs. M'Ilmoyle have a family of five—Mr. R. L. M'Ilmoyle, an engineer in London; Mr. Vincent M'Ilmoyle, who is manager of a bank at Limavady; Mrs. Mitchell, wife of a doctor at Omagh, Co. Tyrone, and Misses Elvena and Kathleen M'Ilmoyle, who are at college.

E. J. SLOAN

Dervock vacancy

Dervock congregation through the retirement of Rev. R. J. McIlmoyle are experiencing their first vacancy for 60 years. Dr. Hugh J. Blair, Ballymoney, will be in charge during the vacancy.

At Mr McIlmoyle's retirement on 18 May 1964 the following were the office bearers in Dervock :

Session—Rev. R. J. M'Ilmoyle (Moderator), James Lyons (Clerk), Robert M'Fall, James Simpson, Robert Bleakley, W. N. M'Conaghie, James Kerr, David Millar.

Committee—John Chestnutt, James Fleming, George Laverty, Robert Laverty, Josiah Lyons, S. B. M'Conaghie, Daniel M'Keeman, A. B. M'Keeman, Alex. M'Conaghie, Robert M'Alister, Craig Millar, Andrew Turtle, William Lyons, George Hunter, W. N. M'Conaghie (Secretary), Samuel M'Conaghie (Treasurer).

C.Y.P.S. meets on alternate Sabbath evenings at 7-30 p.m. President: Mr. Samuel M'Conaghie; Vice-President: Miss Sadie Kerr; Secretary: Miss Dorothy Kerr; Treasurer: Mr. William M'Keeman; Fifth Member: Mr. George Hunter.

W.M.A.—President: Mrs. M'Ilmoyle, R.P. Manse, Dervock; Vice-President: Mrs. James Kerr; Secretary: Mrs. Robert M'Fall, Ballygobbin, Ballymoney; Treasurer: Mrs. D. J. M'Keeman.

NOTICE.

A Public Meeting for the setting apart and commissioning of Mr. Joseph Kerr as Colporteur in connection with our Irish Mission will (D.V.) be held in **the Reformed Presbyterian Church, Dervock, on Tuesday, 11th August, 1964, commencing at 7.30 p.m.**

All welcome.

S. R. ARCHER (Convener).

COMMISSIONED FOR COLPORTAGE WORK IN DUBLIN

Mr. Joseph Kerr.

Irish Mission—At a well attended meeting held on 11th August, 1964, in Dervock R.P. Church, Mr. Joseph Kerr was commissioned as colporteur in connection with our Irish Mission. The Moderator of Synod, Rev. F. S. Leahy, presided and after praise, prayer and the reading of the Word, addressed the meeting emphasising the great need of evangelistic effort and the spread of the Scriptures in our land. The Convener of the Irish Mission Committee gave a brief historical narrative of our Mission and a statement of the events which led up to this commissioning. Rev. R. J. McIlmoyle, M.B.E., led in the commissioning prayer. Rev. A. R. Wright, B.A., addressed words of counsel and encouragement to the new colporteur. Mr. Kerr spoke of the steps by which he had been led to undertake the work of colportage, and asked for the prayers of the Church on his behalf. Rev. H. J. Blair, M.A., PH.D. (minister in charge of Dervock congregation), Mrs. Loughridge (President of the W.M. Union), Rev. R. B. Lyons, B.A. (minister of Limavady, Western Presbytery), and Rev. J. Blair (minister of Kilraughts congregation) to which congregation Mr. Kerr's family formerly belonged, expressed their own good wishes and the good wishes of those they represented to Mr. and Mrs. Kerr. At the close of the meeting a delightful supper was served by the ladies of Dervock congregation. Rev. S. M. Calderwood, M.A. (member of Irish Mission Committee) thanked the ladies on behalf of all present. The offering, which amounted to the splendid figure of £28 14s. 10d. was handed over entirely to our Irish Mission.

. . . . . —Mrs. R. W. McFall, representing the congregation of Dervock and friends, presented Rev. R. J. and Mrs. McIlmoyle with a substantial cheque, as a token of esteem, gratitude and affection, to mark Mr. McIlmoyle's retirement from the congregation of Dervock after more than sixty years of faithful and devoted service. This presentation was made at the meeting for Mr. Kerr's commissioning.

DERVOCK R.P. CHURCH

New Minister Ordained and Installed

Members of the Reformed Presbyterian Church from Monaghan, Cavan and Donegal, were included in the congregation at Dervock on Wednesday, when Rev. Robert Creane was ordained and installed as minister of the North Antrim congregation in succession to Rev. R. J. M'Ilmoyle.

Mr. M'Ilmoyle, well-known in the Reformed Presbyterian Church, and in farming circles, retired recently after sixty years' service in Dervock.

Mr. Crean, who was educated at Dundalk Grammar School and Trinity College, Dublin, also studied in the Reformed Presbyterian Church Theological Hall, Belfast. He is son of Mr. and Mrs. Wallace Crean, Castleblaney, County Monaghan.

The service in the church was conducted by Rev. A. R. Wright, Ballylaggan, Moderator of Presbytery, and the sermon was preached by Rev. Isaac Cole, Drimbolg. Other clergy who took part in the service were Rev. Thomas Donnelly, Ballyclabber; Rev. Professor Adam Loughridge (Portrush) Clerk of Presbytery; Rev. Robert Hanna, Newry; Rev. W. J. Gilmour, Cullybackey; and Rev. F. S. Leahy, Cregagh, Belfast.

Following the service guests were entertained at luncheon in the Holmes Memorial Hall, Ballymoney, when speeches of congratulations, greetings and welcome were made to the new minister.

In the course of his reply, Mr. Crean said that to stand firm in the face of opposition, persecution, and unpopularity because they were Bible believers, required loyalty and courage.

The need for preaching the Gospel with faithfulness and earnestness was urgent, and the need for revival was great.

An International Convention of Reformed Presbyterians was held in Portrush from 15th till 29th August to study the life and teaching of John Calvin the Reformer, and see how the Scriptural principles he re-discovered in his day are related to present day conditions.

Rev. Robert Harold Creane (centre) after his ordination and installation as minister of Dervock Reformed Presbyterian Church. On left is the former minister, Rev. R. J. M'Ilmoyle, and on right is Rev. Dr. Hugh Blair, who was in charge of the vacancy.

DERVOCK

REFORMED PRESBYTERIAN CHURCH

ORDINATION AND INSTALLATION

of

Mr. ROBERT HAROLD CREANE, B.A.

WEDNESDAY, 21st OCTOBER, 1964, at 12 Noon

FACT OR FICTION? As happens to most celebrities, even during their lifetime, legends grew up around RJ McIlmoyle. Amateur raconteurs would blithely attach his name to anecdotes with little or no regard as to whether they were factual or fictional. A good example of this genre is the tale of how he once 'addressed' a meeting. He is reported as having been asked to deliver the main speech at a certain gathering, but an inefficient or misdirected chairman had kept him waiting till almost the end of the programme, and then wearily introduced him with the words: "And now, Mr McIlmoyle, maybe you'll give us your address". "Certainly", replied RJ, stepping briskly up on to the platform. "My address is RP Manse, Dervock, County Antrim, and that's where I'm going now." And with that he disappeared through the door into the night. I had always accepted that as a genuine part of the RJ canon until I heard it related about another popular speaker in Pittsburgh, USA, in the year 1948. Another tale to be taken with the customary prescribed amount of saline condiment is the one which tells of RJ's challenging three commercial travellers to a story-telling contest. He offered to tell three stories to every one of theirs, and the four of them sat round a blazing fire in the small commercial hotel, swapping yarns in the ratio of three to one, from before midnight till after daybreak. This may be one of those incidents which stand on a basis of truth, but which have been honed and embellished by constant repetition till they bear little resemblance to the original reality.

There is, however, one extraordinary tale which I know to be true. It happened during one of RJ's very late homeward journeyings. These were regular occurrences, for he was in great demand as a speaker, especially at farmers' meetings, and there are few corners of the Province from which RJ did not set out for home, sometimes in a blizzard, around midnight or in the small hours. He drove the same car for many years, and his standard of driving was highly individualistic, to put it kindly! He did, however, have sense enough to pull over to the side of the road for a ten-minute nap when he began to feel drowsy, and many a policeman, over the years, after flashing his torch on the recumbent figure, went back to his colleague in the police-car muttering, "It's only RJ McIlmoyle, having a rest". Anyway, travelling home in the small hours, one winter's night, he passed through a small hamlet somewhere in the Sperrins. About two miles farther along the road he felt the arms of Morpheus gently enfolding him; so he did the customary wise thing and pulled over to the side of the road for a nap. Greatly refreshed after a few minutes, he tried to start the car again, to resume his homeward journey, but the engine refused to fire. Fearing that if he pressed the self-starter too much the battery would fail, he got out and walked the two miles back to the village seeking help. Alas, the sleep of those good folk of the village was so sweet and so sound that he couldn't arouse any of them. Realising that there was nothing for it but to spend the night in the car, he walked the two miles back. Before settling himself as comfortably as possible, he resolved to have one more try at starting the car. So he switched on the ignition and pressed the starter. The engine burst into life immediately. It was only then that he realised that, after awakening from his sleep, he had been trying to start the car without having turned on the ignition! (The modern ignition-key starter would make this error impossible nowadays.) I had long been suspicious that this story was just another fairy-tale, so one time, over a dinner-table, I took the opportunity of relating it to him and then

Rev. R. J. M'Ilmoyle

The Rev. R. J. M'Ilmoyle, of Dervock, Co. Antrim, received a great welcome at the Ulster Farmers' Union dinner at Dunmurry.

After a round of handshakes Mr. M'Ilmoyle, who has just recovered from illness, heard glowing tributes paid to his work for Ulster agriculture and the Farmers' Union with which he has been associated for many years.

Mr. A. G. Algeo, president, said that Mr. M'Ilmoyle, who is also a noted prize-winner with his Border Leicester sheep, was a stalwart of the union and also a "tower of strength."

Mr. John Martin and others joined in tributes to Mr. M'Ilmoyle.

Changes

The Rev. R. J. M'Ilmoyle, of Dervock (left), a foundation member of the Ulster Farmers' Union, pictured with Canon C. H. Walsh, of Groomsport, at the U.F.U. dinner.

Rev RJ McIlmoyle was seated at top table (top right hand corner in photograph).

Some of the congregation of Dervock Reformed Presbyterian Church at the reception following the ordination and installation of the new minister asking him, point blank, if this was true. "Yes", he replied, "that is true in every detail, just as you have told it."

It would be a gross injustice to the memory of RJ McIlmoyle to think of him only, or even principally, as a teller of funny stories. He was, of course, unsurpassed in this field, and how one often wishes that some of the purveyors of smut who pollute the airwaves today could be transported back in time to see and hear him in full spate. They could learn valuable lessons from him in the science of making people laugh heartily and uninhibitedly at clean, straightforward humour, totally free from the dirty-mindedness or the leery innuendoes and double meanings with which most of today's comedians insult their audiences. But laughter for laughter's sake was never his chief aim. He was, first and last, a minister of the Gospel, and it was the preparation and delivery of sermons which commanded his best mental and oratorical abilities. The humour was more in the nature of a hobby and a relaxation, strictly for the secular occasion, but often getting in shafts of wisdom and moral lessons which lodged in the hearts and minds of his hearers, even while they laughed.

In these days of public address systems, voice projection is a dying art. RJ's tone of voice and articulation of syllables were such that he came across clearly, even in huge, packed halls. He invariably sat in the back left-hand pew in our Grosvenor Road Church during meetings of Synod, and, when he spoke, he left no-one in any doubt as to what he was saying. This was not true of all the members of Synod. There was one minister in particular whose tones were so gentle that he could scarcely be understood five pews away from where he was standing. One evening, this man, in a speech from the front of the church, proposed a motion which was heard only by those in his immediate vicinity. RJ chose an original way of pointing out this shortcoming. He sprang to his feet with alacrity. "Mr Moderator", he said, "I want to second that motion. Mind you, I wasn't able to make out one word of what was said, but I did hear the general tone of voice in which it was said and it sounded like something I would agree with." This wasn't the only occasion on which RJ was bothered by the acoustics at Synod. After he had complained of not being able to hear speakers two or three times on one particular evening, the Moderator, at the end of his patience, said rather testily, "Mr McIlmoyle, if you have any difficulty in hearing, why don't you come up nearer the front?" RJ replied without hesitation, "Mr Moderator, this meeting of Synod was advertised in the press as taking place in this building at a certain time. I came at the appointed hour. I am inside the building. I have a right to expect to be able to hear what is going on, irrespective of where I choose to sit. You at the front can hear me without any difficulty. I am not suffering from any degree of deafness; so I should be able to hear you and the other speakers at the front." There was no reply.

RJ McIlmoyle's age was always something of a mystery, and it was only after his death that it was firmly established. He claimed, indeed, not to be too sure of it himself." If you want to live long", he would say, "forget all about your age. Don't count your birthdays. Have nothing to do with birthday greetings or cards." He had another recipe for longevity which came to light one evening as he was taking High Tea in the Trocadero restaurant in Portrush. The waitress placed before him a mouth-watering plate of golden-brown chips and milky white cod in breadcrumbs. He ate about half the contents of the plate and pushed the rest aside. "What's wrong?", someone asked. "Isn't it properly cooked?" "It's

R.P. CHURCH TRIBUTE TO REV. R. J. M'ILMOYLE

Presbytery's Special Minute

THE Northern Presbytery of the Reformed Presbyterian Church, meeting in Ballymoney on Wednesday under the chairmanship of the Moderator, Rev. A. R. Wright, placed on record their appreciation of the outstanding service rendered over a period of sixty years by Rev. R. J. M'Ilmoyle, M.B.E., who retired as minister of Dervock R.P. congregation in May last.

Mr. M'Ilmoyle was present at the meeting to hear the following special minute recorded in the records of the Presbytery.

"The Northern Presbytery puts on record its appreciation of the distinguished service rendered during the past 60 years by Rev. R. J. M'Ilmoyle. M.B.E. Mr. M'Ilmoyle entered the Presbytery on the 31st August, 1904 when he was installed pastor of Dervock Congregation. He retired from the active duty of the ministry on the 18th May, 1964.

"Endowed with a keen mind and a brilliant gift of speech, Mr. M'Ilmoyle was a faithful and effective preacher of The Word. His style was unique, his application of the truth pointed and forceful, and his appeal to young and old, fresh and arresting.

Untiring Devotion

"He was untiring in his devotion to his pastoral work. He had a wonderful human touch, and with equal facility, rejoiced with his people in days of gladness and brought them the full consolation of the Gospel and the comfort of his personal sympathy in the dark hours of sorrow.

"Mr. M'Ilmoyle, as one 'who ne'er had changed, nor wished to change his place,' held an honoured position in the whole community. His public services ranged over a wide field, and it is certain that no minister of the Covenanting Church in any generation was better known. It was a fitting climax to a life of outstanding service when Her Majesty the Queen invested him with the dignity of Member of the Most Honourable Order of the British Empire.

The Synod has no better servant. A master in the art of debate, he was able to grasp a situation quickly and resolve a problem by his keen assessment of what was truly worthwhile. He served on numerous Committees of Synod and has had the most remarkable distinction of acting as Moderator of the centenary Synod in 1911 and of the ter-jubilee Synod half a century later, both in Cullybackey.

Without Parrallel

"The Presbytery is pleased to take special account of his services as a member of Court. On one occasion only in 60 years, when in hospital in November, 1963, did he fail to attend a meeting of Presbytery—a record that is possibly without parallel. He bore a full share of Presbyterial activities, and as Clerk of Presbytery for more than 33 years, he was a wise leader and counsellor and most efficient in directing the business of the Court. His brethren found him a willing helper in every time of need, and he travelled widely to supply vacant congregations and to assist ministers laid aside by sickness. He was a welcome preacher in the congregations of the Presbytery and on many occasions addressed congregation social meetings in his own inimitable way.

Presbytery; is gratified that he Mr M'Ilmoyle remains within its bounds and that he has been privileged to see his successor ordained in Dervock church, is gratified that he has recovered a measure of health and prays that he, and Mrs M'Ilmoyle, who has supported him so faithfully in all his work, may enjoy a blessed eventide in retirement."

delicious", he replied, "but that's about all I eat of any meal." He then went on to deliver another nugget of wisdom which was surely validated by his own length of days: "If you want to live long, eat little".

The Rev RJ McIlmoyle preached his first sermon as a student here in Ballyclabber, and his long career as a public speaker ended in the same church when he was principal guest at the annual congregational social on Friday, 8 January 1965, just about four months before his death. Congregational socials were more prestigious events in those days than now, as is shown by the presence of many visiting ministers on this historic occasion. An excerpt from the report of the meeting in the *Covenanter Witness* of February 1965 sets the scene. Visiting ministers who addressed the meeting and brought the greetings of their respective congregations were the Revs AR Wright BA (Ballylaggan); R Creane BA (Dervock); WN McCune BA (Faughan); I Cole BA (Drimbolg); and Prof A Loughridge MA, M Litt (Portrush). There was a special welcome for the Rev RJ McIlmoyle MBE. The Moderator of the Northern Presbytery, the Rev AR Wright, expressed Presbytery's gratification at Mr McIlmoyle's good recovery from his recent lengthy indisposition. Mr McIlmoyle addressed the meeting in his own inimitable and entertaining way. But what the official report doesn't record, and what I, as chairman, remember vividly, was that he could climb on to the platform only with great difficulty and that while he spoke he had to steady himself against the table and the piano. But the fire still burned. The wit and the wisdom shone forth, underlined and made the more memorable by the anecdotes, and his last audience was as appreciative of him as any in his long career. For RJ McIlmoyle's success as a humourist was due, largely, to his ability to hold a mirror up before the people of Ulster and let them see themselves, with all their quirks and idiosyncrasies. And they laughed at what they saw. He was the product of a kindlier, less sophisticated generation, which found its entertainment in the ways and the words of its neighbours and not in an electronic talking-box. We shall hardly look on, or hear, his like again.

RJ usually ended his speeches with one of two monologues which he made his own over the years. One was "The Old Violin" and the other was "The Train Driver". The last lines of each of these monologues could well sum up his message to the world as a preacher of the Gospel and his service to his fellow-man, as he instructed and entertained them with his wisdom and his humour. Of the preacher, it could be said that he showed "the worth of a soul, and the change that is wrought by the touch of the Master's hand". Of the travelling speaker, it could be said: "A good run, Sir, a very good run!" **Tom Donnelly, Ballyclabber Manse**

A VERY GOOD RUN

Mrs Jean McCooke, 10 Fisherwick Gardens, Ballymena, wife of Steve the former athlete, recalls that her uncle, James Sharkey, lived in the house and farm owned by the former athlete, Kennedy McArthur, not far from Dervock. That uncle bought the Rev RJ McIlmoyle's car after he passed away in 1965. It was an old white Austin A40. William Sharkey, only son of James, now owns that same farm.

On Friday 5 February 1965 the Rev RJ returned to his home church, Broad Lane, Limavady, for what was probably the last occasion.

Limavady R.P. congregation's tributes to pastor and his wife

THE Reformed Presbyterian congregation of Limavady held the annual business and social meeting on Friday evening last week when the Crawford Hall was filled with members and children and friends. Rev R. B Lyons, pastor of the congregation, presided.

Reports of the past year's work were presented—From the Session by Mr. J. W. M'Cloy; from the Committee by Messrs. Jas Haslett and James Blair; from the Repair and Building Fund by Mr. Marcus M'Collum; from the W.M.A. by Mrs. A. Blair and Mrs. J. W. M'Cloy; from the J.M.B. by Miss Willis Allen and Mrs. E. Fallows; and from the C.Y.P. Society and the Sabbath School by the chairman.

The reports, which contained many encouraging features, were cordially adopted.

Several additional members were appointed to the Committee, and it was decided to increase the pastor's salary for the coming year.

Completed 40 years

At this point it was proposed that Mr. Lyons should vacate the chair and that the congregational treasurer, Mr. James Blair, should take his place. Mr. Blair explained that their minister had completed 40 years as pastor of the congregation in October 1964. It had been felt that they should mark the occasion in a tangible way, and the proposal had been taken up very heartily by the members and friends.

Mr. John M'Cloy, clerk of Session, testified to the esteem in which Mr. and Mrs. Lyons were held in the congregation He spoke with appreciation of Mr. Lyon's pulpit ministrations and his faithful visitation of the sick and aged.

Mr. Alfred Blair spoke in the same vein about Mr. Lyons' pastoral work and the happy relationships in the congregation and presented him with a wallet of notes.

Mrs. M. Allen presented Mrs. Lyons with a bouquet of flowers. Tribute was paid to Mrs. Lyons for her interest in Mission work and in the children of the Sabbath School.

Mrs Lyons replied, thanking all the speakers for their kind references to her. The presentation had been a well-kept secret and had come as a complete surprise to Mr. Lyons and herself. She thanked them for the spirited efforts they had made in building a hall and a manse, for missionary sale and lately in gathering funds for a sexton's house. She also expressed appreciation of the help received from many good friends.

Mr. Lyons spoke of the happiness of his 40 years' ministry among them and the harmony that had prevailed in the congregation. He paid tribute to the office-bearers past and present with whom he had worked and to their interest in the well-being of the congregation. He thanked the speakers for their words of appreciation of his work and their good wishes for the future.

The chairman read apologies from Rev. R. A. Watson, Londonderry, and Rev. James Blair, Kilraughts, a former member of the congregation.

Congratulations

Congratulatory speeches were delivered by Rev. R. W. Lyttle, Stranorlar, Moderator of Presbytery, Rev. W. N. M'Cune, Londonderry, and Rev. J. W. Calderwood, Bready, who had been a fellow-student with Mr. Lyons and had been ordained in the same month.

A special welcome was given to Rev. R. J. M'Ilmoyle, retired minister of Dervock and a former member of Limavady, and he joined in the congratulations.

Mrs. Greta M'Ilmoyle apoligised for the absence of her husband, Rev. Professor M'Ilmoyle Belfast (both of them former members) and added her tribute to Mr. and Mrs. Lyons.

Messrs. A. F. M'Ilmoyle, Belfast, also a former member, and Vincent M'Ilmoyle expressed their congratulations

Dr. S. M. Lyons voiced the appreciation of his sisters and himself for the tribute the congregation had paid to his mother and father.

A delicious supper was provided by the ladies. A programme of songs and recitations was presented by the children of the two Sabbath schools and some other young friends. A junior choir trained by the precentor, Mrs. W. M'Collum, rendered several items.

A large number of Sabbath School prizes were distributed and after a cordial vote of thanks to all contributors and helpers a happy meeting was brought to an end with the Benediction.

One of the best known figures in Ulster agriculture for more than half a century, the Rev. R. J. M'Ilmoyle, former minister of Dervock Reformed Presbyterian Church, died on Tuesday at the Route Hospital, Ballymoney.

Mr. M'Ilmoyle, who was famed for his expression, "Nobody knows my age, not even myself," had a distinguished career both as a clergyman and an agriculturist. He held a unique church record by constituting the 100th and 150th meetings of the Synod as Moderator on both occasions.

As a farmer, he was a founder member of the Ulster Farmers' Union and secretary of the Ram Breeders' Association.

He took a leading part in organising the Farmers' Union and devoted much of his time and service to the formation of branches throughout the Province.

Mr. M'Ilmoyle, a native of Limavady, was ordained in Ballyclare Reformed Presbyterian Church in September, 1900. After a brief ministry at Ballyclare he was called to Dervock and installed there in August, 1905. Despite frequent invitations to join other congregations he spent most of his life at Dervock. He was often in demand as a preacher on special occasions.

In 1911 he was Moderator of the Synod at its 100th anniversary and was again installed to this high office at the 150th Synod in 1961.

Mr M'Ilmoyle had few equals as a storyteller and was always in demand to speak at functions.

He had many interests and activities outside the Church. One of the best known breeders of Border Leicester sheep in the British Isles, he had a long and distinguished career as an exhibitor. His sheep won for him more than 2,000 cups, medals and rosettes.

He was the only surviving honorary member of the Ulster Farmers' Union, for which body he kept up a heavy programme of lectures.

He was awarded an M.B.E. for his services to Northern Ireland agriculture in 1960.

Often described as the busiest clergyman in Ulster, Mr. M'Ilmoyle was a judge, breeder, lecturer and a leader of the Co-operative movement in Dervock.

Mr. M'Ilmoyle is survived by his wife, Louise.

GARVAGH U.F.U.'s SYMPATHY

The members of Garvagh Branch Ulster Farmers' Union mourn the passing of Rev. R. J. M'Ilmoyle, M.B.E., Dervock, who was a staunch friend. He was president of the branch for a time. Last February he attended the annual social of the branch and entertained the members with his many humorous stories, as he had done on many occasions before.

Mr. M'Ilmoyle was particularly interested in the Garvagh branch and was greatly disappointed if he was not able to attend the annual social.

The sympathy of the branch is extended to his widow and family.

The funeral took place to Ballymoney Cemetery on Thursday following a service in Dervock Reformed Presbyterian Church.

OBITUARY.

REV. R. J. McILMOYLE, M.B.E.

VETERAN NORTH ANTRIM CLERGYMAN

Death of Rev. R. J. McIlmoyle

The following is a summary of the address given at the funeral service by Prof. A. Loughridge:

"The Rev. R. J. McIlmoyle was a man of whom we may fittingly use the words spoken by David of Abner: 'Know ye not that there is a prince and a great man fallen this day in Israel?' For he was a prince among men; great, not after the trivial standards of a fickle world, but great in the possession and use of gifts that were spiritual and enduring.

He loved to be known as a son of the soil. It was in his blood from boyhood. He loved it all through his long life, and a kindly farming community at Dervock gave him a perfect setting for an illustrious ministry. It was a ministry unique in the history of the Church. Among its many distinctions we mention that it was the longest ministry exercised by a Covenanting minister, it was the longest in one congregation; no one else occupied the Moderator's chair twice with an interval of 50 years between; and it is surely without parallel that he did not miss a meeting of the Presbytery until he had entered the 64th year of his ministry.

But while these things are worthy of note they are not the standards by which his life's work is to be measured. He had the right emphasis on the things that really mattered. The advice that he so often gave to others on the care of sheep was a fine illustration of his outlook on life. "Keep a few," he would say, "and keep them good." It was quality and not quantity, on which he placed the emphasis. And this was true of all the service that he rendered to his fellow men. The Congregation of Dervock expressed its appreciation of this service many times. The Ulster Farmers' Union recognised its worth. And the quality of his service was fittingly rewarded when Her Majesty the Queen invested him with the dignity of Member of the Most Honourable Order of the British Empire.

It is our privilege to recall that he was first and foremost "a good minister of Jesus Christ." In whatever sphere we assess his work, it stands the test. In public life, he was a Christian minister all the time. Through his hobby, he reached thousands, and commended the Christian Faith and the principles of the Covenanting Church in a wide circle.

In the Courts of the Church he was a wise counsellor and loyal colleague. A master in the art of debate, he was able to grasp a situation quickly and to resolve a problem by his keen assessment of what was really worthwhile. The Synod had no better servant; a minister of the Church had no better friend.

In the pastoral care of his people he showed untiring devotion. His association with them in joy or in sorrow revealed the true human touch. When he led them in worship he lifted them to the heights in the fervency of his prayers and applied the truth to their hearts in a pointed and fearless manner that arrested old and young alike.

He was a prince of orators. We shall remember gratefully his glorious voice that roused an audience as few could do with a story brilliantly told ; a glorious voice that thrilled the Synod with its vibrant tones and resolute appeal ; a voice that filled this house so often and so faithfully with a well-reasoned presentation of the everlasting gospel of the grace of God. There are those who would say that some of his best sermons were given on the public platform when, after he had made his audience to rock with laughter, he brought his address to a close with a moral and a challenge that was pointedly and personally applied.

I feel that there is no better summary of his life than the words that were so often the climax of a brilliant speech—the words of the railway director to the faithful engine-driver : "A good run sir, a very good run."

The sympathy of the whole church is extended to his sorrowing widow who was his worthy partner for more than 60 years, to his two sons and three daughters, to his brothers and sisters, and to all the family circle.

Services of thanksgiving Rev. R. J. McIlmoyle were held on Sabbath, 23rd May. At the morning service Rev. R. H. Creane paid tribute to Mr. McIlmoyle and expressed the sympathy of the whole congregation to his widow and family. In the evening the church was filled to overflowing when Rev. Prof. Loughridge delivered an inspiring and elevating message.

McILMOYLE—May 18, 1965, at the Route Hospital, Ballymoney, the Rev. Robert John McIlmoyle, M.B.E., dearly-loved husband of Matilda Louise, and former Minister of Dervock Reformed Presbyterian Church. Service in Reformed Presbyterian Church to-morrow (Thursday), at 2-30 p.m., followed by interment in Ballymoney Cemetery. House private. Very deeply regretted.

M'ILMOYLE—The congregation of Dervock Reformed Presbyterian Church regret the passing of their former minister, Rev. R. J. M'Ilmoyle, M.B.E., and offer their deepest sympathy to his sorrowing wife and family.
(Signed)
JAMES LYONS, Clerk.
W. NORMAN M'CONAGHIE, Secretary.

A SPECIAL SERVICE

In memory of the late Rev. R. J. M'Ilmoyle, M.B.E.

to be held (D.V.) in

DERVOCK REFORMED PRESBYTERIAN CHURCH

On SABBATH EVENING, 23rd MAY

At 8 p.m.

Conducted by Rev. R. H. CREANE, B.A., present minister of above Church. Special Speaker: Rev. Prof. A. LOUGHRIDGE, M.A., M.Litt.

Everyone cordially welcome

THE FIRST OF MANY CONTACTS I first saw the Rev RJ McIlmoyle in 1922 when he came to our home. He was Chairman of the North Antrim Milk Recording Association, and, in company with the Secretary, Samuel Killen, was collecting samples of milk to be tested for butter fat content. In this service he showed what was to be a life-long concern for the well-being of the farming community and his desire to improve the quality of the products they provided. That was the first of many contacts that I had with him throughout the rest of his life.

I owe a great deal to Mr McIlmoyle for his advice and encouragement. He was a member of a Committee of the Northern Presbytery that interviewed students and recommended them for acceptance as candidates for the ministry. I recall the warmth and the enthusiasm with which he recommended that Alex Barkley and I should be taken under Presbytery's care. He maintained a close personal interest in our progress. When I returned to the Northern Presbytery as minister of Portrush congregation in 1950 he immediately proposed that I should succeed him as Clerk of Presbytery. In June 1950 he nominated me for the office of Clerk of Synod and in 1957 it was on his proposal that I was appointed by Synod to the Chair of Church History & Pastoral Theology in the Theological Hall. During my ministry in Portrush he was a regular guest at the annual business and social meeting of the congregation. His words of encouragement and exciting humorous speeches are still remembered. He would sometimes phone me and say, "I'll be having tea with my son Vincent this evening. You have had a busy day. I'll take your evening service." I should add that Vincent was our efficient congregational treasurer and a close personal friend.

Reference has been made elsewhere in this book to the Rev RJ's brilliance as a story-teller. He had a little notebook to remind him of the sequence in his stories, but all it contained was a list of words linked by a number of arrows. Each story was told in the fewest possible words. I sat beside him on one occasion when a man, proposing a vote of thanks, told a story and suggested that Mr McIlmoyle might add it to his repertoire. When he was about half way through, Mr McIlmoyle whispered to me, "Far too long"! Mr Harry West, a Minister of Agriculture in the former Stormont regime, knew him well. During Mr West's term as President of the Ulster Farmers' Union he heard him tell the same stories again and again at different meetings. But they were always fresh and he laughed at each one as though he had never heard it before. Mr McIlmoyle never laughed at his own jokes. They were told with a grim seriousness and his punch-line was delivered with perfect timing. In the Courts of the Church he rarely took part in the general debate. He listened while others expressed a variety of opinions and made a number of propositions. Then in a single sentence he would sum up the whole situation and lay a foundation for progress. He was never idle. A favourite statement of his was: "If you want a job done, ask a busy man; the other fellow has no time to do it". He was a practical man. "Service", he would say, "is the rent you pay for the space you occupy." He was very well known, making friends easily and keeping them with loyalty. He did not suffer fools gladly and in a few words could demolish an awkward opponent. A well-documented story illustrates this. At a meeting at which he was guest of honour, the programme was marred by endless petty speeches. When called to give his address as midnight approached, he stunned his audience and taught ineffective chairmen a salutary lesson when he said, "My address is Dervock, County Antrim, and I'm going there right now". The Rev RJ was a family man. All of his children made their mark in their chosen careers and he was proud of their achievements. Commenting on the occasion when, as a small boy, his son Lewis, fell from the train between Dervock and Ballycastle, he said, "It's his first venture into railway engineering".

A kindly Providence took care of the Rev RJ on his own many late-night journeys in the interests of farmers. His patience was sometimes sorely tested when, in remote parts of the Province, he would arrive first and find the caretaker opening the hall and lighting the fire. Of such places he would say, "I would have been time enough the next day"! It was my privilege to chair the meeting held to celebrate the 60th anniversary of his ordination at which a happy people in Dervock paid high tribute to his eloquent preaching, his compassionate pastoral care and his notable standing in the community. When the end of a long and useful life came, I had the sad experience and yet the great privilege of taking part in his funeral service and shortly afterwards to preach to a crowded congregation at a special memorial and thanksgiving service. My text, from Revelation 14:13, summed up his life of devoted service: "Blessed are the dead which die in the Lord from henceforth. Yea, saith the Spirit, that they may rest from their labours; and their works do follow them."

Adam Loughridge, Portrush

MINUTE ON THE DEATH OF
REV. R. J. McILMOYLE, M.B.E.

THE Synod of the Reformed Presbyterian Church of Ireland with sorrow and deep sense of loss records the death of the Rev. R. J. McIlmoyle, M.B.E., who, after a prolonged period of weakness, entered into his rest on the 18th May, 1965.

Mr. McIlmoyle was brought up in connection with the congregation of Limavady, where his family have borne an honoured name for generations. In early years he heard the call of God to the ministry of the Gospel and with the ready response that marked his whole life, he laid all his fine gifts on the altar of service.

He received his education at Magee College, Derry, and the Theological Hall, Belfast, and was licensed to preach the Gospel by the Western Presbytery in 1900. On the 6th September, 1900, he was ordained to the office of the gospel ministry and installed pastor of the congregation of Ballyclare. Four years later, on the 31st August, he was installed pastor of Dervock congregation. Though frequently called to serve in other spheres, he elected to remain the minister of Dervock until his retirement on the 18th May, 1964.

Mr. McIlmoyle was a preacher of unusual ability. Blessed with a wonderful voice and the capacity to hold an audience, he thrilled his hearers with his faithful and well-reasoned presentations of the Gospel of the grace of God. He possessed an outstanding gift for story-telling and he used this medium on the public platform to emphasise a moral and present a challenge that was pointedly and personally applied.

In his pastoral work, he was beloved by young and old. A true man among men, he could share the joys and sorrows of his people with equal facility. In his visitation of the people, he was frequently accompanied by Mrs. McIlmoyle, who shared all his work so nobly and courageously in their long life together.

In his public life, Mr. McIlmoyle showed a genius for friendship, gifts for leadership, and a deep sense of responsibility. The Co-operative movement and the Ulster Farmers' Union benefited from his devoted work. He was frequently honoured by his fellowmen, and the quality of his service was fittingly rewarded when her Majesty the Queen invested him with the dignity of Member of the Most Honourable Order of the British Empire.

In the Courts of the Church he was a wise counsellor and loyal colleague. With consummate skill in debate he could impress the Court and win support for his viewpoint. His was the unique distinction of acting as Moderator twice with an interval of half a century between. His services were greatly appreciated in the Committees of Synod and in some of these he established long-service records. He served the Congregational Aid Fund for fifty-nine years, the Colonial Mission Committee for fifty-seven years, the Ministers' Sick Benefit Fund Committee for forty-five years, and was a member of the Board of Synod's Trustees for thirty-five years. He acted as Clerk of the Northern Presbytery for thirty-three years. This notable record of faithful service is gratefully remembered by the Synod and by the whole Church.

The sympathy of the Synod is extended to Mrs. McIlmoyle, to the two sons and three daughters and to all the family circle.

Respectfully submitted,

ADAM LOUGHRIDGE, *Convener*.

ACCORDING TO DERVOCK FOLK There seems to be a consensus that it is a great pity that such an illustrious figure as the Rev RJ McIlmoyle should pass from the scene with almost no written record left to perpetuate his memory. This has often been on my mind and this brief contribution may clear my conscience to some extent, as it may stimulate others to recall what they remember. How one wishes that they might record from the archives of memory at least some of his proverbs, his deep thoughts and sayings. Those often used in his preaching helped to fix in memory the point being driven home. My earliest recollections of the Rev RJ McIlmoyle seem to be of his coming to our hall-door on a winter's afternoon on pastoral visitation. He was always accompanied by an elder and they would be clad in hats and winter overcoats. I can remember so clearly his dark piercing eyes, his moustache and his glasses. Mother would have a good fire going in the parlour, as it was then called, and the wind always seemed to whistle around the house. The pastoral visit of the Rev McIlmoyle was brief, as he was never one to dawdle on any matter, social or otherwise. He always read from the Scriptures and to do so removed his glasses to his forehead. Prayer followed and here he excelled. He sometimes used the expression, "As a man speaks with his friend", and he seemed on excellent terms with the One with whom he communed. Who that remembers hearing him in prayer by a graveside will ever forget it? If time permitted or the need required, a cup of tea would be served, but the visitors were soon on their way again, as their itinerary was closely packed. It is perhaps in the pulpit that those of us who were his hearers for so long best remember him, especially at a Communion season. Who could forget with what solemnity and reverential awe he led us up the holy hill of Communion, "To a feast of fat things, a feast of wines on the lees, of fat things full of marrow, of wines on the lees well refined" (Is 25:6)?

On occasion the Rev McIlmoyle and his wife would just drop in unheralded and unannounced and share what was on the table for supper. I think that was how they liked it. When tea was served, a white handkerchief was produced from his inside pocket and given a brief flick over his face. I believe that in that flick his false teeth were removed, but, were I in a court of law, under oath, I could not swear that this was so; but, if it were, the dentures were replaced with the same unobtrusive dexterity, when the repast was over. The only clue to this being the case was what one might call a hist in his speech. I remember on one such occasion Mrs McIlmoyle coming in the back door and, without stopping, saying "I want to see your garden" and walking right on through and out the front door. Her comment on one particular flower, the marigold, was "It's just a glorified weed". In my mind's eye I can see her sitting by our parlour fireside, a frail figure with her white hair and bright blue eyes. It was with pride and joy that she would tell us of a new bride or a new baby in the congregation and one remembers the distinctive way in which she pronounced that word "baby". I always thought that there was something almost regal about her. I believe that our daughter Hazel was the only one of our family to have had the honour of being nursed by her. After Mrs McIlmoyle had her accident, she still continued to visit and I can still feel her cling tenaciously to my arm for support as we would assist her to and from the car. I can remember our own Clerk of Session, Mr RJ Bleakly, refer to her incapacity at a church meeting in these words, "She bore a heavy burden with Christian fortitude". I think we might say of her as the famous broadcaster and radio announcer John Snagge said when announcing the death of the late Queen Mary, "And so we mourn the passing of a great and gracious lady".

Mr McIlmoyle said that on his leaving home to go to college for the first time, "My mother was in a terrible way. My father on the other hand was calm and seemingly unperturbed, but, as he drove me to the station, I saw a tear roll down his cheek." He also told how he had stayed at Ballyclabber manse on one occasion, probably in his student days. On the Sabbath afternoon Professor Houston, who was then the minister, went to his room for a time and when he came forth again his face shone with the glory of Heaven. I believe that it was these social calls and visits throughout the congregation that endeared the McIlmoyles so much to us. They seemed to enjoy these visits themselves as much as did those whom they visited and many an evening was spent in this way to the mutual benefit of all concerned. Going back to memories of the tea-table, the Rev RJ had a manner of cutting off small portions of soda scone and buttering each one individually, before transferring it to his mouth. He was not one to eat a big meal and he often said that he liked to leave the table wanting a little more. He also said that what he left did him more good than what he ate. My mother would usually have something to give them as they left, farm produce of some sort, butter, eggs, etc. Once she gave them duck eggs and fadge and someone of our family commented that the Rev RJ had preached with more than usual eloquence on the following Sabbath. Many of us have happy memories of such occasions.

Some will remember the Rev RJ McIlmoyle best for his powers in the show ring. He bred and showed Pedigree Dairy Shorthorn cattle, Border Leicester sheep and, I believe, even goats. I have been told that there was an occasion when he stood in for someone else to speak about goats. The chairman of the meeting, in introducing him, said that it was good of him to do so, since perhaps his knowledge of goats was limited. When he was permitted to take the floor, any fears of his knowledge of the species were quickly dispelled. To quote the narrator, "Man, he could hardly sit". Generally when the Rev RJ came to the platform he had a tendency to rearrange the seating. I never knew him to use a microphone, unless, of course, when he was broadcasting on the radio, as he did on many occasions. I wonder what his rejoinder would have been, should any committee member have had the audacity to suggest that we install a public address system in the church for his benefit. He certainly did not need it. His diction and clarity of speech were unexcelled. Had he missed a word when he was reading the Scriptures, his command of English was such that he had the ability to rearrange the wording, so that the sense was unaltered and, had one not been following the reading closely or not been well versed in the passage, it would have passed entirely unnoticed.

He once said with reference to us all being different, "When God made me, He broke the mould". No-one would question that statement. It was once said of someone, "We shall never see his like again". It certainly applies here. He was known far and wide, not only as a preacher, but as a speaker and representative of the Ulster Farmers' Union and he travelled many miles on winter nights, often in the blackout during the Second World War, and in all weathers, to be present and not disappoint anyone. His presence on a public platform was always eagerly anticipated and much appreciated. He possessed an ability to take his audience to the heights of mirth and ecstasy and yet ever to end on the serious note and turn their thoughts towards more serious things. Many will remember him give a rendering of "The Old Violin". He said on one occasion that he did not judge a Christian so much by the length of his face as by the breadth of it. At times, and as occasion may prompt, there come to mind some of his stories and quaint sayings, but if one sat down to recall them offhand it would be difficult. Here are just a few. "One man is as good as another until he makes himself worse." "The hill always seems steeper when you are late." "Dead fish go with the stream; live ones swim against it." Referring to man as being like marble in the sculptor's studio, "It is the sharp-edged tools that cut the fine lines". "Every wrinkle on the brow, every ache and pain, every funeral bell that tolls reminds us that we pass by sufferance and not by right." On conviction of sin: "When man sees himself as God sees him, a sinner in His sight, then truly he must be of all men most miserable".

On one particular Sabbath towards the end of his ministry, he was present at the service, but someone else had been the preacher (I don't remember who it was). By this time his health was failing and he was feeling the weakness and frailty of the flesh. After the service he went to the front of the church, laid his hand on the post at the end of a seat and addressed the congregation. He referred to the forthcoming Communion season and his physical weakness. He said, "I felt I couldn't do it, I just couldn't do it". Need I say that not every eye in that gathering was dry? On one occasion I asked him his opinion of hymns. This, may I say, was when I was quite young and not so soundly founded or grounded in the Reformed faith. His reply, "I would rather have a good secular song than a trashy hymn that teaches error". I certainly have never had any cause to question his judgment. His standards of integrity and uprightness and honesty were impeccable. On one occasion my father-in-law purchased a Border Leicester ram from him to use for one year and sell again. The Rev RJ told him, "If you don't get your own money for him when you sell him, I'll make up the difference". The ram was sold and didn't make the purchase price. The Rev RJ must have been present at the sale because a cheque for the difference came to my father-in-law through the post. "He honoureth and changeth not, though to his hurt he swear" (Ps 15:4). On one occasion, at a meeting of the Border Leicester Society, when judges for the forthcoming agricultural shows were being discussed, the name of a certain prospective judge was suggested and he said, "I am secretary of the Society and I shall be writing to him and he may come, but, if he does, there will be people get prizes that never got them before".

The Rev RJ had a neighbour who, I understand, had lived next door to him in Dervock. He was Johnnie McGrotty, one of the characters of the district of whom many humorous stories are told, but the Rev RJ said, "If there was anything wrong in my byre, he was in it before I was". The Rev RJ once said, "A lop-sided thing always looks ugly". He certainly was not lop-sided. His interests were wide and varied and he left behind, to a very wide circle of people, many happy memories. He was as well-known in parts of Scotland, to the Howies and by the side of a Sale Ring in Lanark, as he was in Dervock. Of him it truly may be said, "The memory of the just is blessed" (Proverbs 10:7). **George A Hunter (elder)**

I first met the Rev RJ McIlmoyle on the occasion of my wedding in December 1936. I was a Presbyterian and my late husband was a member of the RP Church in Dervock. The Rev McIlmoyle assisted at the wedding and at the reception. In the course of his speech he referred to the fact that the bridegroom that day had freedom of choice in his bride, but that Edward VIII had not. It was just at

In Portrush: Rev RJ McIlmoyle, Nevin Carson, Robbie Bleakly, Maureen Bleakly, Jean Carson, John Fleming & Rae Boyd

that time that the King was renouncing the throne, because he was determined to marry the lady of his choice who was a divorcee and unacceptable to his subjects as Queen. The Rev RJ McIlmoyle was a born orator, both in the pulpit and on the platform. His sermons remained in the memory and his prayers were from the heart. He was always able to strike the right note, whether in a house of mourning or on a joyful occasion. His strong and abiding faith showed through at all times. He was a man of many interests, an advocate of all farmers and he travelled throughout the Province to speak at meetings and socials, where he brought advice and encouragement. He used to relate how on one occasion during the wartime blackout he was driving home late at night from a meeting when he was stopped by the police. The officer, looking into the car and seeing his collar, said, "Drive on, Father". He had a flock of pedigree Border Leicester sheep and he gained many cups and awards at shows. He could often be seen walking up from the village to his fields, leading his flock like the shepherds of old. He had a great helpmeet in his wife and she entered into and encouraged him in all his works. She would always note from her pew who was missing at the Sabbath service and she and Mr McIlmoyle would drop in through the week to see if all was well. They both took a great interest in the young people and encouraged them by their presence at their activities. They are worthy of remembrance. **(Mrs) Agnes B Millar**

I am very pleased to have this opportunity to pen a few words about a former minister and a real friend who had a long and useful life in the service of the Master whom he loved. The Rev RJ McIlmoyle and Mrs McIlmoyle were an outstanding pair and they were much loved by all ages within the congregation. He received several calls from other congregations, but refused all of them and continued to preach in Dervock while health permitted. The whole RP Church was delighted when he was honoured with the MBE. A faithful preacher of the Gospel in Dervock for sixty years (1904-1964), he retired on 18 May 1964 and entered peacefully into his rest on 18 May 1965. He had a long useful and fruitful ministry. Job 5:26 applies very much to our former minister, "You shall come to your grave in a full age like a stock of corn cometh in its season". Mr McIlmoyle was brought up in the Limavady district where his family exercised a godly influence in the community and in the local church. Early in life Mr McIlmoyle responded to God's call to the ministry of the Gospel. He was educated in the historic city of Londonderry and completed his training for the ministry in the Reformed Presbyterian Theological Hall, Belfast. He was licensed to preach the Gospel by the Western Presbytery in the year 1900 and was ordained to the office of minister and installed to the pastorate of Ballyclare congregation by the Eastern Presbytery on 6 September in that year. Four years later Mr McIlmoyle accepted the call from Dervock congregation and was installed by the Northern Presbytery on 31 August 1904. The Rev McIlmoyle was blessed with good health and found much pleasure in his pastime as a farmer with a Pedigree flock of Border Leicester sheep which won many cups at most shows in Northern Ireland. Above all else, he was an excellent shepherd of his congregation of Dervock. It was an exceptional privilege to be brought under his teaching. I am sure that he brought many young people to put their trust in his Saviour, the Lord Jesus Christ. All of us who had the privilege to listen to him explain God's word, Sabbath by Sabbath, have much reason to thank Almighty God.

Robert John Bleakly (former Clerk of Session)

It is my pleasure to recall some of my happy memories of the Rev RJ McIlmoyle who was our minister in Dervock RP Church. I had known him since I was a small boy, living next door to his family in Dervock. His youngest son took me by the hand on my first day going to school. The Rev McIlmoyle was a man of many interests, first as a minister, then as a farmer and stockbreeder. We were visiting in the manse one summer evening when I was a boy and I went with the minister along to the farm to attend to the sheep. He had a bottle of milk with him and a ewe, not a lamb, came to him and he gave it to her. A burn runs along the bottom of the manse farm and there was then, maybe there still is, a little shallow well on the far side of the burn, with stepping-stones leading to it. He lifted water from this well and put it in a drinking-trough for the sheep. He said that they didn't like the black (or burn) water to which they had ready access. He lavished attention on his livestock and spared no effort on their behalf. Any tit-bits of greenery from the garden went to the sheep. He travelled to shows all over the country and had been known to transport his sheep as far as Co Down and be first in the gate when the Showgrounds opened, having had to wait until they did so. He was also a great speaker who championed the cause of the farmers everywhere. He was a man who took a great interest in the Co-operative movement, and was successful in helping to get a Co-op started in Dervock. Many people around the neighbourhood took shares, and got a good dividend at the end of each year. The Rev RJ told the story of a shareholder who came into the shop, and wanted two pork hams and 28lb of the best back bacon. The assistant at the counter said that his order would be very expensive, and said he could give him lots of cheaper cuts, and parings, that would not cost so much. The shareholder said, "You are trying to do me out of my good dividend. Give me the good bacon and charge me plenty for it." I remember delivering loads of pork pigs and at Christmas time fat turkeys which were killed, plucked and dressed there, before being sent to Belfast and other towns to be marketed.

As a stockbreeder RJ was a great judge, both of cattle and sheep. He brought out excellent stock of Dairy shorthorns. I recall a young beast called Dervock Renown which he took to Balmoral bull sales. It was awarded the Championship Prize, awarded a premium and made a record price. A County Tyrone farmer purchased the bull and the premium was granted for a further period. I have many recollections of assisting RJ to show his Pedigree Border Leicester sheep at local and more distant shows all over the North, where he won hundreds of prizes, cups and rosettes. His motto was "Keep a few sheep, but keep them good quality". "A sheep's worst enemy is another sheep" was also often quoted. Many times I drove him to Ulster Farmers' Union meetings where he had been invited to speak. No matter what the distance was, he attended. Banbridge, Larne, Londonderry, Enniskillen or anywhere local, distance was no obstacle. We usually returned in the early hours of next morning. On the journey going many stories were told and many topics discussed, but on the way home he would wrap himself up in the car rug and have a good sleep, usually awakening as we neared Dervock. On returning home, he would look around the sheep to see if they were all right, especially if the ewes were near to lambing. He told me that he often had a sleep in the armchair instead of going to bed. He was kept very busy, with all the different committees and so on. He always said that if you wanted anything done, always go to the busy man. The other fellow has no time. He certainly lived that out, both in the Church and in daily life. He will always be remembered for his ready wit and humour, and for the way he encouraged those in trouble. He was a kind and loving pastor, a faithful preacher of the Gospel and those who were privileged to know him will long remember his gracious words.

W Norman McConaghie (elder)

On the journey through life we meet many different people, some of whom are as "ships that pass in the night" and are soon forgotten. Others because of their example and influence are remembered always. Such a man was the Rev RJ McIlmoyle who had a long and useful ministry in Dervock RP Church. He was first of all a well-loved preacher and pastor whose Church came first in his thoughts. He upheld the principles of the Covenanting Church, but was tolerant of the beliefs of other denominations, as was seen by the fact that Roman Catholics in the village, as well as all the other inhabitants, held him in great respect. Mr McIlmoyle was a very industrious man; his was not an eight-hour day. Often he came home from a Farmers' Union meeting well after midnight; yet he was out as usual in the morning, attending his stock, in which he took great pride. He was a friend and confidant to each member of his congregation and always found a solution to any problem about which he was consulted. The Rev RJ was an outstanding orator who required no microphone to address many large audiences where everyone heard him clearly. His sermons were well prepared and his prayers brought a sense of peace to his listeners. With Mrs McIlmoyle he enjoyed visits to his flock, for a friendly call, but he often said, around ten o'clock, "It's the farmer's bedtime; it's time to go home". Where there was sickness or sorrow, he was present to offer a prayer and support, while on a joyful occasion he was a valued speaker. At the end of a long ministry, when he began to feel the frailty of the flesh, he continued to preach a thought-provoking sermon with the help of elders in the other parts of the service, but eventually the years took their toll and he resigned. After a period of weakness, he was called home to be with the Saviour whom he had served for so long and to hear the words, "Well done, thou good and faithful servant, enter into the joy of thy Lord". **the late (Mrs) Jeannie Millar**

PREACHER & PASTOR RJ McIlmoyle's preaching was characteristic of the man he was. He did not preach unduly long sermons, but he made every word count, and his sermons were delivered not too hastily and yet with a sense of urgency that communicated itself to the hearer. As might be expected from a man with his experience of public speaking, his word-pictures were vividly and graphically drawn. His preaching was always Biblical and applied with direct relevance to the needs of his people. His pulpit prayers were offered with a deep reverence and an obvious awareness of the majesty of God, and at the same time with a clear and practical understanding of the needs of those for whom he prayed. The older members of the Dervock congregation where he served for almost all of his ministry still speak of his devoted pastoral care of all who were committed to his charge. He was indeed a good shepherd of his flock. **Hugh J Blair, Ballymoney Manse**

MINISTERS OF DERVOCK R.P. CHURCH

Rev. James McKinney	1783 — 1793
Rev. William John Stavely, A.M., D.D.	1804 — 1864
Rev. James Brown	1860 — 1878
Rev. Ezekiel Teaz	1886 — 1895
Rev. James Alexander Smyth Stewart	1895 — 1902
Rev. Robert John McIlmoyle, M.B.E.	1904 — 1964
Rev. Robert Harold Creane, B.A.	1964 — 1967
Rev. Edward Donnelly, B.A.	1968 — 1972
Rev. William Young, B.A.	1973 — 1980
Rev. John David Trevor McCauley, B.Sc., B.Agr., M.Div.	1981 — 1984

Rev Prof W Norris S Wilson BA, MAR, MTh 1986 -

Throughout the two hundred years of its existence, Dervock R.P. Church has been blessed in having, as elders, men of wisdom and dedication. A list of those who have served in the eldership of the congregation is given below. It is possible, however, that this may be incomplete, especially in relation to the early years, as records of that period are few and fragmentary.

John Picken
James Clark
Matthew Cathcart
John Craig
Archibald McFadden
George Henry
John Guthrie
Thomas Mitchell
Samuel Jackson
Archibald Rogers
James Nevin
James Lyons
John Kane
Moses Chestnutt
Francis Kane
Robert Clarke
Joseph Mulholland
John Nevin
Richard Gilmore
John McFaul
Hugh McCaw
Samuel Lyons
William Y. Patterson
Andrew L. McCurdy
Robert Carson
Samuel McConaghie
T Ivan McConaghie
Archie McKeeman

Daniel Neill
Robert Clarke (Jun.)
Samuel Chestnutt
John Mullan
David Teggart
Alexander Carson
John Fleming
John McFall
Daniel L. Carson
W. G. Finley
Daniel Carson (Jun.)
James Lyons
Robert Patterson
Neill Fleming
Robert McFall
Robert J. Campbell
Robert J. Carson
John Patrick
James Simpson
David Millar
Robert Bleakly
Norman McConaghie
James Kerr
George Hunter
Daniel J. McKeeman
David Millar
Alan Kerr

POSTSCRIPT

In Hebrews 13.7 we read: "Remember your leaders, who spoke the word of God to you. Consider the outcome of their way of life and imitate their faith" (NIV). I have really only one clear memory of the late Rev RJ McIlmoyle. It was one Sabbath Day when I was a boy in Ballymoney RP Church. Our own minister, Dr Hugh J Blair, was away that day and the Rev RJ was preaching in his place. I and my brothers watched with interest as this elderly, grey, solemn gentleman slowly entered the pulpit. He seemed to me a bit doddery and I wondered, "What will this old man have to say?" However the voice was clear and steady and I remember vividly to this day what he said. His sermon was on Christ and His disciples in the boat on the Sea of Galilee, when the furious storm came on. The Rev RJ's words painted the scene vividly. "Imagine yourselves in that boat that day", he said. And I could! The fishermen in the boat were used to storms, but there was something about that storm that absolutely terrified them. Yet there was Christ asleep, calm and unafraid. They woke him with the words, "Do you not care if we drown?" Then, in a moment, Christ rebuked the elements and brought a great calm. Turning to the disciples, he said, "O you of little faith, why are you so afraid?". In no uncertain terms the message was applied to us. Only with Christ in the boat of our lives, as it were, could we hope to face the storms of life; in the crisis we must exercise faith, instead of giving in to fear. Many remember Rev RJ McIlmoyle for many reasons and rightly so. However, I'm glad that when I think of him I remember that day in my boyhood in the family pew when he spoke the Word of God and it left an impression on my young life. It is good then to remember RJ McIlmoyle as one who warmed to his subject and presented it so tellingly. In his old age he commended to us Christ and the life of faith, a faith that he himself exemplified. Some in old age seem to have lost their zeal and freshness. He had not. The writer to the Hebrews says "Consider such men. Consider the outcome of their way of life and imitate their faith." It is a good word for any young minister, indeed any believer. As I think of him, I am moved to pray that like Paul and like the Rev RJ I may one day be able to say, "The time has come for my departure. I have fought the good fight, I have finished the race, I have kept the faith. Now there is in store for me the crown of righteousness, which the Lord, the righteous Judge, will award to me on that day and not only to me, but also to all who have longed for his appearing" (2 Tim 4: 6-8 NIV).

Norris Wilson, Dervock Manse

OBITUARIES

Mrs. Louise McIlmoyle, widow of Rev. R. J. McIlmoyle, died on 21st November, 1965, just six months after her husband. She was brought up in Limavady congregation, and to the end cherished the ties that bound her there. It was her destiny to be closely connected with the work of the Church during a long life ; and first in Ballyclare and then for many years in Dervock she was an able and devoted mistress of the manse. She maintained a deep interest in the welfare of the church at large, and in her own congregation she was a worthy helpmeet to her husband, and a true friend to any who sought her counsel. Physically handicapped in later years, her indomitable spirit kept her up both in the home and in the courts of God's House. We tender the sympathy of the Church to her three daughters and two sons and many relatives.

ALGEO—[illegible] November, 1967, at the Royal Victoria Hospital, Belfast, Sir Arthur George Algeo, C.B.E., J.P., beloved husband of Rosemary and dear father of Patricia, Ann, Richard and Henry, "The Gables," Ballymoney. Interred in Ballymoney cemetery.

PROFESSOR JOHN McILMOYLE, who has died, aged 76, was a minister of the Reformed Presbyterian Church for over 52 years.

For 25 years he has been Professor of Systematic Theology and Christian Ethics in the Reformed Presbyterian Hall, Belfast, and since 1947 minister of the Dublin Road congregation in the city. He lived at Eglantine Avenue.

A native of Limavady, where he was associated with the Broadlane congregation, Professor McIlmoyle was educated at Magee College, Derry, and Trinity College, Dublin, where he graduated with first-class honours in mental and moral philosophy.

He completed his training for the ministry at the R.P. Theological Hall.

Ordained at Creevaghy, Co. Monaghan, he served in Kellswater and Faughan, Co. Derry, before moving to Belfast.

He served the Church with distinction in many spheres. For many years he was editor of the Church's magazine, "The Covenanter." He was a Dean of Residence at Queen's University.

Surviving him are his wife, two daughters and a son.

McILMOYLE — June 22, 1966 ([illegible]denly), at his residence, 86 Eglantine Avenue, Rev. Professor [illegible] (M.A.), beloved husband of [illegible] McIlmoyle, Minister of Dublin Road Reformed Presbyterian Church, Belfast. Funeral to-morrow (Friday) at 11-30 a.m., to Knockbracken [illegible] flowers by request.

McILMOYLE — March 16, 1973, at her brother's residence, Limavady, Elvina, daughter of the late Rev. R. J. and Mrs. McIlmoyle, Dervock. Cremation took place at Roselawn Crematorium on March 20. No letters, by request. Deeply regretted.

McILMOYLE — January 10, 1976, at her home, 96, Greystown Avenue, Margretta, wife of the late Rev. Professor John McIlmoyle. Service in Dublin Road Reformed Presbyterian Church to-day (Tuesday), at 11 a.m. Funeral afterwards to Knockbracken Reformed Presbyterian Churchyard. House private. Donations in lieu of flowers to Reformed Presbyterian Missions, c/o the Rev. H. Tadley, 11, Cranmore Gar-